Building
Miniature
Furniture

BUILDING MINIATURE FURNITURE

A Treasury of Classic American Styles

Joseph Daniele

Stackpole Books

Published by
STACKPOLE BOOKS
Cameron and Kelker Streets
P.O. Box 1831
Harrisburg, Pa. 17105

Published simultaneously in Don Mills, Ontario, Canada
by Thomas Nelson & Sons, Ltd.

Printed in the U.S.A.

Library of Congress Cataloging in Publication Data

Daniele, Joseph William.
    Building miniature furniture.

    Includes index.
    1. Miniature furniture.   2. Furniture—United.
States.   I. Title.
TT178.D37   1981   749.213   80-22180

ISBN 0-8117-1000-9

To my wife Jean,
who made ''once upon a time'' come true

Contents

Section Two

Early American Furnishings

Section Three

Pennsylvania Dutch Furnishings

Section Four

Victorian Furnishings

Preface

The range of furnishings to make in miniature is just about endless. It encompasses everything from rustic dollhouse furniture up to precise miniature duplication. The cost of a single piece can be anywhere from a few dollars to a few thousand dollars. The ultimate construction, value, and exactness lies within the builder's or owner's intention. For what purpose will the miniatures be used, as a plaything or collector's item? The average public is not always aware of the difference between dollhouse furnishings and miniature collections. While the two are related, they are not always close relatives.

Dollhouse furniture, because it is intended to be played with, used, and handled by children, must be a little more utilitarian in nature. This means heavy basic construction stock with an overall aim of durability. In addition,

dollhouse furnishings are not always confined to a specific scale. Many of them are designed for a certain size doll. The popular "Barbie and Ken" sets are a good example of a furnishing environment made to a specific size and for a specific reason.

This book offers patterns and designs strictly on a one-twelfth, or one inch equals one foot, scale; the universal size for miniature making. While the furnishings of this book were developed or copied from museum pieces and intended for miniature collections, they can be used as dollhouse furnishings. The primary aim was to produce furniture with the close, exact detailing sought in most miniature work. In this respect, a finer degree of workmanship is required. The suggested materials, sizes, and construction were designed to correlate with the full-size antique pieces. Every effort

Victorian house

was made to offer miniature reproductions compatible with the time periods they represent.

Most miniature collectors have a favorite period setting. Early American, Pennsylvania Dutch, and turn-of-the-century Victorian are only a few of the periods sought. However, just as modern, full-size homes are decorated in a particular theme yet incorporate other periods of furniture, the following miniature reproductions can be mixed and matched together or used in a contemporary-style setting. Many Early American and Pennsylvania Dutch pieces are interchangeable, and often, selected

Early American furniture can be integrated into Victorian settings, making the possibilities just about endless.

This book's contents were arranged around the concept of furnishing a complete miniature dwelling or a single room setting. The individual period sections are subdivided into a certain room, such as bedroom, kitchen, or dining room. Here the aim is to provide the miniature furniture needed to decorate the scale-size dwellings offered in *Building Masterpiece Miniatures* (Harrisburg, PA: Stackpole Books, 1980). Combined, I feel these two books offer the most comprehensive, detailed miniature con-

Gingerbread-style house, Chester, Vermont

Early American house and furnishings

struction resource material available on today's market. Everything possible is offered, from the house itself down to the smallest furnishing detail.

Most furniture is made from wood and every species has been used. What makes one piece Early American, another Victorian, and a third Contemporary is how the wood is formed and put together. Once a tree is felled, the eventual outcome is almost predetermined. From the same log one can either make firewood or a Queen Anne style breakfront. The wood itself is the same, it is the forming that makes it unique.

A close look at Early American or Victorian styles displays the same basic raw material. It is how this material is cut and shaped that categorizes the eventual style and/or time period in reproductions. Every furniture era

had characteristics particular to its period. Every effort has been made to incorporate this theory into the following miniature reproductions.

In the designing of the furnishings, a primary concern was that special stock or tools were to be avoided if at all possible. All of the reproductions offered here are made from stock found in the average hobby or craft shop or in regular lumberyards. Of equal importance to the book's format is that special skills and expertise are not required. The beginner or expert craftsman will be equally at home with the offerings. Step-by-step instructions are given for each reproduction. The builder who has no experience can, by following the steps, produce valuable miniature furnishings.

The first section, devoted to construction methods, was developed from teaching miniature making to adult students who had never held a tool before. The procedures show how to make difficult pieces with relative ease.

Miniature making is often a strange hobby. It can become addictive. It leads individual collectors to seek more and more authentic reproductions of heirlooms. While very little can match the ownership of a fine miniature collection, nothing can equal the pride and satisfaction of making one's own complete collection. Taking a rough piece of stock and transforming it into a precise one-twelfth-scale copy of an original through diligence and patience, rewards the maker many times over. A special world is created where in years to come every joint, each brush stroke, all the tender care is remembered, and the personal satisfaction is thereby intensified. As the Pennsylvania Dutch said, "They make music on the eye, and joy in the heart." This book was designed, created, and geared toward the concept of what people can do for themselves if they want to make their own brand of visual music.

As always, I have many people to thank for their help and advice. Many historical organizations provided photographs and ideas on period furnishings, and the Early American Society, publishers of *Early American Life* magazine, allowed me to reproduce in miniature several full-size, authentic designs I made for them. Various local, regional, and national miniature dealers also provided information and possible ideas for the book's contents, and friends with private collections gave freely of their advice and knowledge. My publisher assigned a very competent staff to oversee and work on this book, and the resulting publication is as much theirs as it is mine. To all of these organizations and people, I owe my sincere gratitude and appreciation. To everyone, thank you very much.

SECTION ONE

Construction Notes

1

Scale, Materials, and Tools

SCALE

One of the problems of working on a $1/12$, or one inch equals one foot, scale is that the normal inch or foot does not divide by twelve very easily. Eighth-inch markings are too large to represent a scale inch, and sixteenths are too small.

There are, however, $1/12$ scales available on rulers in hobby and craft outlets or on architectural triangular rulers. Designated as "1" on the side of the architect rule, the $1/12$ scale has a sample foot divided into quarter-, half-, and full-inch markings, plus full- and half-foot measurements (fig. 1–2). Learning to use the $1/12$ scale is easy and important as it will prove valuable for miniature furniture construction and scale conversions.

Reading the $1/12$ Scale

The $1/12$ scale runs from left to right on the architect rule, with another scale, $1/2$, running from right to left along the same edge. Numbered from zero to ten, the $1/12$ full-foot markings are the longest division markings on the rule. The $1/2$ scale is also used to mark the $1/2$ foot or 6 inch measurements on the $1/12$ scale. Remember to discount the numerical value as they are intended only for the $1/2$ equals 1 foot scale.

For example, to find the $2^{1}/_{2}$-foot mark, first

Fig. 1–1. Architectural scale showing ¹/₁₂ scale, with divider and compass

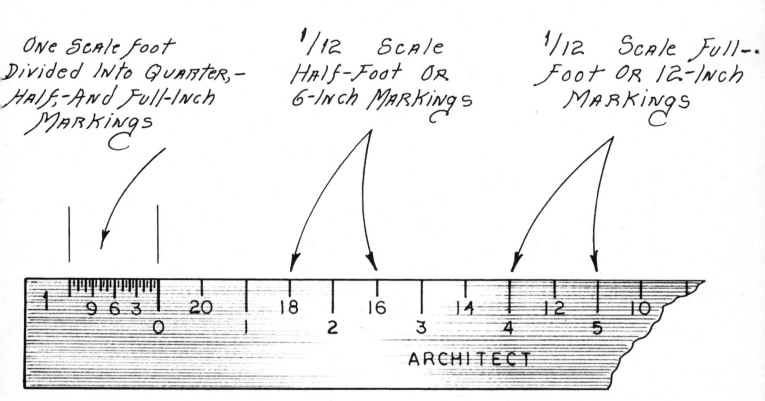

One Scale Foot Divided Into Quarter,- Half,-And Full-Inch Markings

¹/12 Scale Half-Foot Or 6-Inch Markings

¹/12 Scale Full- Foot Or 12-Inch Markings

Fig. 1–2. Section of ¹/₁₂ scale on architect ruler

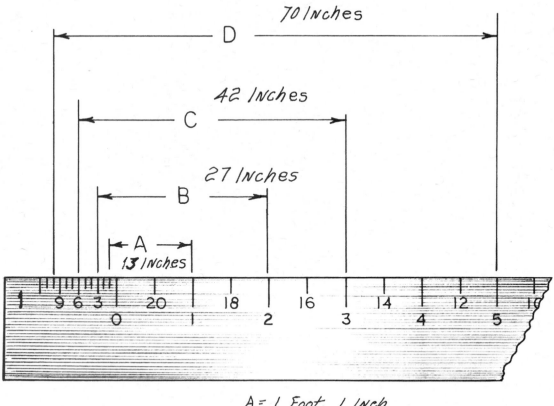

Fig. 1–3. *Measuring odd-inch lengths on a* 1/12 *scale*

locate the 2-foot marking (labeled 2), then move to the 1/2-foot mark (labeled 16).

Finding Odd-inch Dimensions

If an odd-inch size is desired, incorporate the 12-inch or full-foot markings with the inch fraction division markings. Refer to figure 1–3 for the following examples.

Example A equals 1 foot, 1 inch or 13 inches. Measure from the first foot marking (1) or 12-inch marking and add one of the divided scale inches to make the total 13 inches.

Example B equals 2 feet, 3 inches, or 27 inches. This time measure from the 2-foot mark and add 3 of the divided scale inches for a total of 27 inches.

Example C equals 3 feet, 6 inches or 42 inches. Measure from the 3-foot value and add 6 additional inches to equal a 42-inch total.

Example D equals 5 feet, 10 inches or 70 inches. Measure from the 5-foot mark and add 10 of the scale inch markings to total 70 inches.

Dividing an Opening into Equal Spaces

Figure 1–4 shows a space being divided into five equal parts.

Place the rule on any angle that will provide the desired number of equal spaces, in this case five. Any angle or scale can be used, 1/2 inch, 3/8 inch, 3/4 inch, full inch, or whatever fits across the opening and divides to the correct number of spaces. Mark the points as shown, 1, 2, 3, 4.

With a T square and triangle draw a horizontal or vertical line at each marking. This will result in five equal spaces in either direction.

Converting Full-Size Plans to Miniature

Many magazines and books offer plans for full-size period reproductions. Such full-size plans can be quickly converted to miniature sizes by using the 1/12 scale on the architect rule.

Figure 1–5 shows a plan for a full-size cabinet front. By using the 1/12 scale on the rule, such a front can be reduced to miniature size.

The height of the cabinet (A) is 30 inches: Finding the 2-foot marking and adding 6 of the divided scale inches will make the 30-inch total desired.

The length (B) equals 42 inches. The 3-foot mark plus 6 additional inches on the divided scale gives the desired measurement.

The width of the wood (C) is only 2 inches and is therefore found in the divided inch area.

The cabinet opening (D) measures 18 inches. The 1½-foot marking or the 1-foot mark plus 6 scale inches can be used to give this measurement.

WORKING WITH FULL SIZE PATTERNS

Once the reproduction is selected, note the

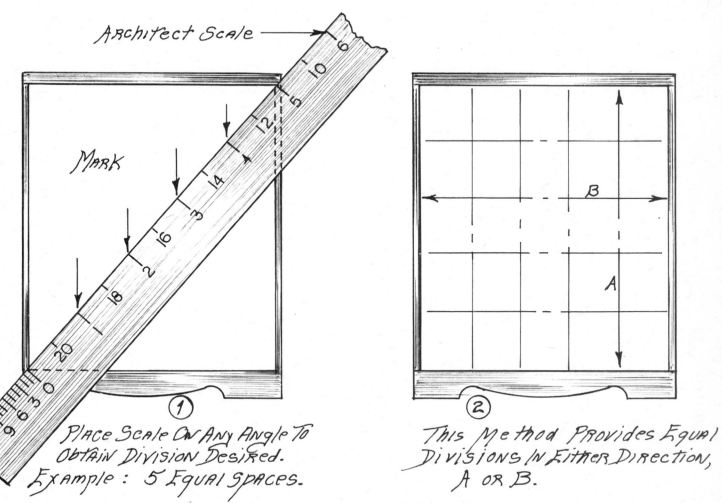

Fig. 1–4. Using a scale to divide a space equally

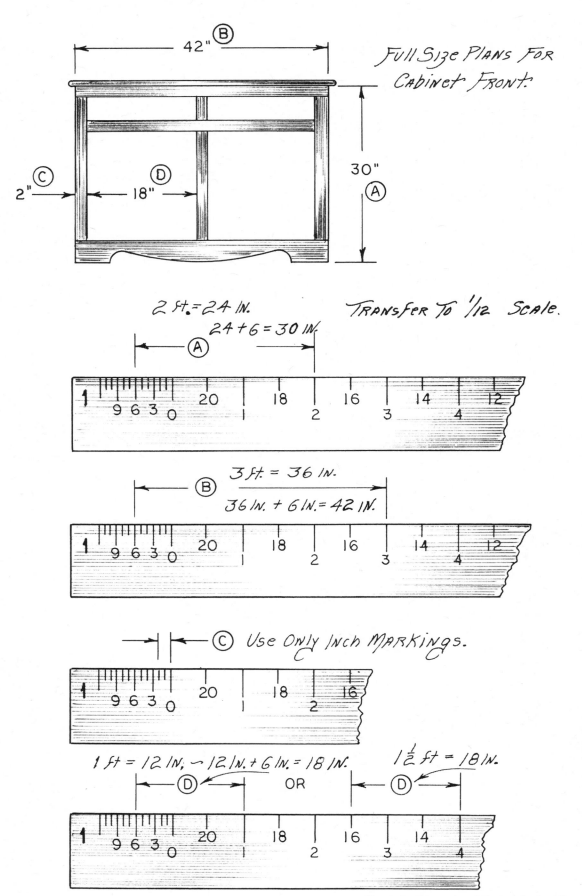

Fig. 1–5. Converting full-size plans to $^1/_{12}$ scale

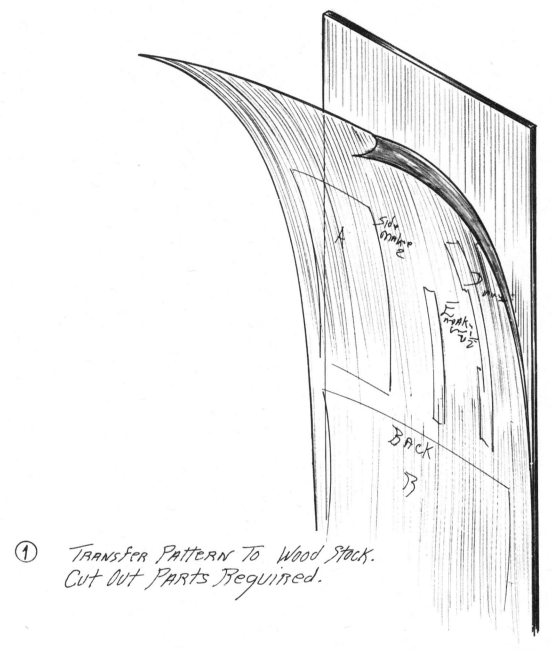

① TRANSFER PATTERN TO WOOD STOCK.
CUT OUT PARTS REQUIRED.

Fig. 1–6. Transferring full-size patterns.

wood thickness required for each piece. The wood thickness is the last measurement given for each piece in the material list.

1. Trace the pattern size onto the selected stock and cut out all the parts required.

It is important to make all cuts square and accurate. Note that most often the side pieces of each reproduction are thicker than the other

parts. This thickness allows for a rabbet along the rear inside edges that receive the back piece. Cut in the suggested $1/16$ inch by $1/16$ inch rabbet into the sides (A) with a knife, file, or saw.

2. Glue the back piece into the rabbets cut into the sides (B into A). (The back piece can be pinned into the side rabbets if preferred.) It is

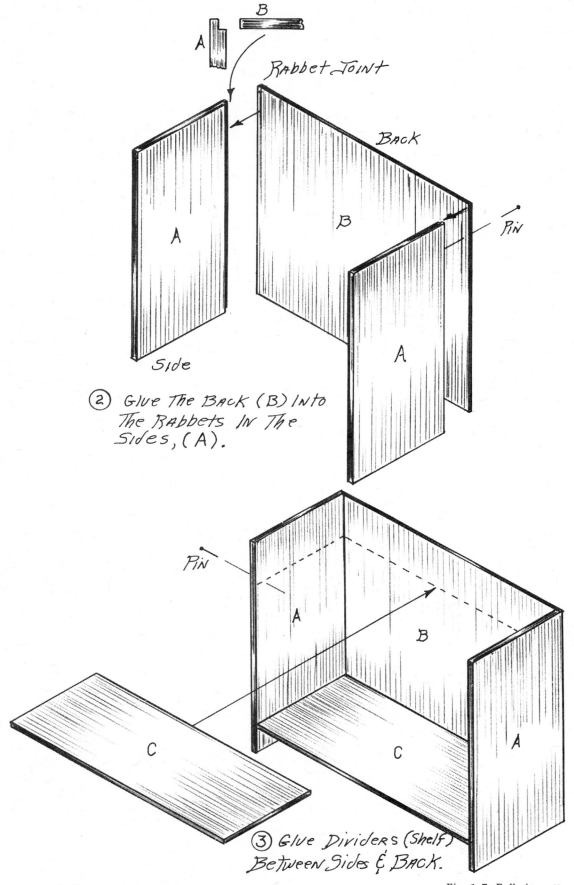

B

A

Rabbet Joint

BACK

B

Pin

A

Side

A

② Glue The BACK (B) Into The Rabbets In The Sides, (A).

Pin

A

B

A

C

C

A

③ Glue Dividers (Shelf) Between Sides & BACK.

Fig. 1–7. Full-size pattern assembly

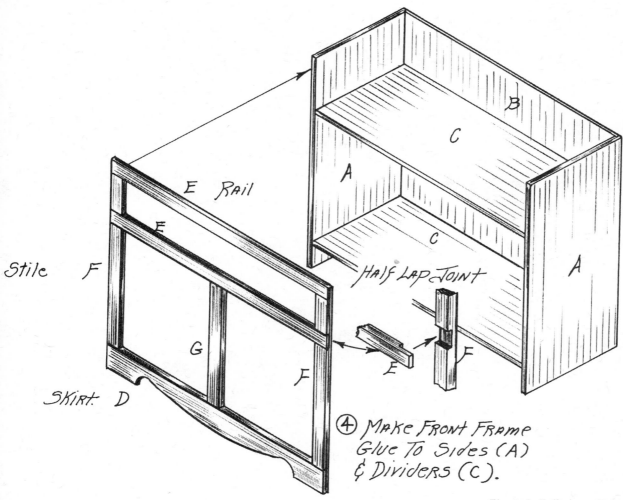

Stile F

E Rail

E

Skirt D

G

F

A

B

C

A

C

Half Lap Joint

E

F

F

A

④ Make Front Frame
Glue To Sides (A)
& Dividers (C).

Fig. 1–8. Full-size pattern assembly

not important for the sides to be perfectly square to the back at this time.

3. Install the shelf or divider where required. The shelf or divider (C) fits between the sides (A) and to the back (B). It is this piece, the divider or shelf, that squares up the reproduction. It is important that these be made the precise size to fit between the two sides. If too long they will force the sides away from the back piece, and if too short, they will force the sides in and make the furnishing out of square.

4. Make the suggested front frame. The frame consists of a skirt board (D), rail, and stiles. It is suggested that half lap joints be employed.

The frame will be more accurate if it is made on a jig or backer board with parts pinned in place until the glue joints have dried. When the frame is finished, glue it to the side-divider-back assembly.

5. Make any drawers or doors required. It is suggested that drawers and doors be made slightly oversize and then sanded to fit the opening exactly.

Make and install the top and the reproduction is ready for finishing.

Finishing

Sand the completed furnishing smooth re-

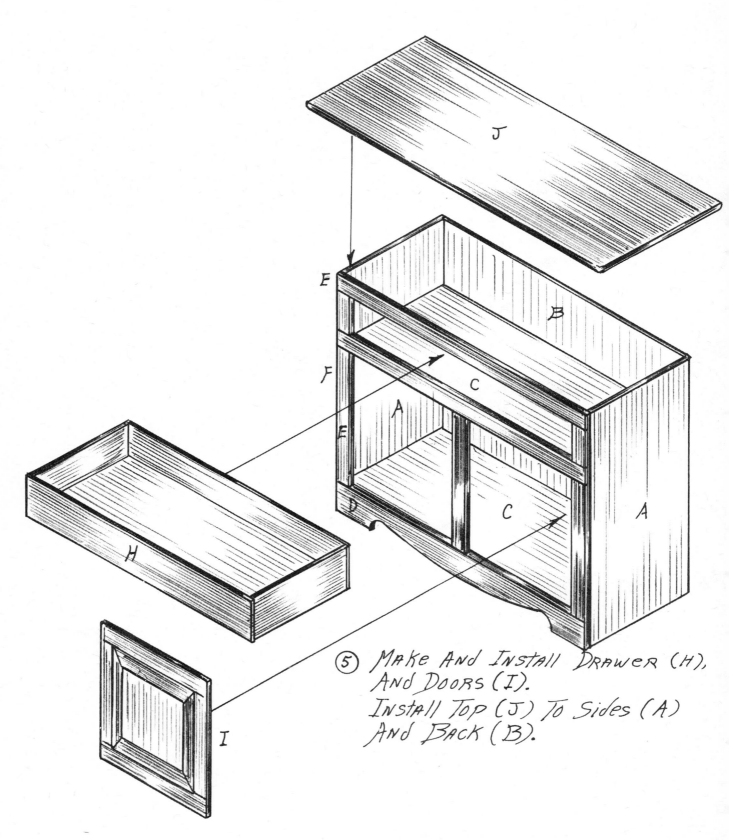

⑤ Make And Install Drawer (H), And Doors (I).
Install Top (J) To Sides (A) And Back (B).

Fig. 1–9. Full-size pattern assembly

Fig. 1–10. Miniature-size lumberyard (Courtesy H. L. Childs)

moving any trace of glue. Stain or paint to a color selection of choice. Cover the stain or paint with several coats of lacquer or similar finish. Complete the furnishing with a coat of paste wax.

MATERIALS

Wood sheet stock of different thicknesses and shapes can be obtained from three sources. It can be purchased from miniature supply outlets or hobby stores. If local retail outlets do not have such stock, it can be ordered from mail-order companies that deal in miniature or model railroad supplies. Check local hobby,

model, or miniature stores before seeking these mail-order outlets though.

The woods available include basswood, mahogany, cherry, walnut, maple, and clear select pine. Hardwood dowels from $1/16$-inch diameter up to $3/8$-inch diameter are also available for leg turnings.

The third source of sheet stock is to create your own from normal lumberyard materials. This method is the least expensive alternative and only requires the use of an average table saw and any species of wood you want to use.

Most often $1/16$-inch or $1/8$-inch thick stock is suggested for miniature furnishing reproductions. This material can be obtained from full-size lumber by resawing or cutting. The total width of such sheet stock is limited to slightly under twice the table saw blade height, therefore individual widths will be determined by the type of table saw used. For example, if the table saw blade is 3 inches, the maximum stock width will be 5⁷/₈ inches.

Resawing Stock

Step one. Secure a piece of protective wood facing to the table saw rip fence. This will pro-

tect the fence and the saw blade from accidentally touching.

Step two. Set the blade at its maximum height.

Step three. Set the rip fence away from the raised blade for the desired amount of thickness. In figure 1–12, the thickness desired is ¹/₈ inch, therefore, the fence is set ³/₁₆ inch away from the blade. This will allow stock for sanding and finishing to size.

Step four. Rip saw the selected stock on both

Fig. 1–11. Typical table saw (Courtesy Rockwell Company)

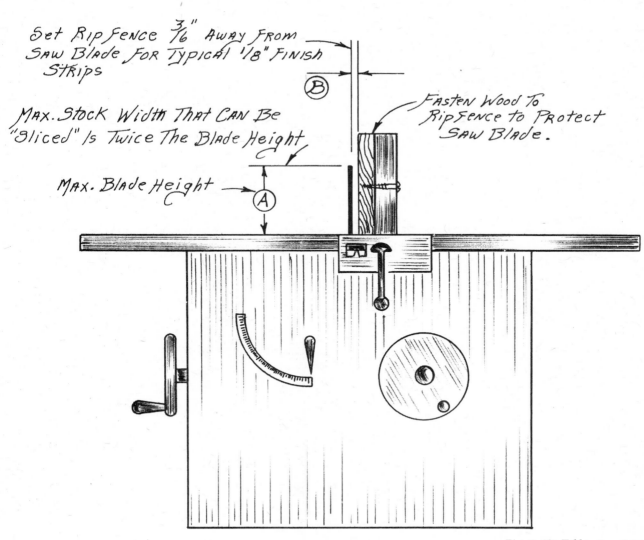

Set Rip Fence $\frac{3}{16}$" Away From Saw Blade For Typical $\frac{1}{8}$" Finish Strips

Max. Stock Width That Can Be "Sliced" Is Twice The Blade Height

Max. Blade Height →

Fasten Wood To Rip Fence to Protect Saw Blade.

Fig. 1–12. Table saw set-up

outside surfaces. See figure 1–13, A. Notice that the saw kerf (blade cut) takes a good deal of stock thickness. This thickness will depend upon the type of blade used. The center section or slice in this example will be slightly thicker than the side slices and will require sanding and finishing on both sides. The outside cuts will require refinishing on only one side.

Step five. Turn the selected stock over after the first cuts and make the intersecting second cuts (fig. 1–13, B). The resulting slice may leave a slight saw bead where the two cuts meet (fig. 1–14). This will be sanded off during finishing.

Step six. Lay the cut slices on a workbench and sand the sawed edge or surface until it is

smooth and the desired thickness is achieved. Thinner thickness stock slices can be obtained by following the same basic procedures but using a closer rip fence setting. Remember to allow for sanding. For example, for a 1/16-inch finish, start with a 3/32-inch-thick slice.

TOOLS

The miniature reproductions offered in this book can be made with a minimum of specialized tools. Many of these tools can be found in the average household. It is recommended that beginning miniaturists start off with the tools listed on the Basic Tool List. If they enjoy

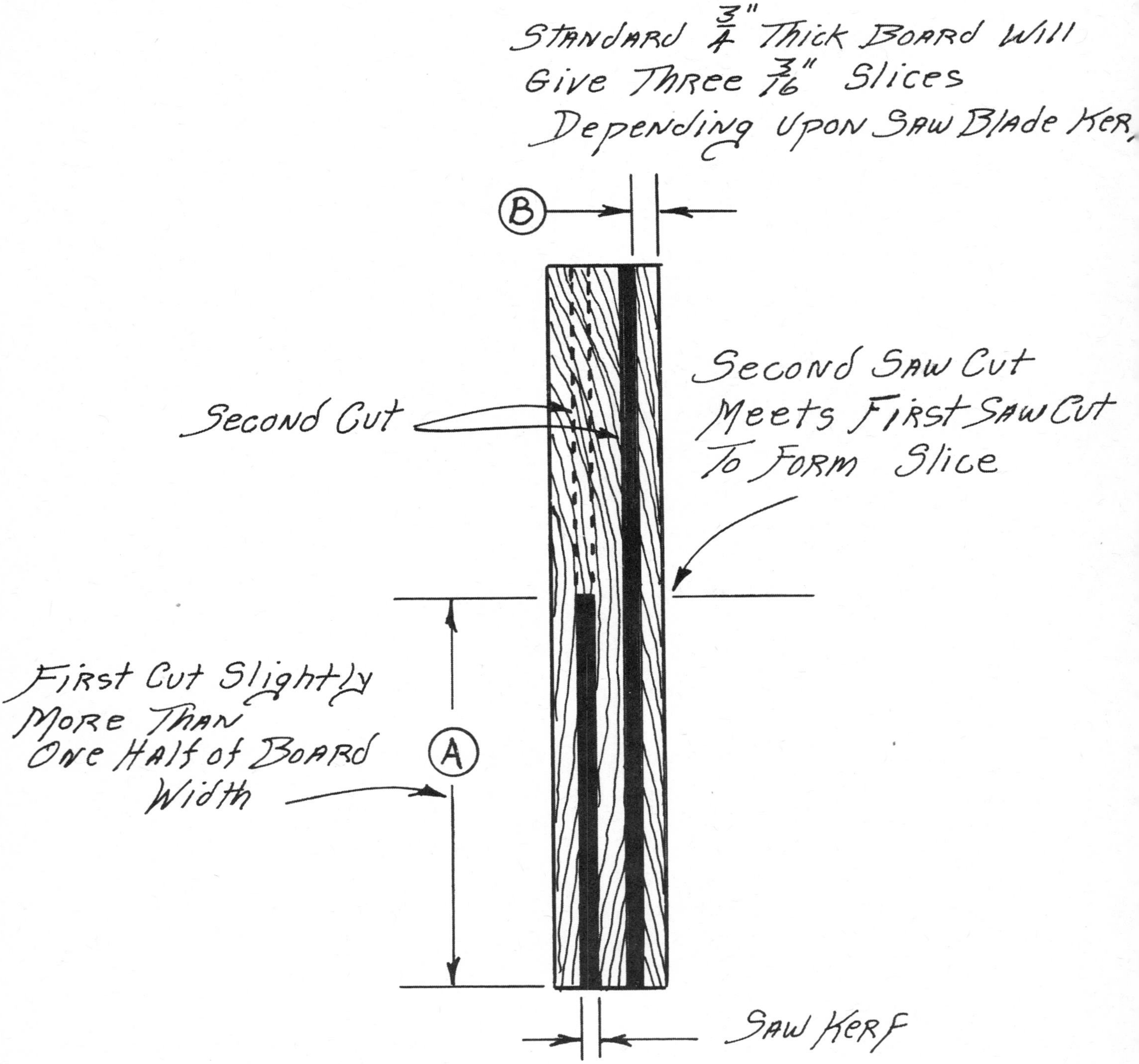

Standard $\frac{3}{4}$" Thick Board Will
Give Three $\frac{3}{16}$" Slices
Depending Upon Saw Blade Ker,

(B)

Second Cut

Second Saw Cut
Meets First Saw Cut
To Form Slice

First Cut Slightly
More Than
One Half of Board
Width

(A)

Saw Kerf

Fig. 1–13. Resawing steps

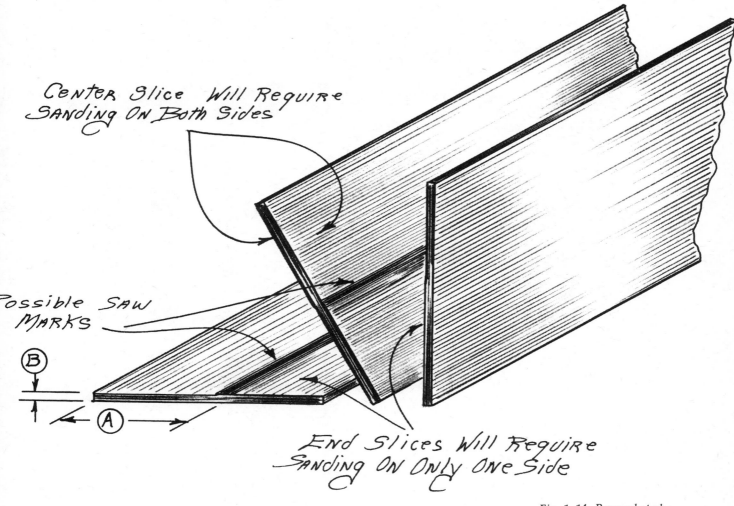

Center Slice Will Require Sanding On Both Sides

Possible Saw Marks

End Slices Will Require Sanding On Only One Side

Fig. 1–14. Resawed stock

working on a $^1/_{12}$ scale, they can add specialized tools from the Secondary Tool List as needed. Hand and power tools for miniaturists are carried as stock items by most hobby and miniature outlets. Larger retail stores, such as Sears Roebuck Co., Montgomery Ward and Co., or J.C. Penney Co., often have such tools in their hardware departments or through their catalog sales. Mail-order miniature vendors offer a wide selection of hand or power tools. Many of these offer their catalog of tools and millwork for a nominal charge.

Basic Tool List

1. Combination square, 90 degree and 45 degree angles

2. Divider and/or compass

3. T square and triangles, 45 degree and 30/60 degree

4. Substitute clamps: rubber bands, snap-type clothespins, alligator clips

5. Long-nose pliers with side cutter

6. X-ACTO knife or set of knives

7. Shop-made or purchased miter box with fine-tooth saw

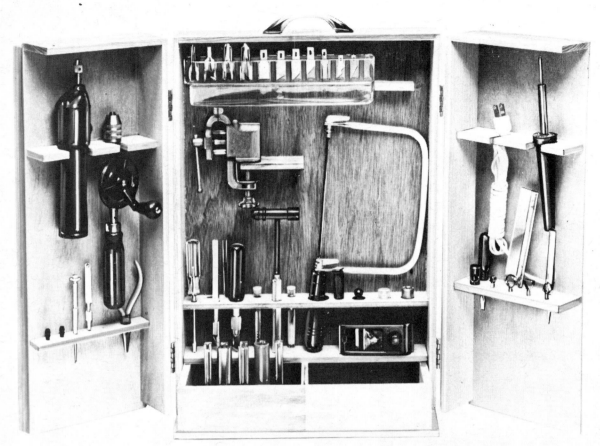

Fig. 1–15. Tool chest (Courtesy X-ACTO Company)

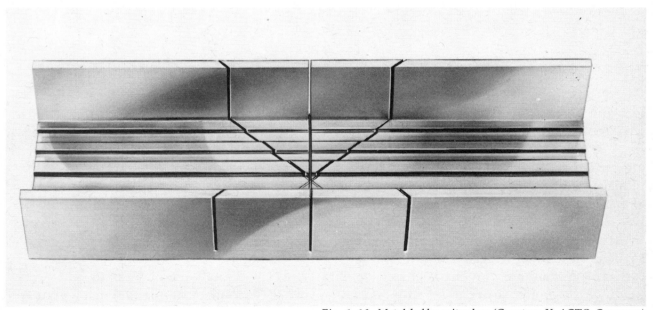

Fig. 1–16. Metal hobby miter box (Courtesy X-ACTO Company)

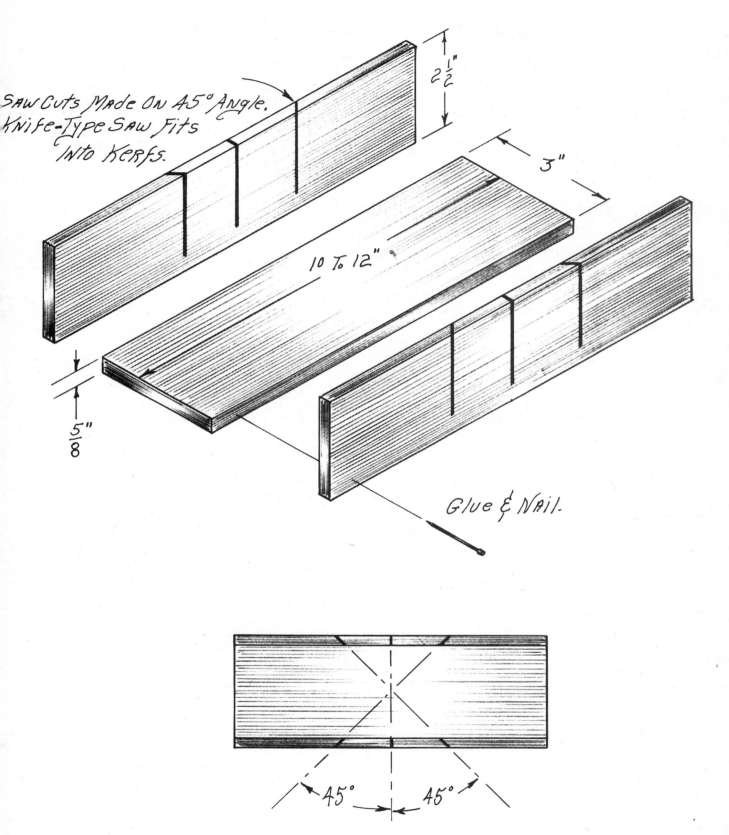

Saw Cuts Made On 45° Angle.
Knife-Type Saw Fits
Into Kerfs.

$2\frac{1}{2}$"

3"

10 To 12"

$\frac{5}{8}$"

Glue & Nail.

45°   45°

Fig. 1–17. Shop-made miter box

8. Back, dovetail, miter box, or razor saw
9. Files: small flat, half-round, rat-tail
10. Block plane
11. Sanding blocks and assorted grit sandpaper
12. Twelve-inch steel rule for straight edge
13. Architect scale or miniaturist scale
14. Hand (eggbeater-type) or finger drill
15. Assorted size twist drills, $1/32$-inch to $3/16$-inch diameter
16. Coping saw or jigsaw

Secondary Tool List

1. Circle templates
2. Mat knife
3. Files: jeweler's assortment
4. Jeweler's screwdriver set
5. Small C clamps
6. Metal spring clamps, assorted sizes
7. Plastic pressure clamps (X-ACTO)
8. Soldering iron and 50/50 core solder
9. Oil stone for sharpening

Power Tools and Machines

1. Portable electric drill, $3/8$-inch chuck cap (can double as lathe for round turnings)
2. Jigsaw
3. Circular saw, miniature or full size, 4- to 8-inch blade
4. Orbital sander
5. Belt and disk sander
6. Miniaturist's lathe
7. Hand-held electric grinder with flexible feed and assorted bits, rotary files, burrs, rasps
8. Hand-held router and bits

Finishing Accessories

1. Stains, oil- or water-based
2. Paints, assorted colors, latex or oil base, flat semi-gloss or gloss
3. Finishing covering: lacquer, Deft, polyurethane, varnish
4. Glaze, shop-made or antiquing kit
5. Thinners
6. Assorted artist's brushes
7. Paste wax
8. Steel wool, fine and very fine grades

Shop-made Miter Box

A miter box is a unit that contains slots or saw kerfs (cuts) at predetermined angles. Most often these slots are on a right- and left-hand 45-degree angle and a square or 90-degree angle. The stock to be cut is inserted into the box bottom and held tightly against one side while a back, razor, or dovetail saw blade is inserted into the desired slots. The sawing action is contained in the direction of the slots, and a miter or straight cut results.

While most hobby or miniature stores sell small miter boxes, an inexpensive one can be made in the home workshop from small scraps of lumber.

The sizes given in figure 1–17 are approximate and can be scaled larger or smaller as necessary. Begin by cutting the base and side pieces from scrap lumber. Nail and glue the two matching side pieces to the base. After the glue has dried, cut in the required 45- and 90-degree saw kerfs. Insert a common back, dovetail, or razor saw into the kerfs.

2

Fasteners and Finishes

FASTENING

Miniature work, because of its scale, eliminates a great deal of normal fastening methods. Normal-size nails or screws, no matter how small, are too large to use. Because miniatures are too fragile for nails, over 95 percent of all miniature fastening is completed by gluing.

Glue jointing has a few drawbacks, one of which is that the end grain joints require special attention. The danger is that the glue can soak into the open pores at the end grain joint making a glue-starved or weak joint. When gluing the end grain, rub the glue into the grain to fill up the open pores. Apply a second, light coat after the first coat has set for a few moments and attach the two parts.

Another problem encountered in glue jointing is that the glaze left by wiping a glue joint and the glue bead created by clamp pressure will not accept stain because the glue seals the grain or pores much like a coat of paint. The stain, oil- or water-based, will wipe right off the area leaving a white or yellow splotch.

With this in mind, all glue joints should be wiped clean. After the glue has dried, the joint or area should be well sanded to remove all traces of glue. To help overcome this problem, some manufacturers offer precolored glue to match their stains.

The miniaturist can make colored or pretinted glue by mixing a universal or water-based color tint in with regular white glue. The tint will not weaken the glued joint. Normal care should be taken anyway to remove any excess or beads and to sand the area after drying. Any major brand of glue, such as Sobo, Elmer's, X-ACTO, Titebond, Franklin, Ross, or most hobby-type glues, will work equally well.

Remember, for a glued joint to work and hold well, they must be made under some type of pressure. Allow ample time for the glue to dry before removing the pressure.

Bank Pins

Bank or sequin pins look like small, 1/2-inch-long straight pins. They can be used in place of nails without fear of splitting the thin stock. Bank pins can be used to hold glued pieces together until the glue sets and then removed. The pins can also be used and left in place where the heads will not show.

FINISHING

Many hobby or miniature outlets sell stains, paints, and finishes in small containers. You can, however, use normal everyday stains, paints, and finishes with equally excellent results.

Fillers

Fillers are not normally used in miniature work unless a very open, large pore grain wood is used. Suggested fillers are Minwax Wood Filler, Plastic Wood, Wood Dough, and Minwax Blend in pencils.

Stains

Any water- or oil-based stain will work on miniatures. It is suggested that the stain be applied with a brush and wiped down with a soft cloth. Allow ample time before wiping for the stain to penetrate the wood. Typical stains include most name brands: Minwax, Martin Senour, Watco, Deft, X-ACTO.

Finish Coverings

Any finish will work on miniatures. Many finishes are available in spray cans which offer many advantages over the brush-on types. It is easier to cover small pieces and hard-to-get-at areas using a spray finish. Sprayed finishes dry very quickly, and several coats can be applied in one day. They are self storing and require no cleaning thinners or brushes. Hobby, craft, and hardware stores carry spray finishes.

Suggested finishes are Deft Clear Wood Finish, Deft Wood Armor, Zip Guard, any

Fig. 1–18. Victorian ice cream parlor made from resawed stock and finished using normal materials

polyurethane or Waterlox finish coat. Gloss or semi-gloss varnishes can be used. All the furnishings in this book were finished with Deft Clear Wood (lacquer-based) finish.

Paints

Any water- or oil-base paint, flat, semi-gloss, or gloss paint works well. Many hobby or model outlets sell oil- or water-based paints in very small containers. Common wall paints have also been used with excellent results.

Finishing Procedure

There are sequential steps to take in finishing miniature or full size furniture pieces.

After completing the construction, fill the pin holes and voids with filler. Sand the entire reproduction smooth, removing all traces of glue and filler. Stain or paint it the color of your choice.

If the reproduction is to be stained first sand the entire miniature smooth removing any trace of glue. Stain is best applied with a small brush and allowed to soak or set on the wood surface to allow for penetration. Wipe the miniature down with a soft clean cloth and allow the stain to dry overnight before finishing.

If paint is used, apply the paint with a fine brush. Very often two coats of paint will be required. Allow the first coat to dry before applying the second coat. If paint is to be used as a wash coat or as a type of stain, apply the first coat and, while the paint is still wet, wipe the miniature down with a soft cloth until the desired covering is achieved.

Allow the stain or paint to dry overnight. Then cover with a coat of finish such as lacquer or polyurethane.

If Pennsylvania Dutch designs are to be used, apply them with ink or paint and allow them to dry thoroughly.

Apply another coat of clear finish.

If an aged look is preferred, apply a glaze of half flat black paint and half thinner. Wipe this glaze down while it is still wet. The amount of wiping will determine the darkness of the age glaze.

Cover with two or more coats of finish, allowing it to dry thoroughly between coats.

Complete the finishing process by applying a coat of paste wax with very fine steel wool and buffing to a gloss.

3

Drawers, Doors, and Furnishings

There are many assembly techniques that are common to the construction of miniature furniture of every period. This chapter presents some of the basic methods you will need to use when making the miniature furnishings in this book.

DRAWERS

Miniature drawer construction differs a little from the assembly of full-size drawers in that the miniature drawer is made with simple butt joints. Strength is not a factor in such drawers; therefore, simpler methods are employed.

The total drawer height should be slightly larger than the opening it will occupy. After the drawer is assembled, it can be sand-fitted to the size of the individual opening. If the open-

ing is a little off in size or squareness, the drawer unit can be fitted to compensate.

1. Begin by cutting all the required parts to the size suggested in the pattern (fig. 1–19). It is important that all cuts be square.

2. Glue the two side pieces (B) to the back piece (A). Bank pins can be used to hold the parts together while the glue sets.

3. Glue the bottom piece (C) to the sides (B) and the back (A). Since the bottom is square, it will square up the whole drawer assembly.

4. Glue the front piece (D) to the sides (B) and bottom (C).

DOORS
Pin-Hinged Doors

An alternative to scale-size hinges, which

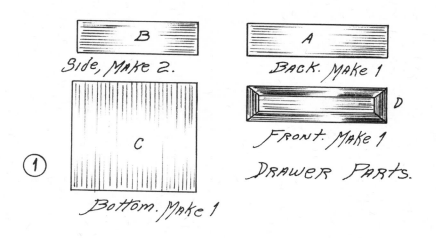

① Side, Make 2.

B

A
Back. Make 1

D
Front. Make 1

C
Bottom. Make 1

DRAWER PARTS.

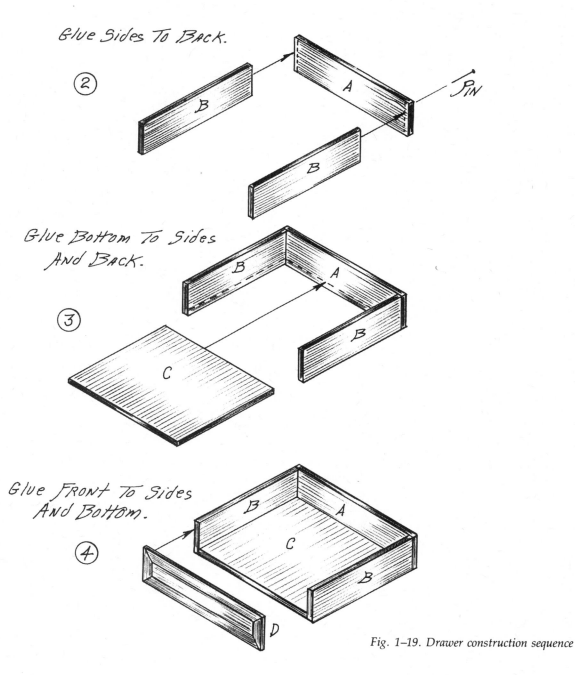

Glue Sides To Back.

② B   A   Pin
B

Glue Bottom To Sides
And Back.

③ B   A   B
C

Glue Front To Sides
And Bottom.

④ B   A
C
B
D

Fig. 1–19. Drawer construction sequence

① *Make Door Slightly Oversize.*
Sand Fit Door to the Opening.

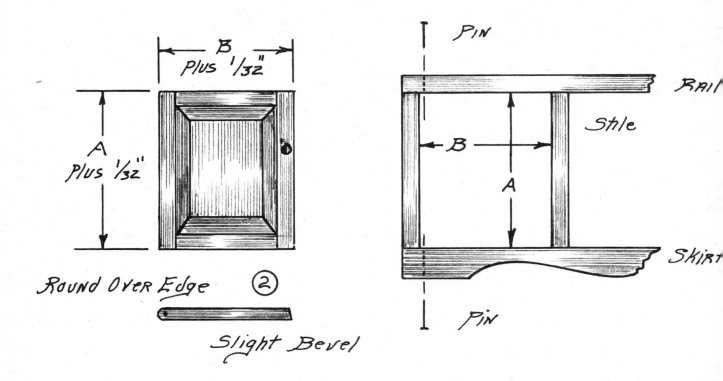

B
Plus 1/32"

A
Plus 1/32"

Round Over Edge

② *Slight Bevel*

Pin

Rail

Stile

B

A

Skirt

Pin

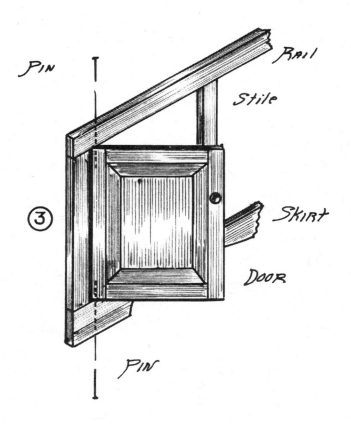

Pin

Rail

Stile

③

Skirt

Door

Pin

Fig. 1–20. Pin-hinged doors

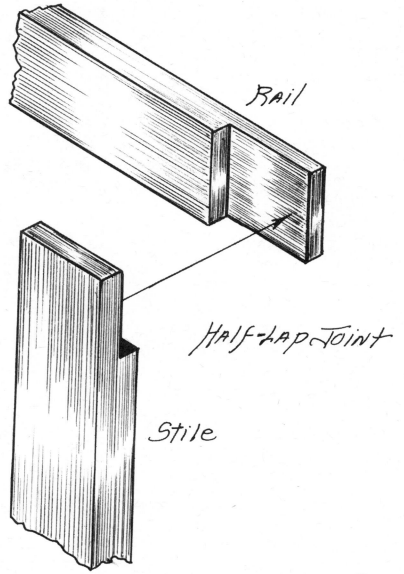

Rail

Half-lap Joint

Stile

Fig. 1–21. Half-lap joint construction

often prove to be too large or the wrong design, is the concept of vertical top and bottom pins which act as pivot points. In order to employ a pin hinge concept, prior planning must take place.

1. Measure the opening. Make the door according to the pattern instructions and slightly larger than the space it will cover (fig. 1–20). Fit the door to the opening by sanding it.

2. Make a slight bevel on the inside door edge that will receive the hinge pins. This will prevent sharp corners from interfering with the swing action of the door.

3. Insert the door into the opening and push bank or straight pins through the rail at the top and the skirt board at the bottom so that the pin point plus at least $1/4$ inch of shank projects into the door. This pin *must* be placed very near the extreme edge of the door for proper operation. The top and bottom pins must also be in as straight a line as possible.

Operate the door very carefully the first

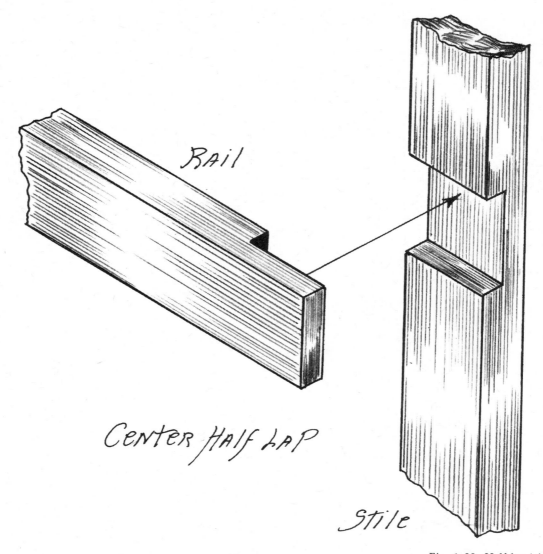

RAIL

CENTER HALF LAP

Stile

Fig. 1–22. Half-lap joint construction

time. If the pin alignment is slightly off, the initial operation will complete any required adjustment.

Half-lap Cabinet Doors

Cabinet doors, mirror frames, panels, or some built-in furnishings require door frames made with half-lap (ship-lap) joints. When many such frames must be made and precise uniformity is desirable, the stiles and rails can be made in large blocks and then cut or sliced into the desired widths.

A half-lap joint is one where half the stock thickness is removed from each piece of mate-rial to be joined together. When the two pieces of stock are glued or otherwise fastened to-gether, the two half thicknesses will make up the "whole" thickness again. The half-lap or ship-lap joint affords a wide area for fastening and is much stronger and durable than a butt joint.

The half-lap joint can be made on the end of the stock as shown in figure 1–22 or it can be made in the center of a stile as shown in figure 1–23.

1. Lay out the shape on a piece of precut selected stock (fig. 1–23). The markings should be for the desired length (A) of either the rail or stile. Cut the half-laps (B) with a table saw,

backsaw, or file. Slice the stock into required widths (C).

2. When all the rails and stiles are cut to size, make the door frames by gluing the members together.

Raised-panel Doors or Wainscoting

Decoration can be found everywhere in Victorian-style homes, including on the doors. To construct a raised-panel door or wainscoting panel, add stiles, rails, and panels to a solid backing.

1. Cut the backing stock to the desired size. On another piece of stock, lay out the stiles (A), rails (B), and panel (C) in the desired shape and size. The combined thicknesses of the backing and stiles, rails, and panel should not exceed 1/8 inch. Cut out the stiles and rails. The half-round shape shown in figure 1–24 can be made with a round or half-round file.

2. Glue the stiles (A) and rails (B) to the backing. Cut the raised panel (C) to shape and finish sand. Glue it to the backing between the rails (B) and stiles (A).

Note: The stiles and rails can be allowed to extend over the edges of the backing thereby making a rabbet-type offset cabinet door if desired.

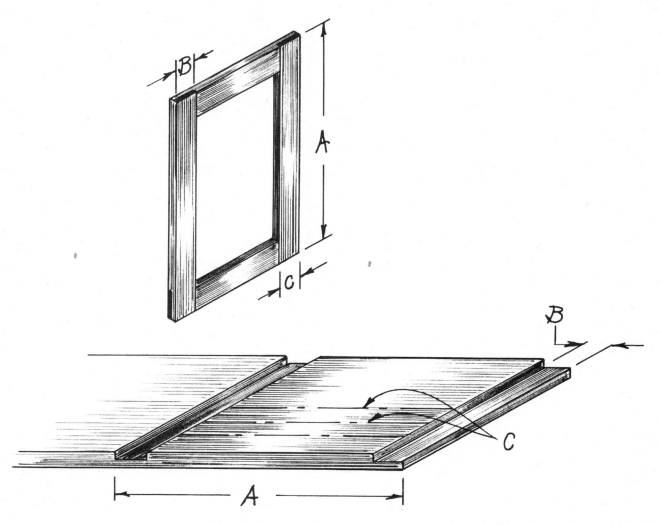

Fig. 1–23. Half-lap cabinet door construction

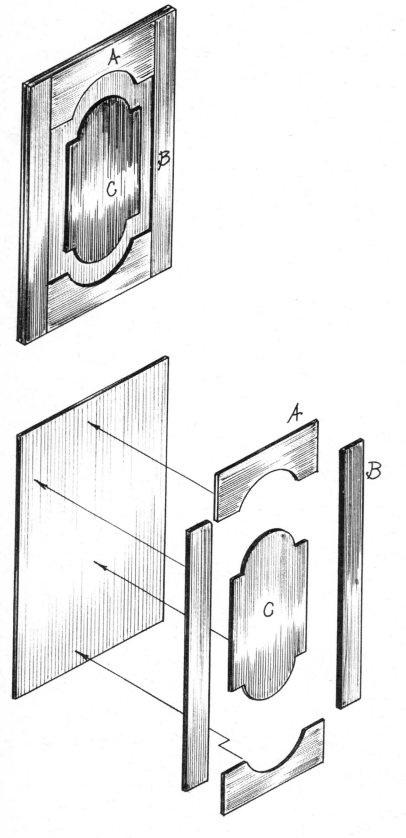

Fig. 1–24. Raised-panel doors or wainscoting

CHAIRS
Contour-style Chair Seat

The contour chair seat has a predesigned body shape cut into or hollowed out of the stock.

1. Transfer the pattern to the selected seat stock (fig. 1–25). Cut the seat stock larger than needed so it can be nailed to the workbench. This will keep it still while you are working on it.

2. With a gouge chisel, ball rasp, or corebox router bit cut the seat to the desired shape. The ball rasp bit fits into an ordinary drill, and the corebox bit will fit a normal electric router.

3. Sand to the final shape and design. Cut the seat free from the holding block and finish the exterior design. Mark and drill the required seat spoke mortise holes.

Plank-style Chair Seats

A common Early American and Pennsylvania Dutch style chair seat is the plank design. This chair seat employs a body contour design that is more pronounced than the molded seat.

1. Transfer the design to the selected stock. It is recommended that this seat block be larger than needed, so that the stock can be secured in a clamp or vise.

2. Rough cut the proposed design with a band, jig, or saber saw. With half-round, round, or flat file finish the proposed contour.

3. Sand the final shape and cut the seat free from the holding block. Complete the exterior design and drill in any required spoke mortise holes.

Rush Chair Seat

Rush has been used for chair seats from colonial times to the present. String or twine is used for miniature chairs to resemble the rush. Waxing the string or twine before rushing will stiffen the material making it hold its shape better. The coating will also prevent reaction to atmospheric conditions.

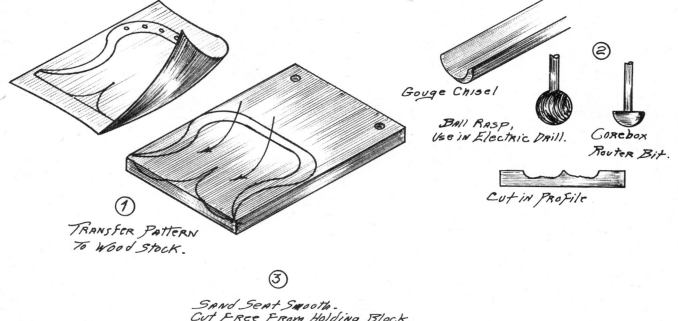

① TRANSFER PATTERN To Wood Stock.

Gouge Chisel

BALL RASP, Use in Electric Drill.

② Corebox Router Bit.

Cut in Profile

③ SAND SEAT SMOOTH. Cut FREE FROM Holding Block. FINISH EXTERIOR DESIGN. DRIll Mortise Holes.

Fig. 1–25. Molded chair seat

The average miniature-size chair seat will require approximately 25 feet of string or twine depending on the thickness of the material chosen. If in doubt, it is better to have an excess of material as knots are to be avoided if possible.

1. Note the numbering of the chair legs and lettering of the chair rails in figure 1–27. Follow the direction arrows. Note that each operation is exactly the same, only the direction changes at the different leg positions. Each time the twine will come from under the seat rail, make a right-angle turn, go up and over the previous turn, and continue under and then over the next rail in turn. Keep the twine rows even and matched.

2. The detail in figure 1–27 shows the basic procedure. Secure the twine to the inside of a seat rail and string it over rail A. Wrap it around the rail to exit under the bottom. Proceed to cross the twine over the first wrap and then over rear chair rail D. Continue the material around to exit under rail D and proceed to the front rail B. Continue to repeat the steps.

FURNITURE LEGS

Most Victorian furnishings made great use of highly decorative legs, the cabriole being one of the most popular.

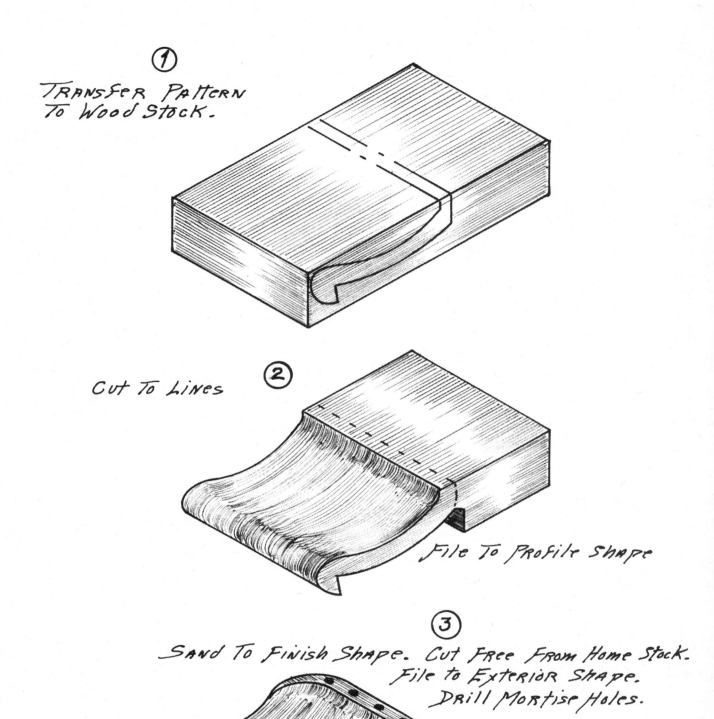

① TRANSFER PATTERN TO WOOD STOCK.

② Cut To Lines

File To Profile Shape

③ Sand To Finish Shape. Cut Free From Home Stock.
File to Exterior Shape.
Drill Mortise Holes.

Fig. 1–26. Plank-style chair seat

44

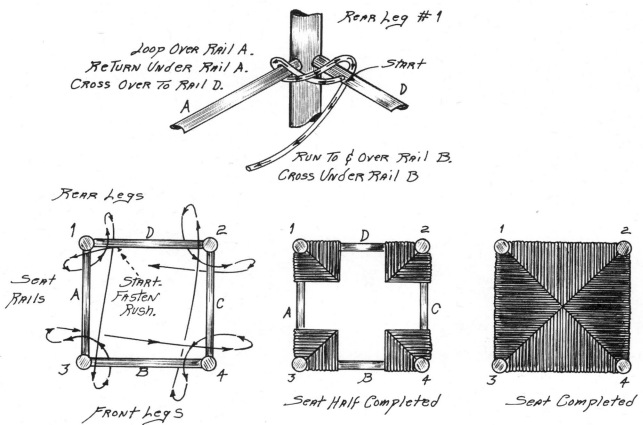

Fig. 1–27. Rush chair seats

Victorian Furniture Legs

1. One of the best methods of making decorative legs is to lay out the proposed design on the edge of a selected board. Most often a 3/4-inch-thick board will be more than adequate. The stock should be wide enough to allow for slicing into the number of legs desired, plus an extra in case of an accident. Such a method insures perfectly matched leg sets (fig. 1–28).

2. Rough cut the design with a scroll, jig, or band saw, allowing excess stock for finishing. With half-round files (A), file the final shape on the wood block.

3. Wrap sandpaper (B) around half-round files (A), and sand the legs into final shape. Use several grits to achieve the desired finish. Slice the block width into the number of legs de-

sired, and sand the saw cuts smooth. Carefully cut the legs from the board (D).

Scroll or Scallop Legs

Victorian furniture design often employed the scroll-type table leg. These legs offered the effect of decorative turnings yet were made on a band or jig saw.

1. Lay out the proposed leg shape on selected stock (fig. 1–29). The width of the stock (A) should allow ample material for slicing into the number of legs required; most period tables have three or four legs. Remember to allow for an extra leg, just in case.

2. Drill holes (B) wherever the design calls for sanding with a compatible-sized round. Rough cut the design with a band, jig, or scroll saw.

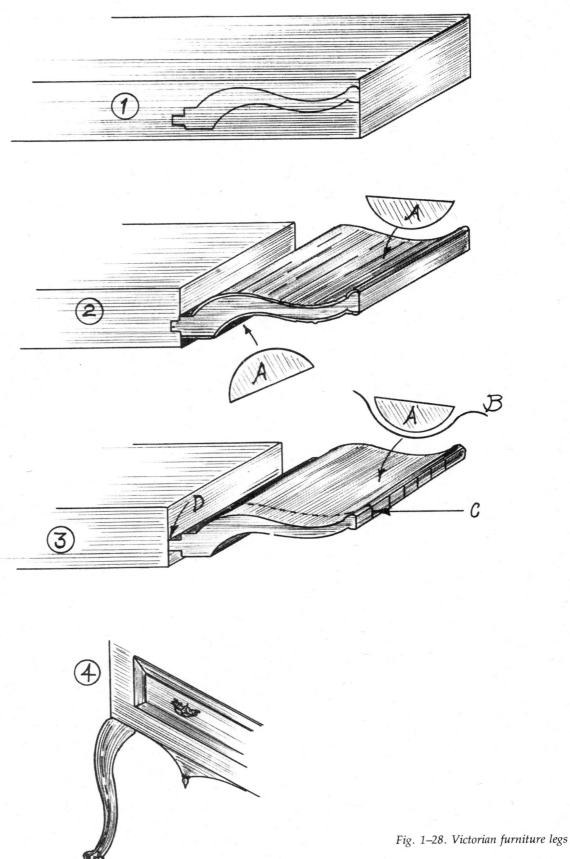

Fig. 1–28. Victorian furniture legs

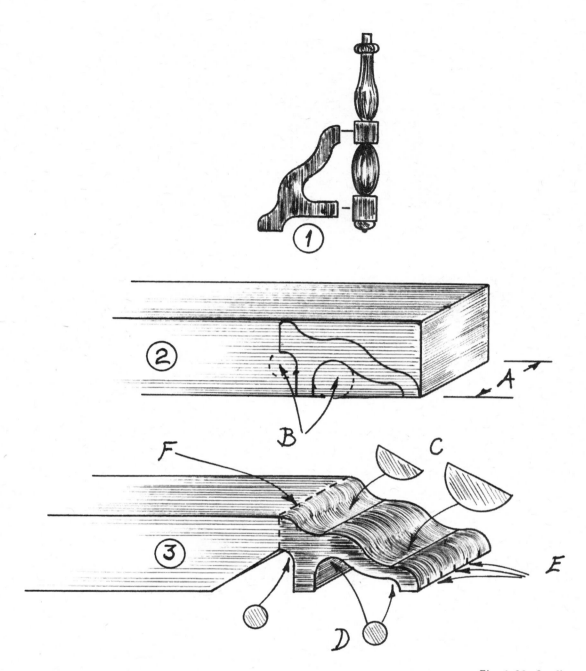

Fig. 1–29. Scroll or scallop legs

3. With half-round files (C), finish the exterior curves. Use round (rat-tail) files (D) to smooth and finish interior rounds. Finish sand the leg shapes with sandpaper wrapped around the various files. Slice into the number of legs desired (E). Cut the legs free from the home stock (F).

Small Molded Chest Legs

The Victorian washstands, dressers, and other cabinets often had small molded legs. The following were designed for several pieces in this book.

1. Lay out the proposed cove design on small blocks of selected stock. With a round file

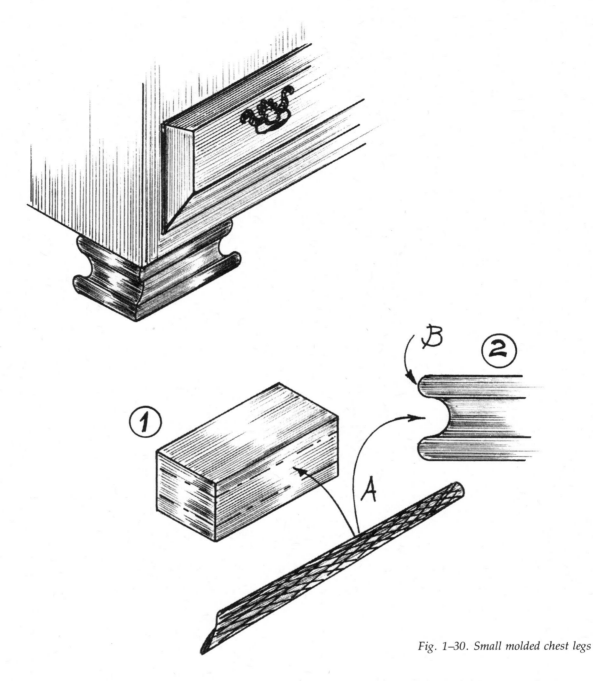

Fig. 1–30. Small molded chest legs

(A), cut the cove relief molding (fig. 1–30) on all surfaces.

2. Round off the top and bottom beads with sandpaper and cut to the desired length. Cut the cove face into the end cuts and finish sand.

FURNITURE CROWNS
Bonnet Top

In addition to elaborate legs, Victorian fur-nishings often had decorative crowns, or tops. Curved bonnet tops could be found on many different household items.

1. Lay out the proposed bonnet-top design on the edge of selected stock. The wood should be wide enough (A) to accommodate the depth of the item of furniture the finished bonnet top will attach to (fig. 1–31). Most often 3/4-inch stock will suffice. However, thicker stock can be obtained by gluing two or more pieces to-

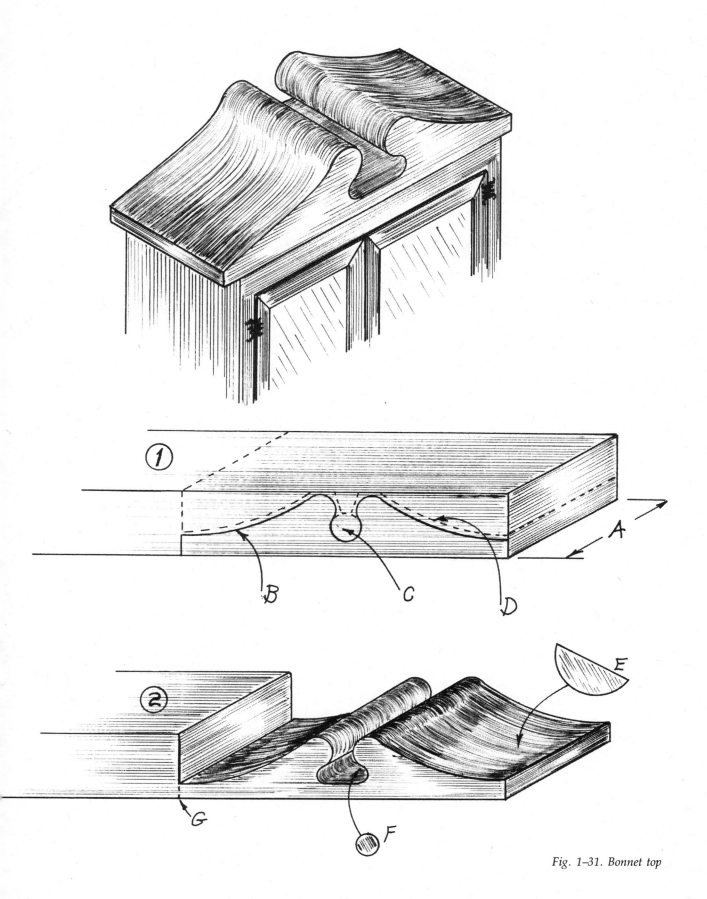

Fig. 1–31. Bonnet top

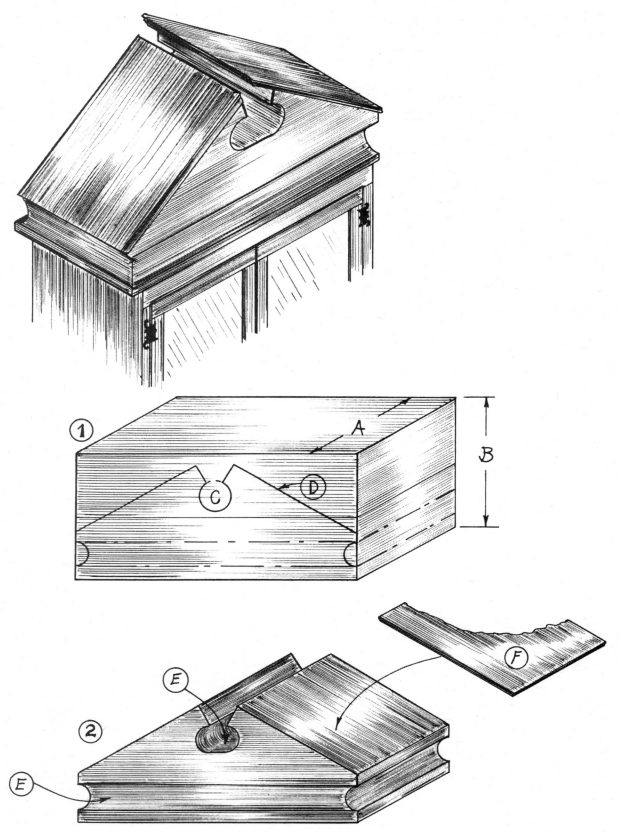

Fig. 1–32. Broken pediment top

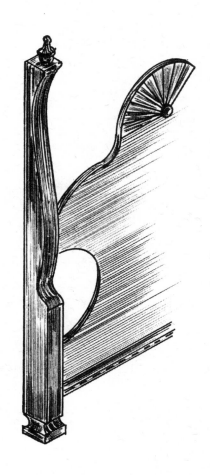

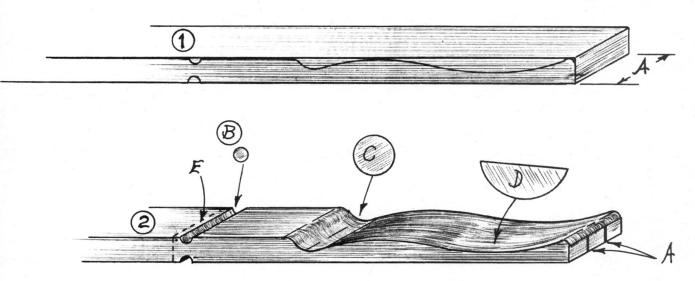

Fig. 1–33. Nonturned scalloped bedpost

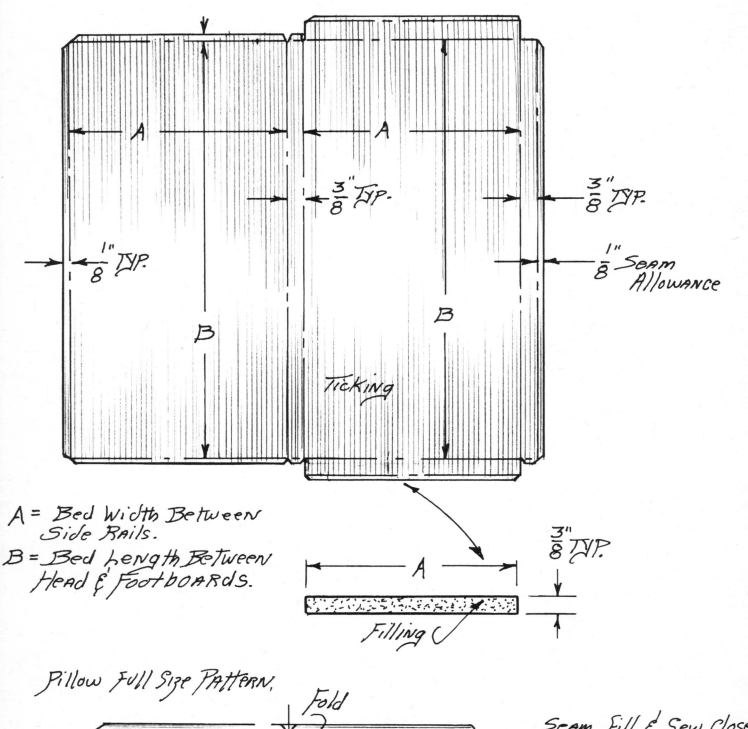

$\dfrac{3}{8}"$ TYP.

$\dfrac{3}{8}"$ TYP.

$\dfrac{1}{8}"$ TYP.

$\dfrac{1}{8}"$ Seam Allowance

Ticking

A = Bed Width Between Side Rails.
B = Bed Length Between Head & Footboards.

A

$\dfrac{3}{8}"$ TYP.

Filling

Pillow Full Size Pattern.

Fold

Seam, Fill, & Sew Close.

$\dfrac{1}{8}"$ Seam Allowance Typical

Fig. 1–34. Bed mattress and pillow

52

gether. Drill a hole (C) in the center. Rough cut the shape (D) with a band, jig, or saber saw.

2. With half-round files (E), file the scroll to the finished shape. The predrilled hole can be elongated with round files (F). Sand the bonnet design smooth and cut free from the parent stock (G).

Broken Pediment Top

The companion of the bonnet top is the broken pediment top which was adopted from the Early American period. This type of crown often requires a thicker width than the bonnet top. If more width is needed, glue two or more blocks together. Small, thin ($1/16$-inch) roof boards are applied to the roof angle and allowed to overhang.

1. Lay out the design on the selected stock. Note that A should be the necessary width, and B should be slightly more than the desired height. Drill a hole (C) through the center point. Rough cut the shape (D) using a band, jig, or saber saw (fig. 1–32).

2. With a round file, cut the cove relief molding on the lower section and elongate the center hole into an oval (E). Cut the roof pieces (F) and glue them to the slopes allowing them to overhang slightly.

NONTURNED SCALLOPED BEDPOSTS

Lathe-turned bedposts have been used in all furnishing periods. Victorian furniture also employed large scroll-type posts that were cut with a band saw, but not turned. Very often the foot posts were smaller versions of the main head posts, incorporating the same basic design.

1. Cut the selected stock to the necessary thickness. The stock width (A) should be enough for the desired number of posts plus an extra. Most often a $1/4$-inch or $3/8$-inch size will be sufficient. Lay out the design on the edge of the wood stock (fig. 1–33).

2. Rough cut the design with a band, jig, or saber saw. A small rat-tail file (B) will form the foot cove reliefs. With a round file (C), round out any small curves. With half-round files (D), finish form the larger curves. Slice the form into the desired widths for the bed posts. Cut from the parent stock (E).

BED MATTRESS AND PILLOWS

Use these instructions to make either mattresses or pillows.

Materials

Mattress or pillow cover: soft linen or polyester. Filler: cotton batting, rubber or polyester fiber fill.

Construction

1. Cut the fabric to the suggested size (fig. 1–34). Note hem allowance on all sides. With a medium-heat iron, press the folds. Sew the cover together on three of the four sides. Trim off excess hem material and turn the cover inside out.

2. Fill the cover with the selected material. Do not overstuff. Sew the remaining hem with invisible stiches and trim any excess hem fabric.

3. Install the mattress on the bed slats. A piece of heavy gauge cardboard laid over the bed slats will act as a box spring and help hold the mattress in shape.

SECTION TWO

Early American Furnishings

There is often not a clear, precise line between furnishing periods. Every period shows the influences of the periods before it and they seem to flow together with no exact beginning and no exact ending.

The Colonial period is often thought of as that time up to the Revolutionary War when the Early American era is considered to have begun. These two periods of furniture have lost the clear lines of departure and seem to blend into a general singleness. For the purpose of this book, therefore, they are referred to as one period, Early American.

Perhaps two of the main influences guiding period furniture were the geographic and economic factors concerning origin. These conditions dictated the type of material used and the quality of workmanship in furniture construction; it was the difference between homemade and artisan-made goods. Evidence of this is found in the contrast between the simple, functional furnishings produced by local artisans in the north and the decorative, sophisticated furnishings found in the south where the economy was much more solid.

The Early American miniature reproductions in this section have been developed from many furnishing pieces located in historical settlements such as Williamsburg, Sturbridge, Shelburne, or Strawberry Bank. They represent a middle ground between the elaborate European imports (or copies) of the southern colonies and the rustic, home-spun furnishings of the north.

As such, they really do transcend any separation line between Colonial and Early American designation. These miniatures are suitable for use in scale-sized houses of the early seventeenth to the early eighteenth century.

While partly designed for the Richardson House, Paul Revere style or colonial ranch house, like those featured in *Building Masterpiece Miniatures* (Stackpole, 1980), these miniature furnishings will enhance a miniature house or room setting from any similar period.

4

Bedroom Group

The following miniature bedroom furnishings were designed for a wide range of Early American settings. The particular designs are compatible to any geographic region for an eighteenth century or contemporary Colonial-style house or room.

They represent an achievement of craftsmanship and display the technical advancement in the woodworking field brought about by the growth and stability of established colonies. Because most miniature houses have several bedrooms and in order to offer a selection, several possible bed styles are presented. The other bedroom furnishings can be duplicated for different sleeping areas using different species of wood and finishing colors to achieve diversity.

FOUR-POST CANOPY BED

The bed canopy was designed for comfort and warmth. Often the only central heat in Early American homes was the fireplace. The bed canopy and side curtains helped hold body heat within the sleeping area. Coupled with deep goose down mattress and coverlets, the only problem encountered by the settlers was who would leave this warm haven and light the fireplace for another day.

Material

Cherry, maple, birch, pine, or basswood. Cherry is preferred.

Fig. 2–1. Four post bed with arch canopy

Material List

	Part	Number	Size
A	Posts	4	$5/16'' \times 5/16'' \times 6^{1}/2''$
B	Headboard	1	$1^{3}/4'' \times 4^{3}/4'' \times 3/16''$
C	Footboard	1	$4^{1}/2'' \times 1/2'' \times 3/16''$
D	Side Rails	2	$1/2'' \times 6'' \times 3/16''$

Construction

1. Lay out and cut posts (A) to basic shape and size. Mount on a lathe and turn posts to shape suggested. Make four matching bedposts.

2. Lay out and cut headboard (B) to suggested shape and size. Note the tenon areas shown in figure 2–2. Mark two posts (A) to receive the tenons on the headboard (B). Glue the headboard tenon into the bedposts.

3. Lay out and cut footboard (C) and side rail (D). Note the rabbet cut on the side rail. Drill a $1/8$-inch-diameter hole into both ends of the footboard and the side rail. Glue a small piece of $1/8$-inch-diameter dowel into each hole allowing $3/16$-inch projections to act as tenons. Line the footboard up to the two remaining bedposts (A). The bottom of the footboard (C) should be even with the bottom of the headboard (B). Drill a $1/8$-inch-diameter mortise holes into the bedposts (A). Glue the footboard (C) between the bedposts (A). Line up the side rails (D) between the headboard and footboard assemblies with the rabbet cut toward the bed interior. Glue the side rails (D) to the bedposts (A).

4. Cut several $1/8$-by-$3/16$-inch slats from scrap wood. Lay these slats into the rabbets on the side rails (D). These slats will support the mattress or spring.

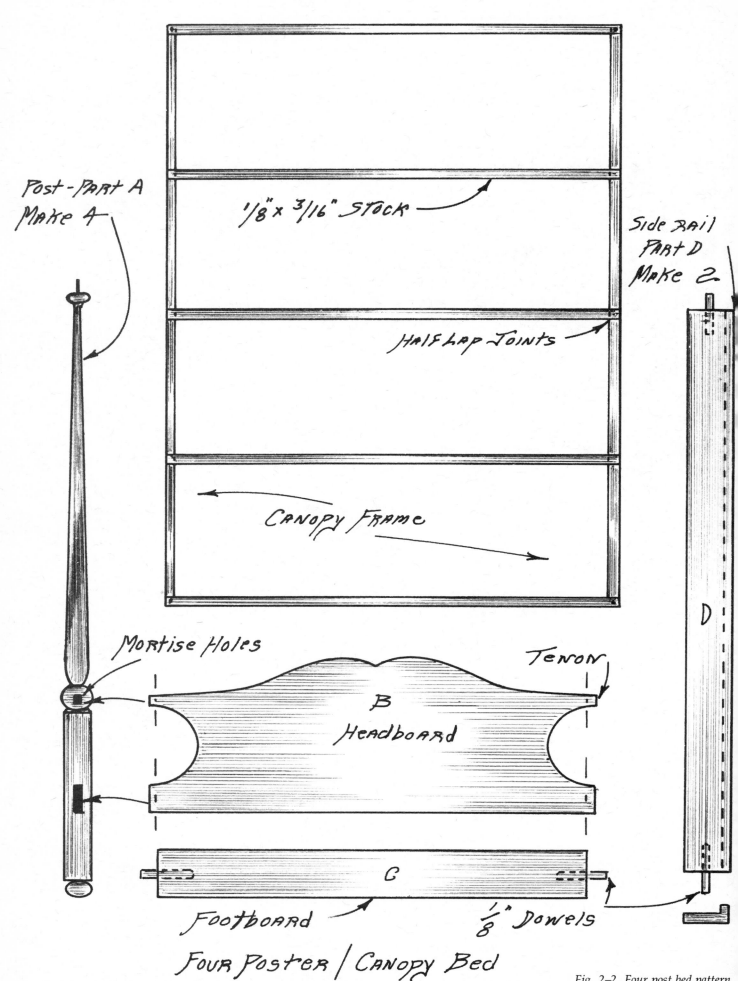

Post - Part A
Make 4

1/8" x 3/16" STOCK

Side Rail
Part D
Make 2

Half Lap Joints

Canopy Frame

Mortise Holes

Tenon

B
Headboard

D

C

Footboard

1/8" Dowels

Four Poster / Canopy Bed

Fig. 2–2. Four post bed pattern

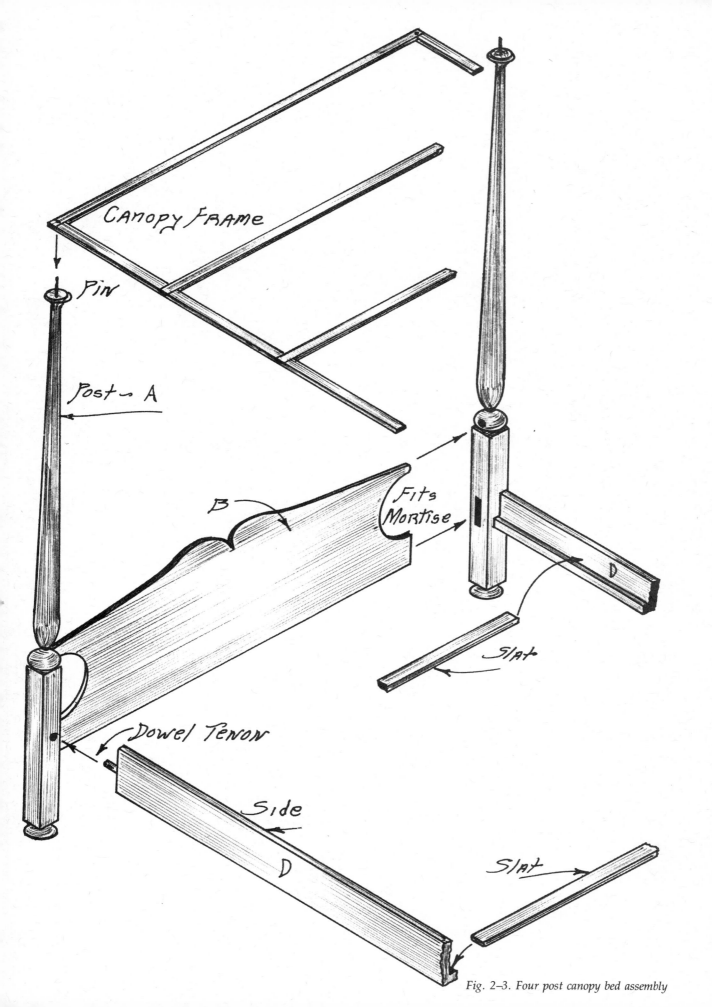

CANOPY FRAME

Pin

Post — A

B

Fits Mortise

D

Slat

Dowel Tenon

Side

D

Slat

Fig. 2–3. Four post canopy bed assembly

Fig. 2–4. Sheraton-style tester bed pattern

5. Canopy frame. Lay the frame pattern out on paper. Place scrap wood under this pattern. Cut 1/8-by-3/16-inch stock to the suggested size. Pin the length pieces to the paper pattern. With a file, cut the required half-lap joints on the ends and where each crosspiece enters. Glue the crosspieces as suggested in figure 2–2. When the glue has dried, remove the frame and sand carefully. Push a pin into the top of each bedpost (A) allowing 1/4-inch extensions. Cut off the pin head. Drill matching holes into the corners of the canopy frame. The finished frame will slide on over the pins.

Finish

Sand the entire reproduction smooth removing any trace of glue. Stain if desired, and cover with several coats of lacquer or similar finish. Finish with paste wax.

SHERATON-STYLE TESTER BED

The tester (covered) bed was used as an open four-post bed in fair weather and with a canopy cover when the air turned cold. The following miniature can be made as a single bed as shown in the pattern, or the headboards and footboards can be lengthened to the sizes for a double bed.

Material

Cherry, maple, mahogany, pine, or basswood. Cherry is preferred.

Material List

	Part	Number	Size
A	Posts	4	$1/4''$ x $1/4''$ x $6''$
B	Headboard	1	$3^3/8''$ x $2''$ x $1/8''$
C	Blanket Roll	1	$3^1/2''$ x $1/4''$ dia. dowel
D	Footboard	1	$3^3/8''$ x $3/4''$ x $1/8''$
E	Side Rail	2	$6^1/2''$ x $1/2''$ x $3/16''$
F	Finial	5	$1/8''$ dia. x $1/4''$

CANOPY

	Part	Number	Size
G	Ends	2	$1/8''$ x $1/8''$ x $3^1/2''$
H	Sides	2	$1/8''$ x $1/8''$ x $6^3/8''$
I	Slats	3	$1/8''$ x $1/16''$ x $3^1/2''$

CANOPY FRAME

Part	Number	Size
Sides	2	$1/8''$ x $3/16''$ x $6^3/8''$
Ends	5	$1/8''$ x $3/16''$ x $4^3/4''$

Construction

1. Lay out, cut, and lathe-turn bedposts (A) and blanket roll (C) to shape and size. Lay out and cut headboard (B) and footboard (D) to suggested shape and size. Note the tenons on the headboard. Match the tenons on the headboard (B) to two bedposts (A). Mark and cut the mortise holes in the bedposts (A). Glue the headboard (B) between the bedposts (A).

2. Drill a $1/8$-inch-diameter hole into the ends of the footboard (D). Glue $1/8$-inch-diameter dowels into these holes allowing $1/4$-inch-long tenon projections. Line up the footboard (D) between the other two bedposts (A). Mark and drill mortise holes in the bedposts (A) in order to receive the blanket roll (C). Glue the blanket roll and footboard between the bedposts.

3. Make the side rails (E) to suggested shape and size. Drill a $1/8$-inch-diameter hole into the ends of the side rails allowing $1/4$-inch-long tenon extensions. Line up and mark the side rail tenons on the bedposts (A). Drill a $1/8$-inch-diameter hole into each bedpost. Glue the side rails (E) to the bedposts (A). Cut several slats from $1/16$-by-$3/32$-inch scrap stock. Glue the bed slats into the rabbets on the side rails.

4. Canopy. Cut the stock to size. Make a male-female jig block in the profile shape (arched) of the canopy frame. Boil or steam the two long canopy pieces (H) for a few moments and place them between the jig members. Tighten the members together. Allow the frame stock to dry in the jig for 24 hours.

Make half-lap joints on the ends and where the crosspieces intersect.

Glue the long, curved pieces (H) and crosspieces (G) together. After the glue has dried, sand the canopy very carefully. Push a pin into the top of each bedpost (A), allowing $3/8$-inch projections. Drill a $1/32$-inch-diameter hole into the ends of the canopy frame. Place the finished frame over the pins. Make five finials (F) on a lathe or drill. Drill a $1/32$-inch-diameter hole into the bottoms of each finial. Place one finial over each pin. Glue the last finial in the center of the headboard (B).

Finish

Sand the entire reproduction smooth removing any trace of glue. Stain if desired. Cover with several coats of lacquer or similar finish. Finish with a coat of paste wax.

CANOPY

There are hundreds of different types and styles of bed canopies. Some are more decorative than functional and every type of material can be used. In the past the canopy often had side curtains that could be tied open in warm weather or drawn shut for sleeping in cold weather. The following canopy was designed for appearance and is a light covering.

Materials

Wide lace, soft linen (handkerchief), nylon,

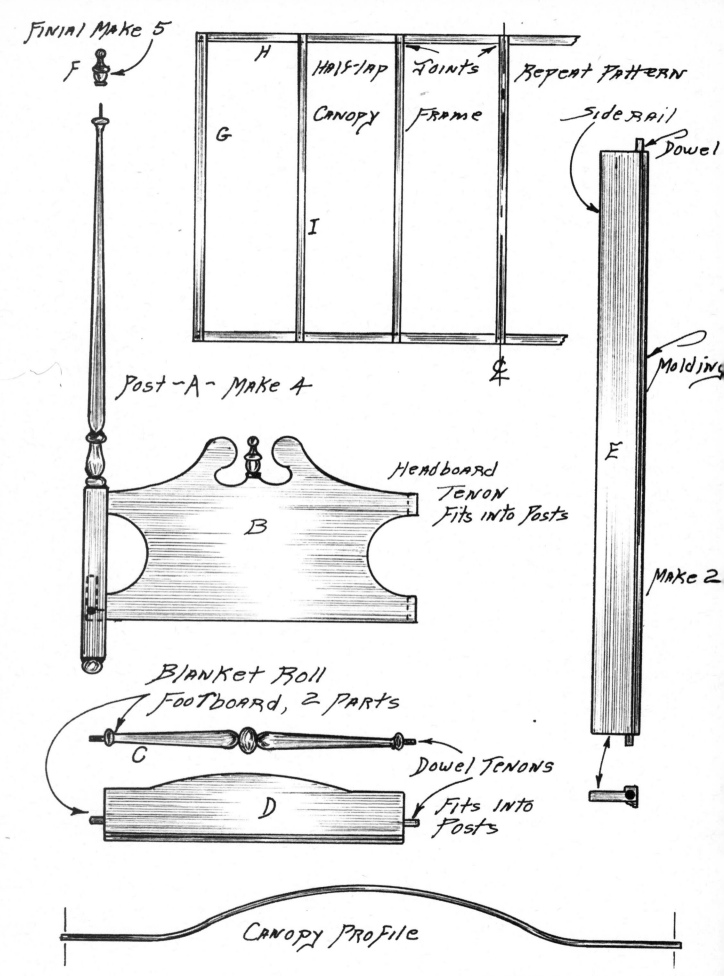

FINIAL MAKE 5

F

Post -A- Make 4

Half-lap   Joints   Repeat Pattern
Canopy   Frame

H

G

I

¢

Headboard
TENON
Fits into Posts

B

Side Rail

Dowel

Molding

E

Make 2

Blanket Roll
Footboard, 2 Parts

C

D

Dowel Tenons

Fits into
Posts

Canopy Profile

Fig. 2–5. Sheraton-style tester bed assembly

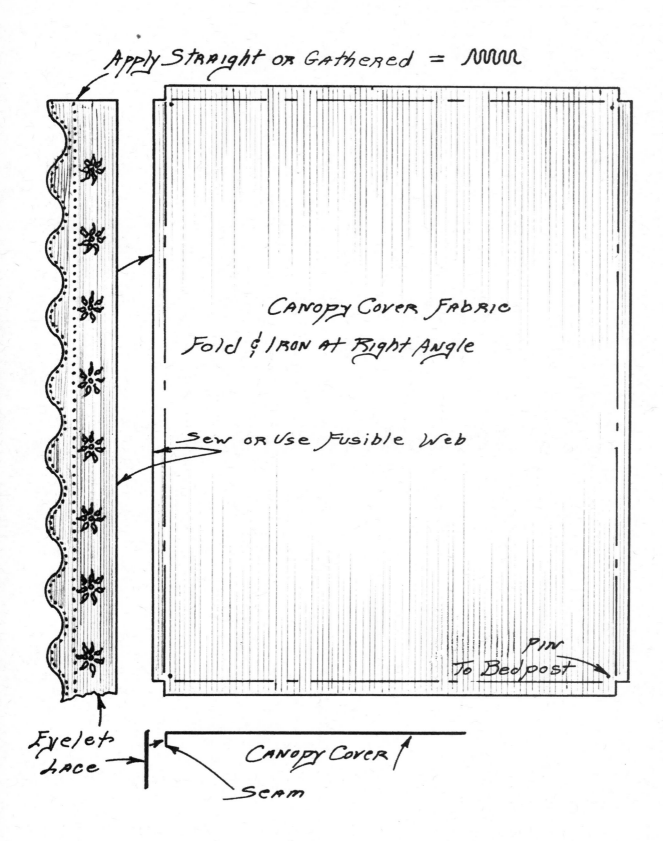

Apply Straight or Gathered = ⋀⋀⋀⋀

Canopy Cover Fabric

Fold & Iron At Right Angle

Sew or Use Fusible Web

Pin
To Bedpost

Eyelet Lace

Canopy Cover

Seam

Fig. 2–6. Canopy pattern

or polyester. The scalloped edge can be any type of eyelet lace.

Construction

1. Lay out the fabric to the pattern size (fig. 2–6). Note the hem allowance on all four sides. With a medium-hot iron, press the hem under.

2. The scalloped edging can be gathered or applied flat. With right sides together, stitch the edging to the canopy hem or attach them with a fusible webbing like Stitch Witchery. Remember to make right-angle corners so the canopy trim hangs properly. Re-press the canopy so that the hems fit neat and tight. Attach the canopy to the canopy frame over the bedpost pins.

BLANKET CHEST

Some experts say the blanket chest developed from the old sea chest, but in truth, Early American homes contained very little closet or storage space. In the warmer months, heavy blankets had to be put away in a protected place and the chest became the best answer.

Material

Cherry, maple, mahogany, basswood, or pine. Cherry is preferred.

Material List

	Part	Number	Size
A	Side	2	$1^3/8''$ x 3" x $1/8''$
B	Back	1	3" x 3" x $1/16''$
C	Shelf	3	$1^1/4''$ x $2^7/8''$ x $1/16''$
D	Skirt	1	$3^3/16''$ x $3/8''$ x $1/16''$
E	Front	1	$3^3/16''$ x $1^1/2''$ x $1/16''$
F	Drawer Back	2	$2^7/8''$ x $1/2''$ x $1/16''$
G	Drawer Side	4	$1^1/8''$ x $1/2''$ x $1/16''$
H	Drawer Bottom	2	$1^1/8''$ x $2^3/4''$ x $1/16''$
I	Drawer Front	2	$3^1/8''$ x $1/2''$ x $1/16''$
J	Top	1	$3^3/8''$ x $1^3/4''$ x $1/16''$

Construction

1. Lay out and cut the sides (A), back (B), and shelves (C) to the suggested shapes and sizes (fig. 2–7). Cut a $1/16$-by-$1/16$-inch rabbet on the sides (A). Glue the back (B) into the rabbets on the sides. Mark the shelf locations on the sides. Glue the shelves (C) between the sides (A) and the back (B).

2. Lay out and cut the skirt (D), front (E), and top (J) to the suggested size and shapes. Glue the skirt (D) to the sides (A) and the bottom shelf (C). Lay out and cut the sunburst design on the front (E) with a mat or hobby knife. (Medallions can be purchased and glued on if preferred.) Glue the front (E) to the sides (A).

3. Make the two hinge blocks (K). Drill a $1/16$-inch hole where marked on figure 2–7. Line up the hinges to each side (A) as shown in the detail in figure 2–8 and drill the required holes. Lay top (J) on top of the chest assembly and mark where the hinges will fit. Allow a slight clearance between the hinges and the sides. Glue the hinges (K) to the top (J). When the glue has dried, install the top to the sides (A) with a section of $1/16$-inch dowel pin.

4. Lay out and cut the drawer back (F), side (G), bottom (H), and front (I) to the suggested sizes and shapes. Make two drawer units to fit the available openings. Sand fit the drawers in place.

Finish

The blanket chest can be stained or painted. Green, blue, light red, or yellow paints are often found on full-size antiques. Cover with several coats of lacquer or similar finish.

WASHSTAND OR COMMODE

Early American houses did not have indoor plumbing. The only furnishing that came close was the bedroom washstand or commode. A pitcher and bowl set and fresh linens were

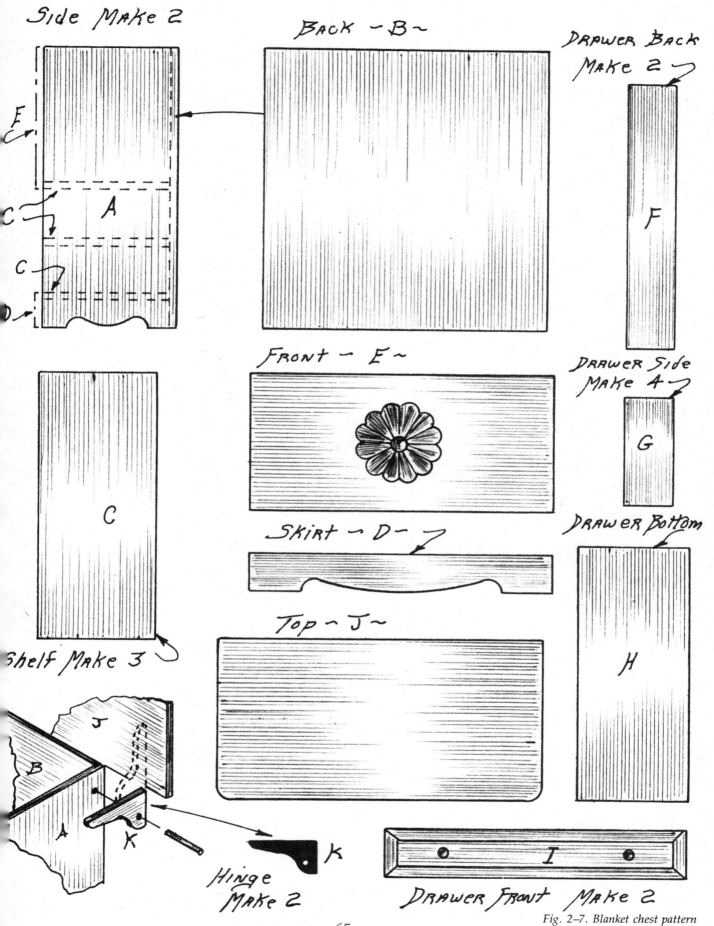

Side Make 2

BACK ~B~

DRAWER BACK
Make 2

F

E

C

C

D

A

Front ~E~

DRAWER SIDE
Make 4

G

C

Skirt ~D~

DRAWER Bottom

H

Shelf Make 3

Top ~J~

J

B

A

K

Hinge
Make 2

K

I

DRAWER FRONT Make 2

65

Fig. 2-7. Blanket chest pattern

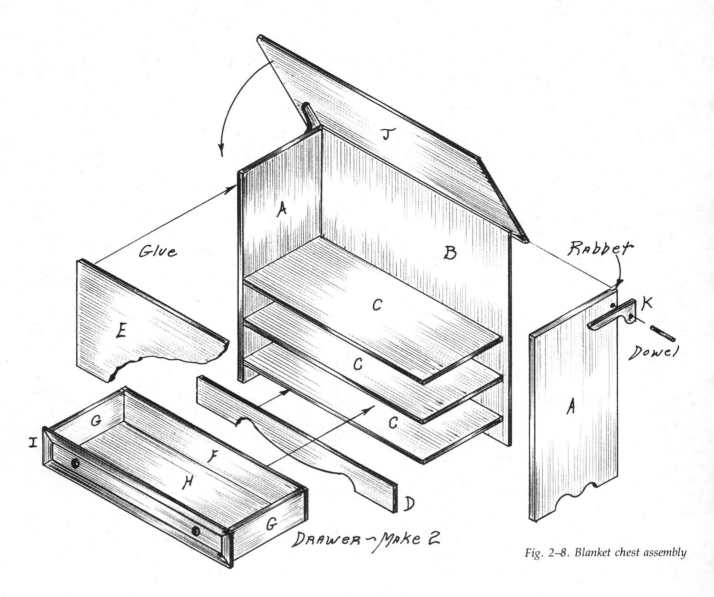

Fig. 2–8. Blanket chest assembly

always on hand while other items were stored in the drawer. This reproduction has a top decorative skirt and a towel bar on each end.

Material

Cherry, maple, mahogany, basswood, or pine. Cherry is preferred.

Material List

	Part	Number	Size
A	Side	2	$1^{3}/_{8}$" x $2^{1}/_{2}$" x $1/_{8}$"
B	Back	1	$2^{1}/_{4}$" x $2^{1}/_{2}$" x $1/_{16}$"
C	Bottom Shelf	1	$2^{1}/_{8}$" x $1^{1}/_{4}$" x $1/_{16}$"
D	Skirt	1	$2^{3}/_{8}$" x $3/_{8}$" x $1/_{16}$"
E	Top Shelf	1	$2^{1}/_{2}$" x $1^{1}/_{2}$" x $1/_{16}$"
F	Top	1	$3^{1}/_{8}$" x $1^{3}/_{4}$" x $1/_{16}$"
G	Bar	2	$1^{1}/_{4}$" x $1/_{8}$" dia. dowel
H	Door	2	$1^{1}/_{4}$" x $1^{3}/_{8}$" x $1/_{16}$"
I	Drawer Front	1	$2^{1}/_{2}$" x $1/_{2}$" x $1/_{16}$"
J	Drawer Side	2	$1^{1}/_{8}$" x $1/_{2}$" x $1/_{16}$"
K	Drawer Back	1	2" x $1/_{2}$" x $1/_{16}$"
L	Drawer Bottom	1	$2^{1}/_{16}$" x $1^{1}/_{8}$" x $1/_{16}$"
M	Top Skirt	1	$2^{3}/_{16}$" x $1/_{4}$" x $1/_{16}$"
N	Side Skirt	2	1" x $1/_{4}$" x $1/_{16}$"

Construction

1. Lay out and cut the side (A), back (B), lower shelf (C), and divider (E) to the sizes and

Fig. 2–9. Washstand or commode

shapes suggested (fig. 2–9). Note that the divider (E) extends beyond the edges of the sides (A). Cut a ¹/₁₆-by-¹/₁₆-inch rabbet on the rear edges of the sides. Glue the back (B) into these rabbets. Glue the lower shelf (C) between the sides (A). Glue the divider (E) to the back (B) and between the sides.

Lay out and cut the skirt (D) to shape and size suggested. Glue the skirt to the sides (A) and lower shelf (C). Lay out and cut the top (F). Cut the end notches for the towel bars. Make two towel bars (G) from ¹/₈-inch dowel. Glue the bars (G) into the notches on the top (F). Glue the top (F) to the sides (A) and back (B).

3. Cut the drawer front (I), sides (J), back (K), and bottom (L) to shapes and sizes suggested. This drawer unit is made to fit the opening between the upper shelf divider (E) and the top (F). Sand fit the drawer unit to fit the opening. Make two raised-panel doors, (H) (see "Construction Notes"). Sand fit the doors to the space between skirt (D) and divider (E). Hinge pin the doors to the openings. Attach scale-size pulls to the doors and drawers.

4. Lay out and cut the side (N) and top (M) skirts. Glue these skirts to the top (F).

Finish

Sand the entire reproduction smooth removing all traces of glue. Stain or paint if desired. Cover with several coats of lacquer or similar finish.

BLOCK FRONT CHEST OF DRAWERS

Most chests of drawers follow the same basic pattern, three or four stacked drawer units combined in a chestlike front. In order to achieve different styles, the drawer or front design is changed. This block front chest of drawers contains a series of rounds, projections, and recesses to produce a late Early American motif.

Material

Cherry, maple, mahogany, basswood, or pine. Cherry is preferred.

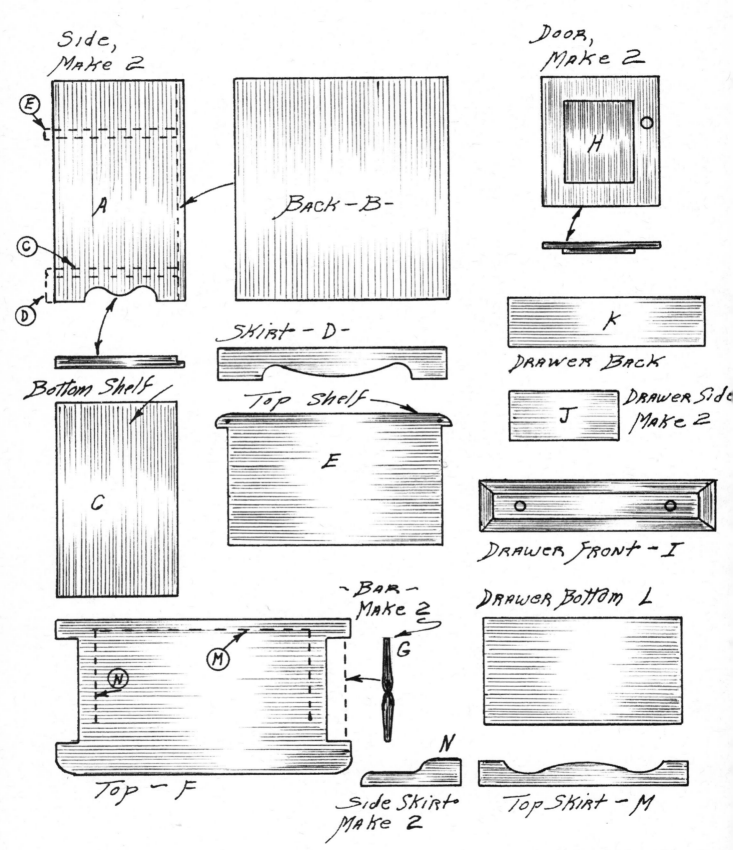

Side, Make 2

E

A

C

D

Back -B-

Bottom Shelf

C

Skirt -D-

Top Shelf

E

Top -F

M

N

Door, Make 2

H

K

DRAWER BACK

J DRAWER Side Make 2

DRAWER FRONT -I

DRAWER Bottom L

-Bar-
Make 2

G

N

Side Skirt
Make 2

Top Skirt -M

Fig. 2–10. Washstand or commode pattern

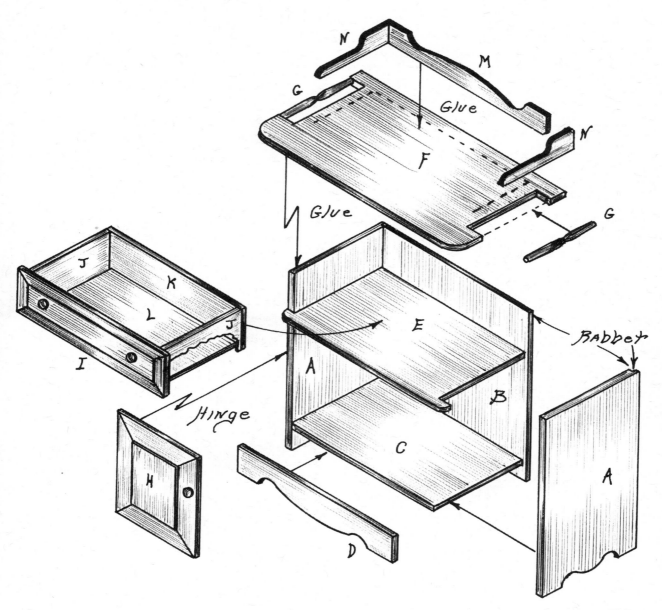

Fig. 2–11. Washstand or commode assembly

Material List

	Part	Number	Size
A	Side	2	$1^{1}/_{2}$" x $2^{3}/_{4}$" x $^{1}/_{8}$"
B	Back	1	3" x $2^{3}/_{4}$" x $^{1}/_{16}$"
C	Divider	4	$2^{7}/_{8}$" x $1^{5}/_{8}$" x $^{1}/_{16}$"
D	Front Skirt	1	$2^{7}/_{8}$" x $^{3}/_{8}$" x $^{1}/_{4}$"
E	Side Skirt	2	$1^{1}/_{2}$" x $^{3}/_{8}$" x $^{1}/_{16}$"
F	Small Drawer Side	2	$1^{1}/_{4}$" x $^{1}/_{2}$" x $^{1}/_{16}$"
G	Small Drawer Back	1	$2^{3}/_{16}$" x $^{1}/_{2}$" x $^{1}/_{16}$"
H	Drawer Bottom	4	$2^{13}/_{16}$" x $1^{3}/_{16}$" x $^{1}/_{16}$"
I	Large Drawer Side	6	$1^{1}/_{4}$" x $^{5}/_{8}$" x $^{1}/_{16}$"
J	Large Drawer Back	3	$2^{13}/_{16}$" x $^{5}/_{8}$" x $^{1}/_{16}$"
K	Small Drawer Front	1	$2^{15}/_{16}$" x $^{1}/_{2}$" x $^{1}/_{4}$"
L	Large Drawer Front	3	$2^{15}/_{16}$" x $^{5}/_{8}$" x $^{1}/_{4}$"
M	Top	1	$3^{1}/_{2}$" x $1^{7}/_{8}$" x $^{1}/_{16}$"

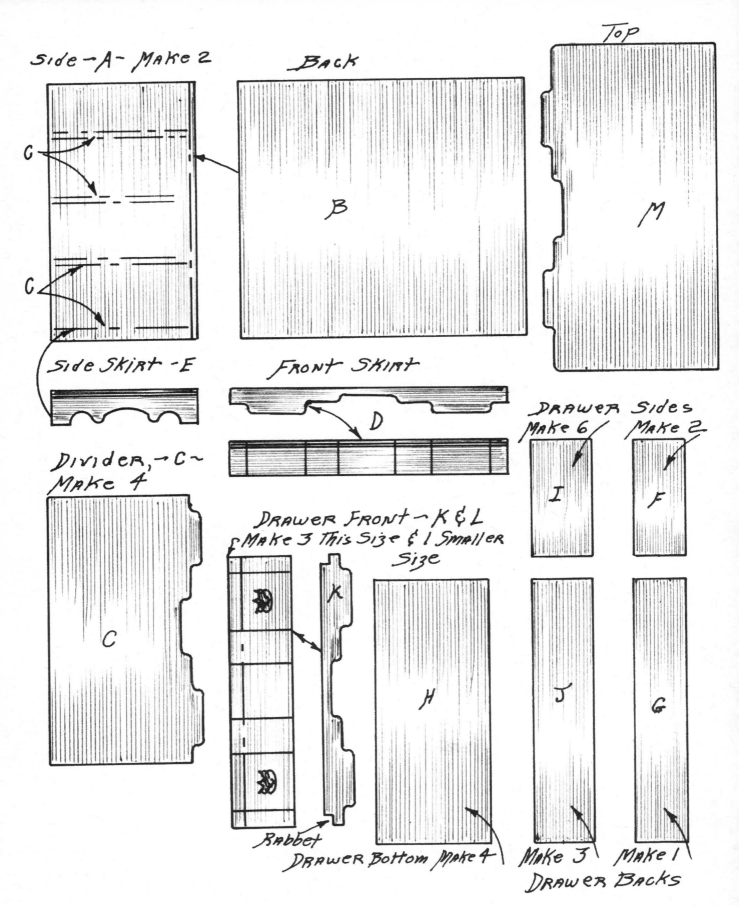

Side -A- Make 2

C

C

Back

B

Top

M

Side Skirt -E

Front Skirt

D

Divider, -C- Make 4

C

Drawer Front ~ K & L
Make 3 This Size & 1 Smaller
Size

K

Rabbet

Drawer Bottom Make 4

Drawer Sides
Make 6 / Make 2

I

F

H

J

Make 3

G

Make 1

Drawer Backs

Fig. 2–12. Block front chest of drawers pattern

70

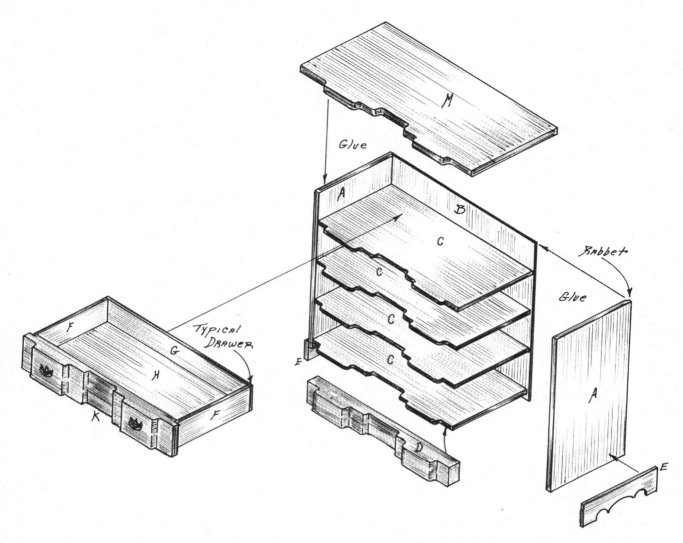

Fig. 2–13. Block front chest of drawers assembly

Construction

Note: The same basic design is used for the dividers, skirt, drawer front, and top.

1. Lay out and cut the sides (A), back (B), and dividers (C). Cut a $1/16$-by-$1/16$-inch rabbet on the back edges of the sides (A). Glue the back (B) into these rabbets. Glue the dividers (C) between the sides (A) and to the back (B).

2. Lay out and cut the front skirt (D), drawer front (K), and top (M) (see "Construction Notes" for suggested techniques). Glue the skirt (D) under the bottom divider. Glue the top (M) to the top of the sides (A) and back (B).

Cut a $1/8$-by-$1/16$-inch rabbet on the drawer fronts (K). Make four drawer units to fit the openings on the chest. Sand fit the drawers to each individual opening. Make the side skirts (E). Glue these skirts to the bottom of the sides.

Finish

Sand the entire reproduction smooth removing any trace of glue. Stain or paint if desired. Cover with several coats of lacquer or similar finish. Attach two drawer pulls (maple leaf design) to each drawer unit.

Fig. 2–14. Wall mirror

WALL MIRROR

A wall mirror hung over the chest of drawers. This reproduction is made from one piece stock.

Material

Use the same wood as for the chest of drawers. Bevel-edged, 1/32-inch mirror.

Material List

Part	Size
A	2¹/₈″ x 3¹/₄″ x ³/₃₂″

Construction

1. Lay out the mirror frame on a piece of ³/₃₂-inch thick stock. Cut out the pattern and carefully sand it smooth. Carve the medallion design. A purchased medallion can be used in place of the carving if desired.

2. Glue the mirror to the wood frame. A regular section of glass mirror can be beveled by hand by sanding the edges on wet and dry emery paper using a water bath as a lubricant. Sand the glass edges until uniform, smooth bevels are obtained.

Finish

Finish to match the chest of drawers.

5

Kitchen Group

GATELEG TABLE

Scores of different methods have been devised to hold up drop-leaf tables. Rudders, butterfly, swing arm, pull stocks, and gatelegs are only a few. This table dates back to the late 1600s, and deviations were still being made in the late 1800s.

Material

Cherry, maple, mahogany, basswood, or birch. Cherry is preferred.

Material List

	Part	Number	Size
A	Main Legs	6	$3/16''$ x $3/16''$ x $2^3/8''$
B	Gate Leg	2	$3/16''$ x $3/16''$ x $1^1/2''$
C	Top Side Stretcher	2	$2^1/2''$ x $5/16''$ x $1/8''$
D	Top End Stretcher	2	$1^3/8''$ x $5/16''$ x $1/8''$
E	Bottom Side Stretcher	2	$2^1/2''$ x $3/16''$ x $1/8''$
F	Bottom End Stretcher	2	$1^3/8''$ x $3/16''$ x $1/8''$
G	Gate Stretcher	4	$1^1/4''$ x $3/8''$ x $1/16''$
H	Tabletop	1	$3/32''$ x $4^3/4''$ dia. circle

Construction

1. Lathe-turn the table legs (A) and the gatelegs (B) to the suggested shape and size. Cut the required mortise slots into the four table legs (see dark area in fig. 2–15).

2. Lay out and cut the stretchers (C, D, E, F). Note the $1/16$-by-$3/16$-inch notches in the top (C) and bottom (E) side stretchers. When installed between the table legs (A), these notches will be opposite each other, one right and one left. Glue the stretchers (C, D, E, F) between the table legs to form a rectangle.

Fig. 2–15. Gateleg table

3. Make the gates using table legs (A), gate-legs (B), and two gate stretchers (G). The gate-legs should fit between the top (C) and bottom (E) side stretchers. Cut matching notches in the gate table leg (A) so that it will fit flush into the notches on the top (C) and bottom (E) side stretchers when closed. Cut mortise slots into the table legs (A) and gatelegs (B) and glue the gate stretchers (G) into these mortises to form two gates (see detail fig. 2–17).

4. Place the gate table leg (A) into the notches in the top (C) and bottom (E) side stretchers, and pin hinge the gateleg (B) between them (C, E). This allows the gate assembly to swing out at a right angle and hold the table leaf or to fit right when the leaf is down (see top fig. 2–17).

5. Cut a ³/₄-inch-diameter circle for the table top (H). Slice the circle as shown in figure 2–16 to form two leaves. Attach the leaves to the center section with scale-size H hinges. Glue the table center to the leg assembly. Test the two leaves and gatelegs for proper operation. Sand adjust if required.

Finish

Sand the reproduction smooth removing any trace of glue. Stain if desired. Cover with several coats of lacquer or similar finish.

SETTLE BENCH/TABLE

The settle bench/table is a prime example of functional design. When a table is desired the top is put down and a large area is available. When the table is not needed, the top is raised to form a suitable bench.

Storage space is provided under the bench top. A drawer under the bin stores specialized items. You can almost see the Early American housewife sitting on the settle working on her mending, which she stores in the drawer.

This reproduction was developed from a piece in the Early American Society office.

Material

Pine, cherry, mahogany, maple, or basswood. Basswood or pine are preferred.

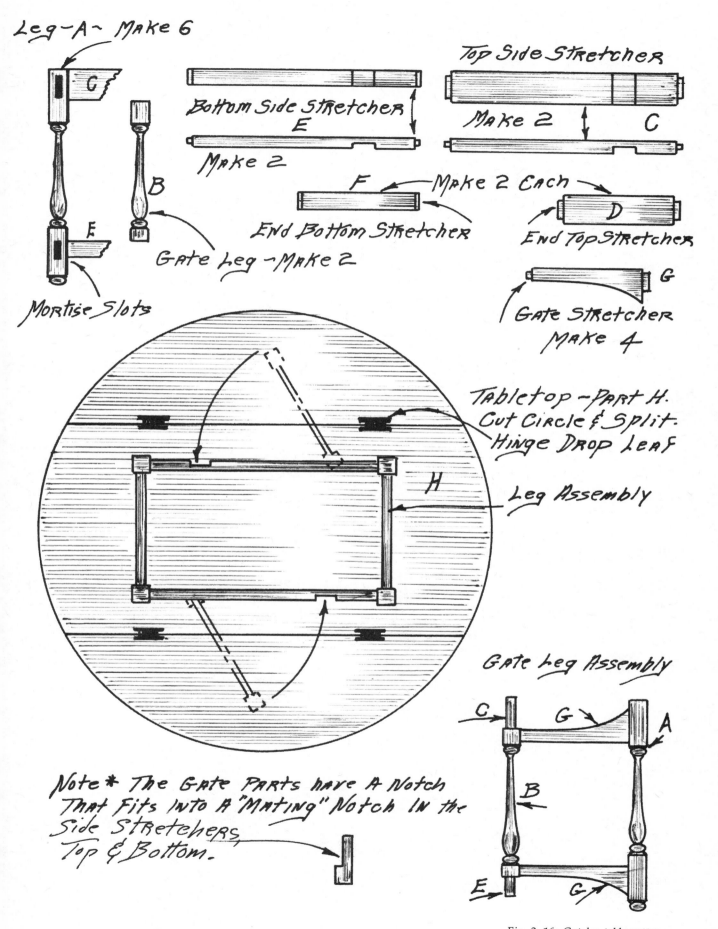

Leg-A- Make 6

G

B

Bottom Side Stretcher
E

Make 2

F

Mortise Slots

Gate Leg - Make 2

End Bottom Stretcher

Make 2 Each

Top Side Stretcher

Make 2   C

D

End Top Stretcher

G

Gate Stretcher
Make 4

Tabletop - Part H.
Cut Circle & Split.
Hinge Drop Leaf

H

Leg Assembly

Gate Leg Assembly

C   G   A

B

E   G

Note* The Gate Parts have A Notch
That Fits Into A "Mating" Notch In the
Side Stretchers,
Top & Bottom.

75

Fig. 2–16. Gateleg table pattern

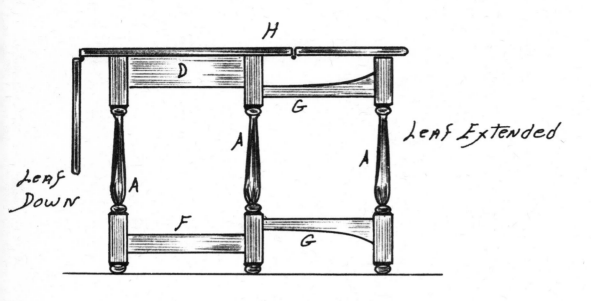

H

D

Leaf Extended

G

A

A

Leaf
Down

A

F

G

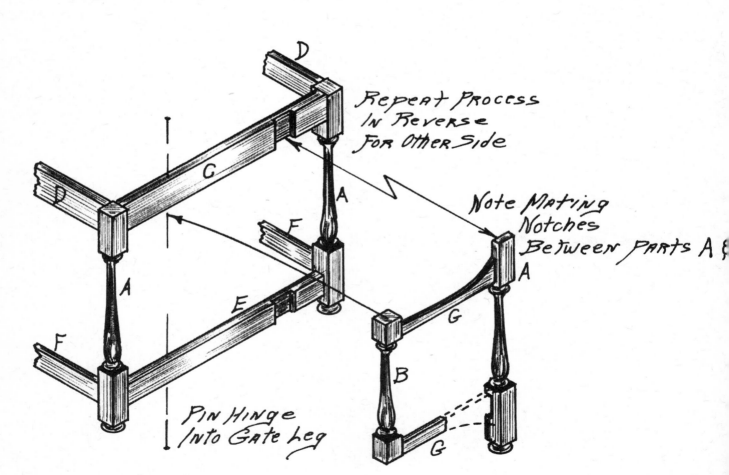

D

Repeat Process
In Reverse
For Other Side

G

A

Note Mating
Notches
Between Parts A

D

A

F

A

F

E

G

B

Pin Hinge
Into Gate Leg

G

Fig. 2-17. Gateleg table assembly

Material List

	Part	Number	Size
A	Side	2	$1^1/_2$″ x $2^1/_2$″ x $^1/_8$″
B	Leg	2	$2^1/_4$″ x $^3/_{32}$″ x $^1/_4$″
C	Stretcher front/back	2	$3^1/_8$″ x $^3/_8$″ x $^1/_{16}$″
D	Bin Bottom	1	$2^7/_8$″ x $1^3/_8$″ x $^1/_{16}$″
E	Bin Top	1	$2^7/_8$″ x $1^3/_4$″ x $^1/_{16}$″
F	Drawer Side	2	$1^1/_4$″ x $^5/_{16}$″ x $^1/_{16}$″
G	Drawer End	2	$^3/_4$″ x $^5/_{16}$″ x $^1/_{16}$″
H	Drawer Bottom	1	$1^1/_4$″ x $^5/_8$″ x $^1/_{16}$″
I	Drawer Guide	1	$^3/_{32}$″ x $^3/_{32}$″ x $1^1/_4$″
J	Drawer Run	2	$^1/_{32}$″ x $^1/_{32}$″ x $1^1/_4$″
K	Top Support	2	$2^1/_2$″ x $^1/_4$″ x $^1/_8$″
L	Hinge Pin	2	$^3/_4$″ x $^1/_8$″ dia. dowel

Construction

Note: The right-hand side (A) has a $^1/_{16}$-by-$^1/_{16}$-inch rabbet cut into it for a drawer guide. See detail in figure 2–19.

1. Lay out and cut the sides (A) to shape and size. Cut the notches to receive the back (C). Cut the drawer-guide rabbet as suggested. Lay out and cut the legs (B). Glue the legs (B) to the sides (A).

2. Lay out and cut the back (C), bin bottom (D), and top (E). Glue the back (C) into the premade notches in the sides (A). Glue the bin bottom (D) to the inside bottom of the back (C) and sides (A). Sand fit the bin top (E) to a loose fit. Pin hinge the bin top (E) to the sides (A) so that the bin top operates like a door top.

3. Lay out and cut the tabletop support (K) and tabletop (M). Drill a $^1/_8$-inch hole into the tabletop support (K) and the sides (A) as marked. Glue the support (K) to the tabletop (M) where indicated. Turn out two hinge pins (L). Insert the hinges (L) through the supports (K) into the sides (A). The tabletop hinges on these pins. Similar pins can be used in the front also if preferred.

4. Drawer Unit. Make a drawer unit of F, G, and H. Cut $^1/_{16}$-by-$^1/_{16}$-inch-square drawer runs (J). Glue the drawer runs (J) to the top edges of the drawer sides (F). Cut a L-shaped drawer guide (I). Line the drawer unit up under the bin bottom (D) so that the right hand drawer run (J) fits into the rabbet cut into the sides (A), and mark where the drawer guide (I)

Fig. 2–18. Early American settle bench-table and dry sink

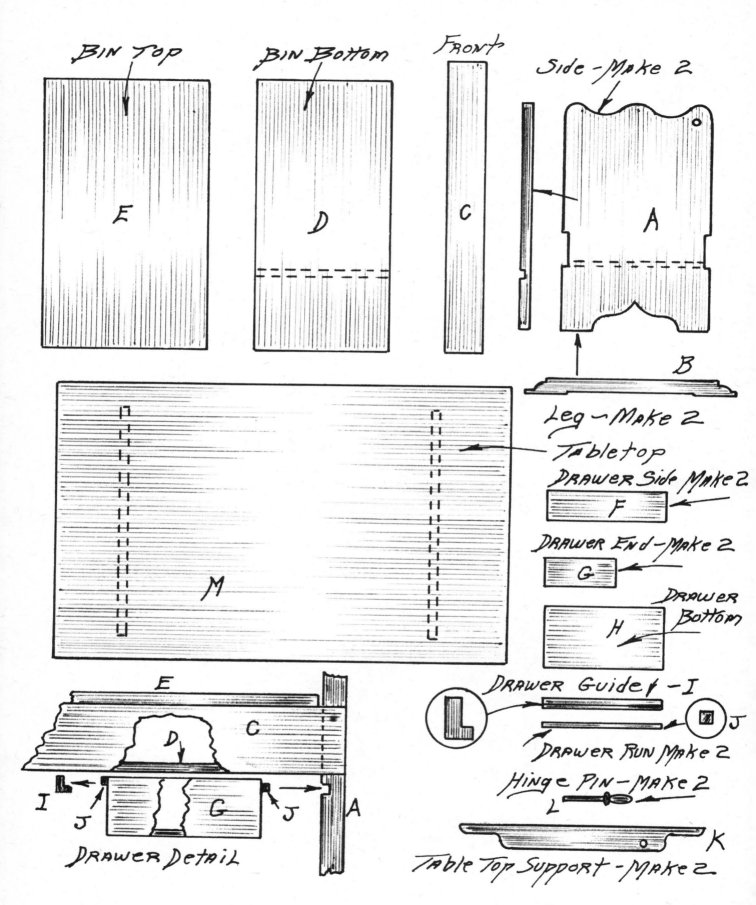

BIN TOP

BIN BOTTOM

FRONT

Side–Make 2

E

D

C

A

B

Leg–Make 2

Tabletop

DRAWER Side Make 2

F

DRAWER End–Make 2

G

DRAWER Bottom

H

M

DRAWER Guide–I

DRAWER RUN Make 2

J

Hinge PIN–MAKE 2

L

E

D

C

I

J

G

J

A

K

DRAWER Detail

Table Top Support–Make 2

Fig. 2–19. Settle bench-table pattern

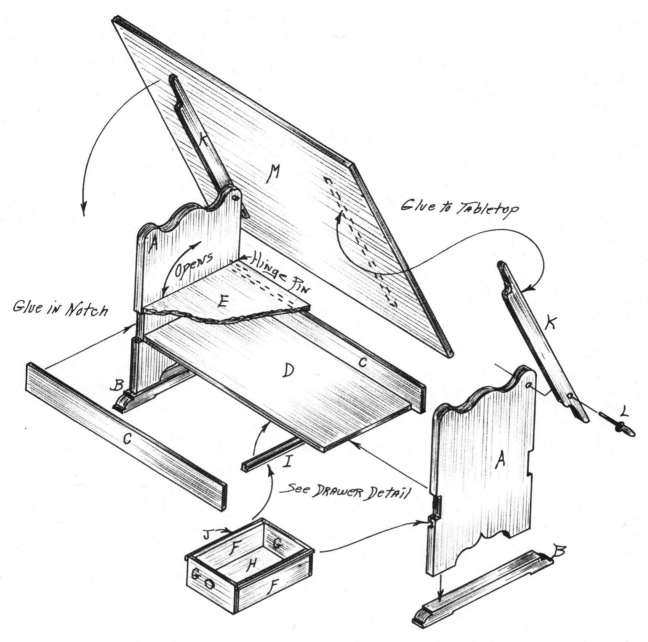

Fig. 2–20. Settle bench-table assembly

will contain and operate the other drawer run (J). Glue the drawer guide (I) to the bin bottom (D) on this mark. The drawer unit will operate either way, from the front or from the rear.

Finish

Remove the top. Sand the entire reproduction smooth removing any trace of glue. Stain or paint if desired. Cover with several coats of lacquer or similar finish. Attach drawer pulls to each drawer front (G).

DRY SINK

Early American housewives did not have running water. Their kitchen work center was the dry sink. Water was carried in, the chore performed, and the water was carried out.

The dry sink was designed in many shapes,

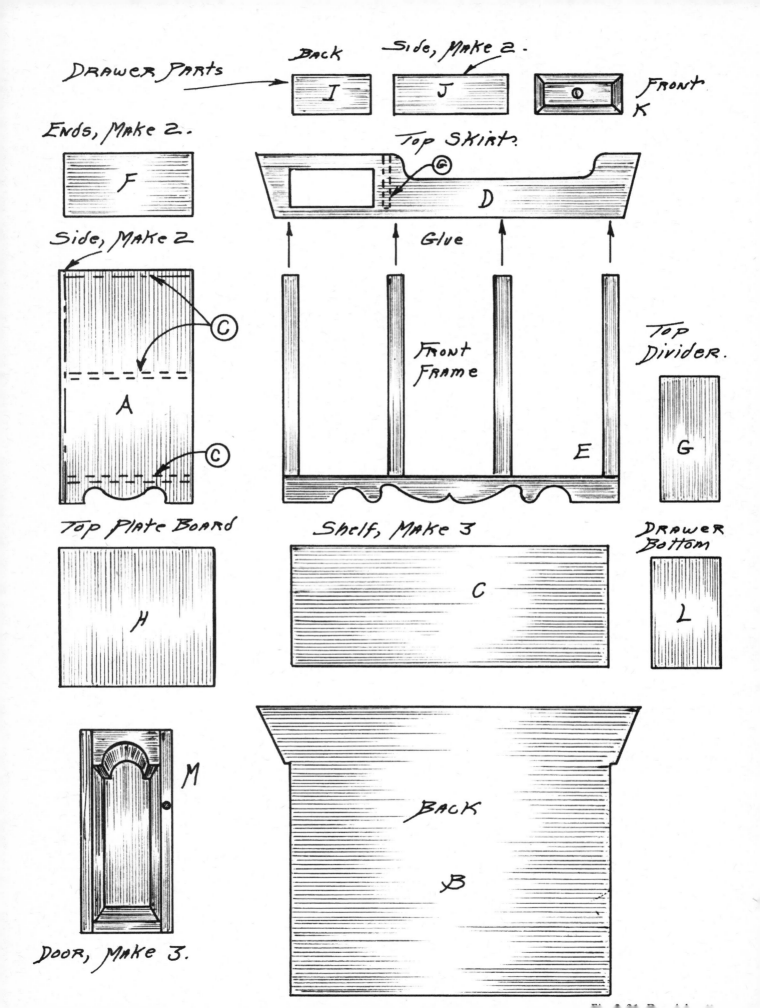

DRAWER PARTS

BACK — I

Side, Make 2. — J

FRONT. K — ⊙

Ends, Make 2. — F

Top Skirt. — G — D — Glue

Side, Make 2 — C — A — C

FRONT FRAME — E

Top Divider. — G

Top Plate Board — H

Shelf, Make 3 — C

Drawer Bottom — L

Door, Make 3. — M

BACK — B

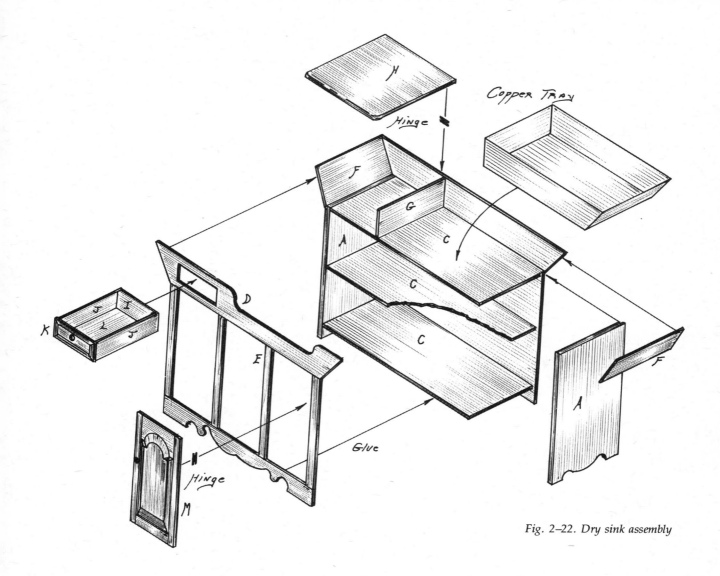

Fig. 2–22. Dry sink assembly

sizes, and styles, all with the basic fundamentals of a work area, sink area, and storage area (see fig. 2–18).

The following miniature reproduction offers a composite of most dry sinks of that time period.

Material

Cherry, maple, birch, pine, or basswood. Cherry or basswood is preferred. Heavy-gauge copper foil is available in most hobby or train outlets.

Material List

	Part	Number	Size
A	Side	2	$1^3/8$" x $2^1/2$" x $1/8$"
B	Back	1	4" x $2^1/2$" x $1/16$"
C	Shelf	3	$3^1/4$" x $1^5/16$" x $1/16$"
D	Top Skirt	1	4" x $^{11}/16$" x $1/16$"
E	Bottom Skirt	1	$3^1/2$" x $1/4$" x $1/16$"
	Stile	4	$3/16$" x $2^1/8$" x $1/16$"
F	Top End	2	$1^3/8$" x $^{11}/16$" x $1/16$"
G	Top Divider	1	$1^5/16$" x $5/8$" x $1/16$"
H	Top Plate	1	$1^5/8$" x $1^1/2$" x $1/16$"
I	Drawer Back	1	$^{13}/16$" x $7/16$" x $1/16$"
J	Drawer Side	2	$1^3/16$" x $7/16$" x $1/16$"
K	Drawer Front	1	$7/8$" x $7/16$" x $1/16$"
L	Drawer Bottom	1	$3/4$" x $1^3/16$" x $1/16$"
M	Door	3	1" x $2^1/8$" x $1/8$"

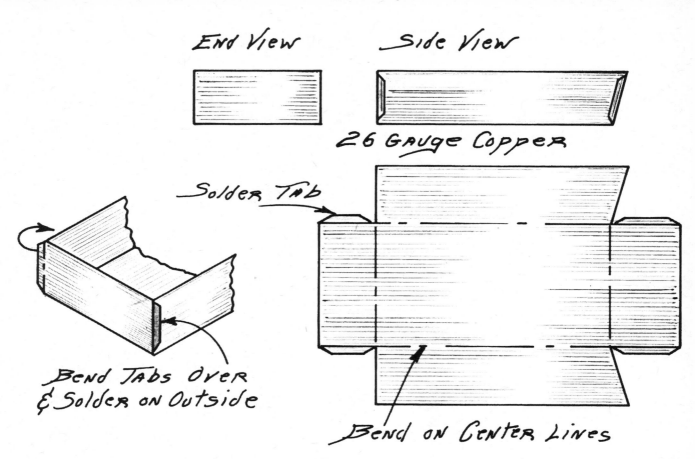

End View   Side View

26 Gauge Copper

Solder Tab

Bend Tabs Over
& Solder on Outside

Bend on Center Lines

Fig. 2–23. Copper tray pattern

COPPER PAN

1 Piece 2³/₄″ x 3³/₄″

Construction

1. Lay out and cut the sides (A) and back (B). Cut a ¹/₁₆-by-¹/₁₆-inch rabbet on the back edges of the sides (A). Lay out and cut the shelves (C). Glue the shelves between the sides and to the back. See location in figure 2–21.

2. Lay out and cut the top skirt (D) and construct the front frame (E). (See "Construction Notes" for frame-making instructions). Glue this assembly as shown in figure 2–21. Glue the skirt board to the bottom shelf (C), the two end stiles to the sides (A), the top skirt (D) to the top shelf (C), and the last two stiles between the skirt board and the top skirt to complete the front frame.

3. Lay out and cut the ends (F) and the top divider (G). Glue the ends (F) between the top angles on the back (B) and the top skirt (D). Glue the top divider (G) between the back (B) and the top skirt (D) in the location shown in figure 2–21.

Lay out and cut the top plate board (H) to the size suggested. Glue the top plate board (H) to the back (B) as shown in figure 2–22.

4. Make a drawer unit from parts I, J, K, and L. Sand fit the drawer unit to fit the opening in the top skirt (D). Drawer containment guides can be made from scrap wood and glued to the top shelf (C).

5. Make three raised-panel door units to fit the openings in the front frame (see "Construction Notes"). Hinge the doors to the openings and attach scale-size pulls.

6. Copper tray. Lay out the pattern on heavy gauge copper foil. Bend the copper on the center lines as shown in figure 2–23. The solder tabs are placed on the outside of the pan. Dry-fit the copper pan in place in the dry sink and, if acceptable, solder the tabs in place.

Finish

Sand the reproduction smooth removing all

traces of glue. Stain or paint a color of your choice. Cover with several coats of lacquer or similar finish. Polish the copper tray with fine steel wool and preserve the sheen with a coat of brushing lacquer.

TRESTLE TABLE

The long, flat tabletop resting upon two or more T-trestles has been seen in every shape, size, and design. It is offered here in two styles; as a Colonial harvest table, and as an Early American side table. The major difference between the two versions is the serpentine top and lathe-turned legs and stretchers of the Early American side table design. The construction is otherwise the same for both tables.

Material

Cherry, maple, birch, walnut, or basswood. Cherry is preferred.

Material List

	Part	Number	Size
A	Leg	2	$3/16''$ x $2 1/8''$ x $1/8''$
B	Top	2	$3/16''$ x $1 1/2''$ x $1/4''$
C	Bottom	2	$3/16''$ x $1 1/2''$ x $1/4''$
D	Stretcher	1	$4 1/2''$ x $3/16''$ x $1/8''$
E	Tabletop	1	$5''$ x $2''$ x $3/32''$

Construction

1. Lay out and cut the legs (A), tops (B), and bottoms (C) to suggested shapes and sizes. Cut the stretcher mortise slots into both legs (A). Drill a $1/16$-inch hole into the ends of the legs, and glue a section of $1/16$-inch dowel into each, allowing $1/8$ inch to extend to create a tenon. Drill matching mortise holes into the tops (B) and bottoms (C). Glue the dowel tenons in the legs (A) into the mortise holes in the tops and bottoms.

2. Lay out and cut the stretcher (D) making a tenon on each end. Fit the stretcher tenons to the mortise slots on the legs (A). Drill a $1/16$-inch hole where the stretcher tenon clears the edge of the leg when inserted in place. Insert a section of $1/16$-inch dowel into these holes. This action locks the stretcher to the two trestle legs.

3. Lay out and cut the tabletop (E). Glue the tops of B to the underside of the tabletop. See figure 2–24 or 2–25 for placement.

Finish

Sand the reproduction smooth, removing any traces of glue. Stain or paint to a color of choice. Cover with several coats of lacquer or similar finish.

DEACON'S BENCH-ROCKER

The deacon's bench is similar to the wagon seat or the popular mammy bench. They all have the same basic lines and design; a double-spaced seat, decorative spoke back, and turned legs. The following reproduction is offered as a plain, four-legged bench or as a rocker, complete with child guard.

Material

Cherry, oak, maple, or walnut. Cherry is preferred.

Material List

	Part	Number	Size
A	Seat	1	$4''$ x $1 1/4''$ x $1/8''$
B	Back	1	$4 1/4''$ x $5/8''$ x $1/8''$
C	Primary Spoke	2	$1/8''$ dia. dowel x $1 1/4''$
D	Secondary Spoke	13	$1/16''$ dia. dowel x $1 1/4''$
E	Arm Rest	2	$1/4''$ x $1''$ x $3/32''$
F	Primary Arm Rest Support	2	$1/8''$ dia. dowel x $3/4''$
G	Secondary Arm Rest Support	4	$1/16''$ dia. dowel x $3/4''$
H	Leg	4	$3/32''$ dia. dowels x $1 1/2''$
I	Stretcher	2	$4''$ x $3/16''$ x $1/16''$
J	Rocker	2	$2''$ x $1/4''$ x $3/32''$
K	Guard Post	2	$1/8''$ dia. dowel x $1''$
L	Guard Top Slat	1	$3/16''$ x $1 1/16''$ x $1/16''$
M	Guard Slat	2	$1/16''$ x $1 1/16''$ x $1/16''$

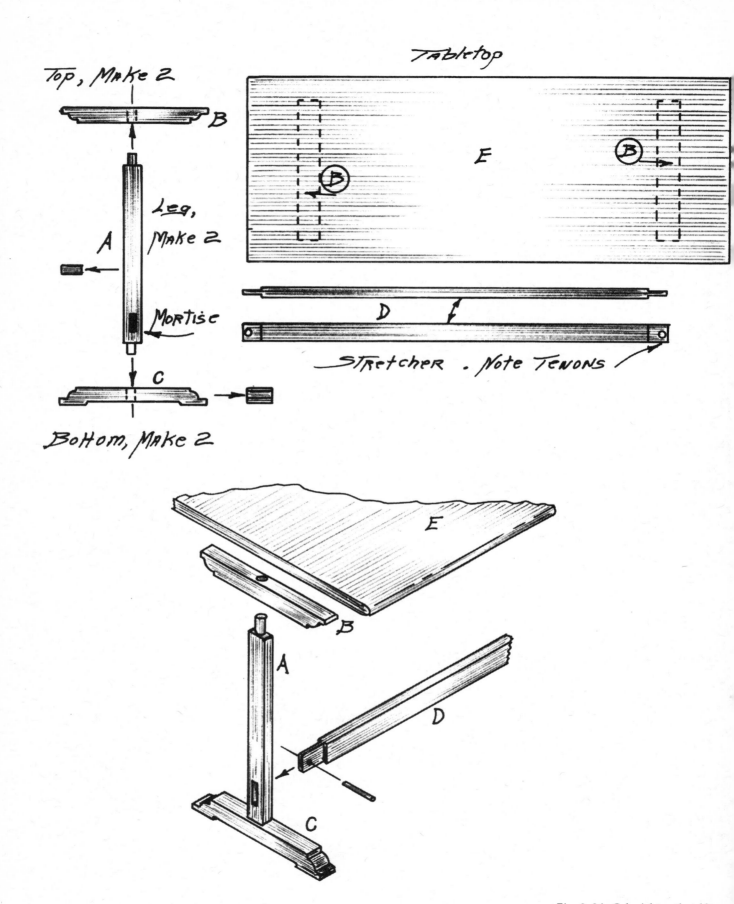

Top, Make 2

Leg, Make 2

A

Mortise

C

Bottom, Make 2

Tabletop

B

E

B

B

D

Stretcher . Note Tenons

E

B

A

D

C

Fig. 2–24. Colonial trestle table

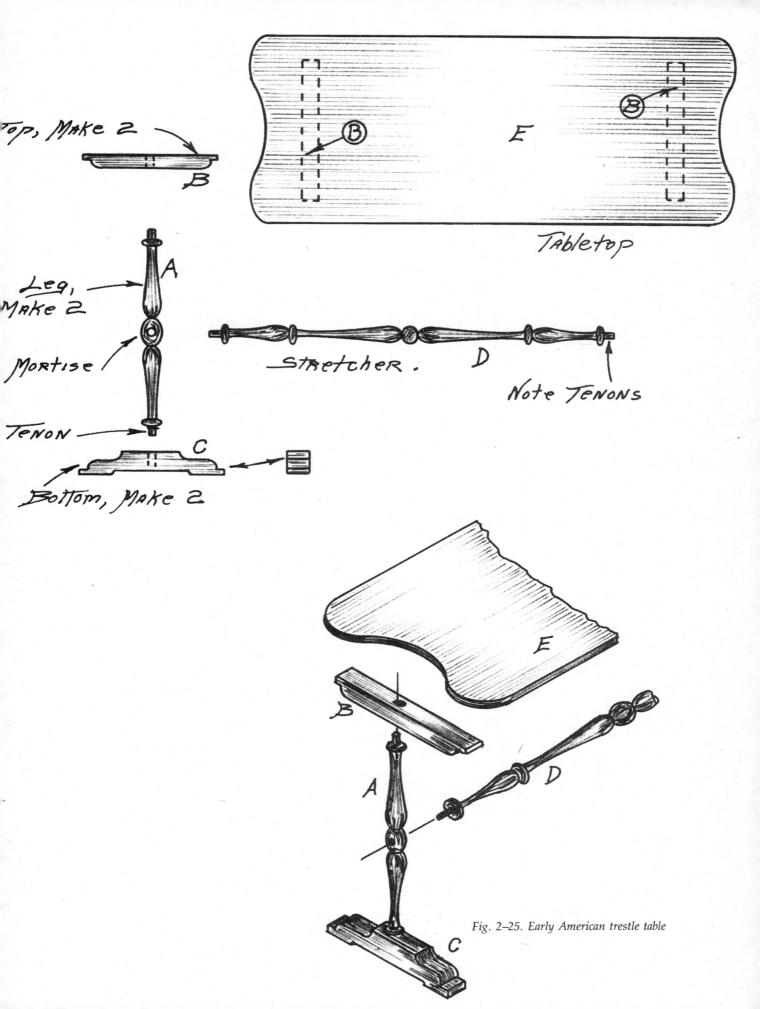

Top, Make 2

B

E

B

B

Tabletop

Leg,
Make 2

A

Mortise

Stretcher. D

Tenon

Note Tenons

C

Bottom, Make 2

E

B

A

D

C

Fig. 2–25. Early American trestle table

Fig. 2–26. Deacon's bench with child guard and Boston rocker

Construction

1. Lay out and cut the seat (A) and back (B). Note that two different backs are offered, one has a carved eagle as part of the design while the other has a painted motif.

Cut out the seat profile (see shaded area in fig. 2–27). (See "Construction Notes" for detailing.)

Mark the seat (A) and back (B) for the required mortise holes. Note the splay angle for the back spokes in figure 2–28. (Note placement in fig. 2–27.) Drill the required holes using a ⅛-inch drill for the primary spokes (C and F) and a ¹⁄₁₆-inch drill for the secondary spokes (D and G).

2. Lathe-turn the spokes (C, D, F, and G) to suggested shape and length. Glue the bottom tenons of the back support spokes (C and D) into the seat holes. Glue the tenon tops of C and D into the holes in the back (B).

Glue the arm supports (F and G) into the holes in the seat (A). Cut out the armrests (E). Drill the required mortise holes into the armrests (check fig. 2–28 for placement and splay).

Glue the top tenons of F and G into the holes in the armrest, and glue the armrest to the primary spoke (C).

3. Lathe-turn the legs (H), making a tenon on each end. Drill a ¹⁄₁₆-inch mortise hole into the center ball on each leg in order to receive the stretcher (I). Drill the leg-mounting mortise holes into the bottom of the seat (see fig. 2–28 for location and splay angles).

Dry-fit the legs to the seat and the stretchers between the legs. If the bench "sits" even and smooth, remove these parts and glue them in place. If rockers (J) are to be used, lay out and cut them to shape and size. Drill mortise holes for the tenons on the bottom of the legs (H). Dry-fit the rockers in place and check for proper action. If satisfied, glue the leg tenons into the rocker mortise holes.

4. Child guard. Lathe-turn the guard posts (K) to shape and size. Lay out and cut the backs (L and M) to size. Glue the parts (K, L, and M) together as shown in figure 2–27. Drill the two mounting holes into the seat (fig. 2–28) and glue the child guard into place.

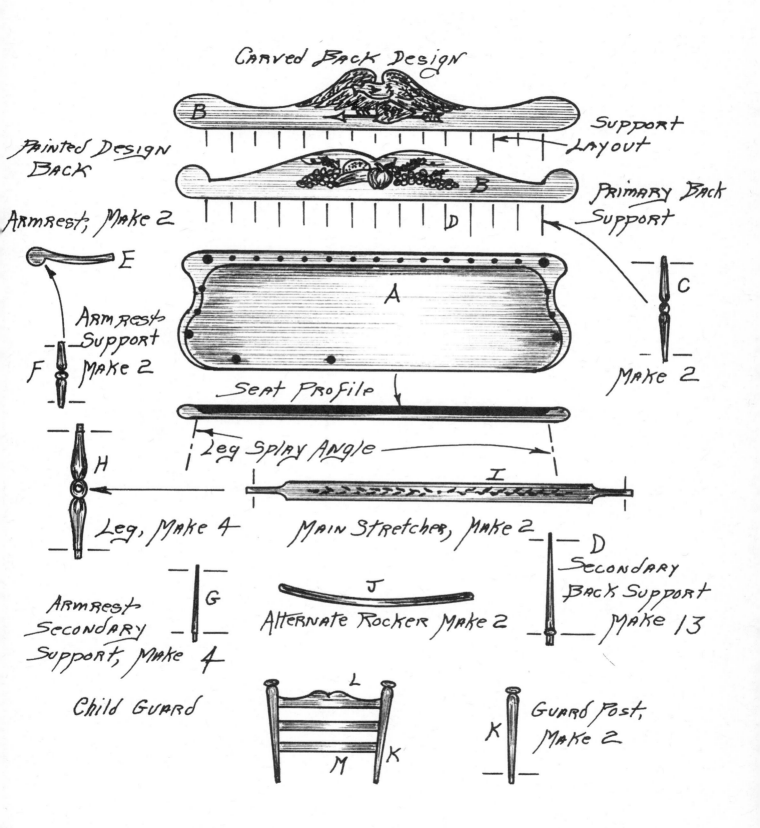

Carved Back Design

Painted Design Back

Support Layout

Primary Back Support

Armrest, Make 2

E

Armrest Support Make 2

F

B

B

D

A

C

Make 2

Seat Profile

Leg Splay Angle

H

I

Leg, Make 4

Main Stretcher, Make 2

D

Secondary Back Support Make 13

G

Armrest Secondary Support, Make 4

J

Alternate Rocker Make 2

Child Guard

L

M   K

K

Guard Post, Make 2

Fig. 2–27. Deacon's bench pattern with alternate back design

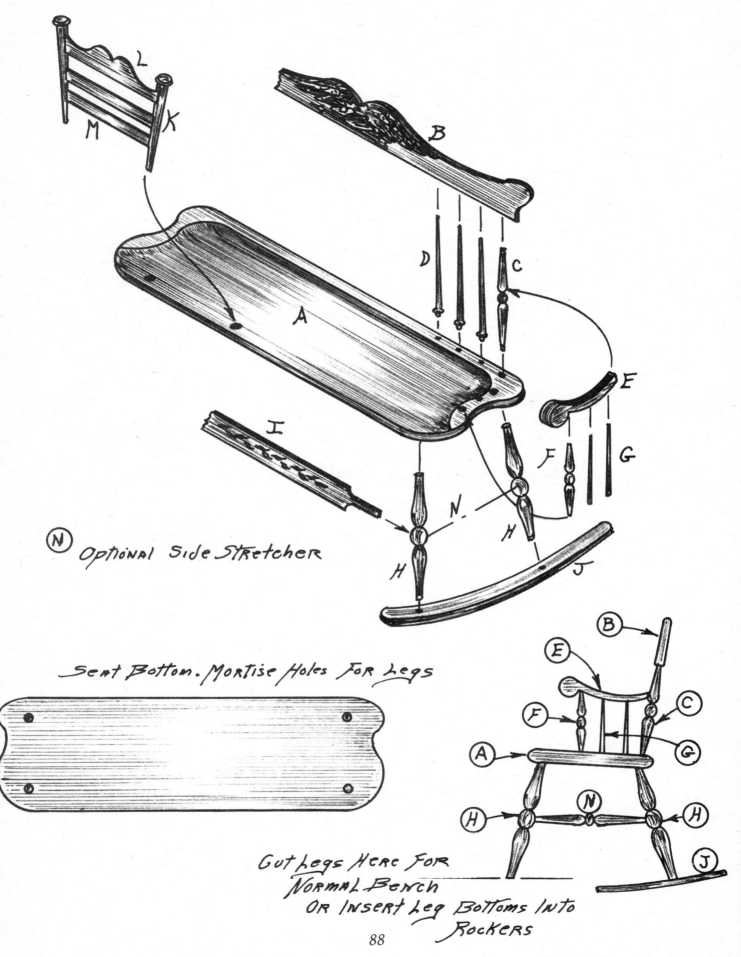

(N) *Optional Side Stretcher*

Seat Bottom. Mortise Holes For Legs

Cut Legs Here For Normal Bench Or Insert Leg Bottoms Into Rockers

88

Fig. 2–28. Deacon's bench assembly

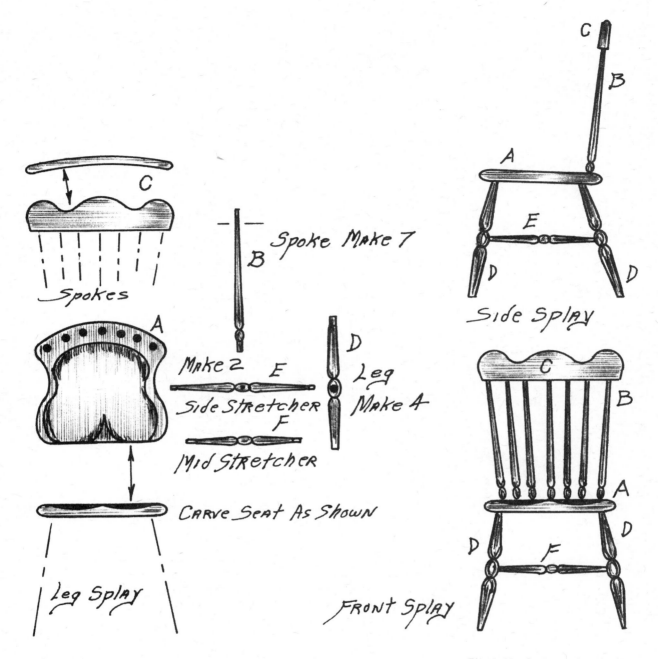

Fig. 2–29. Governor Carver chair

Finish

The bench-rocker may be stained and finished, painted, or stained and painted to resemble Hitchcock styling. Cover with several coats of lacquer.

GOVERNOR CARVER CHAIR

There are a dozen or more different style chairs that go under the name, Governor Carver. The following reproduction is an excellent example of Early American styling.

Material

Cherry, maple, birch, basswood, or walnut. Cherry or maple are preferred. The dowels are maple.

Material List

	Part	Number	Size
A	Seat	1	1½" x 1³/₈" x 1/₈"
B	Spoke	7	1/₁₆" dia. x 1⁹/₁₆"
C	Back	1	1⁹/₁₆" x ³/₈" x ³/₁₆"
D	Leg	4	1/₈" dia. x 1½"
E	Side Stretcher	2	1/₁₆" dia. x 1½"
F	Mid Stretcher	1	1/₁₆" dia. x 1¼"

Construction

1. Lay out and cut the seat (A) to suggested shape and size. Carve out the depressed seating area as shown in figure 2–29. A ball rasp held in an electric hand drill is an excellent tool for such an operation (see "Construction Notes"). Drill the back spoke mortise holes (see splay angle in fig. 2–29).

2. Lathe-turn spokes (B), legs (D), side stretchers (E), and mid stretchers (F) to suggested shape and sizes. Make tenons as shown in figure 2–29. Glue the tenons of the spokes (B) into the mortise holes in the seat (A).

3. Lay out and cut the back (C). Mark splay angles and drill the required mortise holes. Glue the tops of the spokes (B) into these holes.

4. Turn the chair over and drill the leg mounting holes into the bottom of the seat (A) using the splay angles shown in figure 2–29. Drill the required stretcher mortise holes into the legs (D). Glue the stretchers (E and F) into the mortise holes cut into the legs as you glue the leg tenons into the seat mortise holes. This assembly must be completed as a single step.

Finish

Sand the entire reproduction smooth removing all traces of glue. Stain or paint to a color of choice. Cover with several coats of lacquer or similar finish. A design can be applied to the center of the back if preferred.

Fig. 2–30. Early American chairs, left to right: captain's chair, Hitchcock chair, plank seat chair

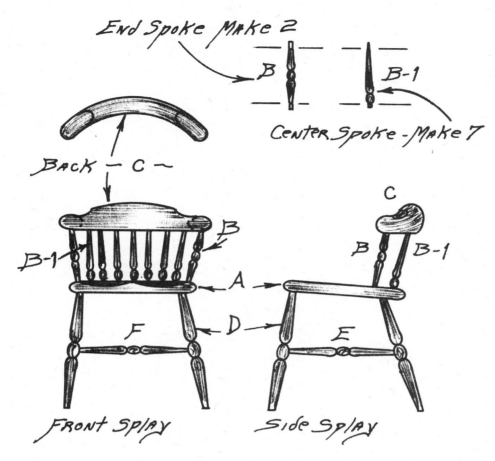

Fig. 2–31. Captain's chair pattern

CAPTAIN'S CHAIR

The captain's and mate's chairs have low, curved backs and can be made from the same basic parts as the Governor Carver chair.

Material

Cherry, maple, birch. The dowels are maple.

Material List

	Part	Number	Size
A	Seat	1	$1^{1/2}$" x $1^{3/8}$" x $^{1/8}$"
B	End Spoke	2	$^{1/16}$" dia. x $^{3/4}$"
B–1	Mid Spoke	7	$^{1/16}$" dia. x $^{3/4}$"
C	Back	1	$1^{5/8}$" x $^{5/16}$" x $^{1/2}$"
D	Leg	4	$^{1/8}$" dia. x $1^{1/2}$"
E	Side Stretcher	2	$^{1/16}$" dia. x $1^{1/2}$"
F	Mid Stretcher	1	$^{1/16}$" dia. x $1^{1/4}$"

Construction

1. Follow the general directions given for the Governor Carver chair. The seat, legs, and stretchers will be the same size and shape as those given in figure 2–29. The end spokes (B) and the center spokes (B–1) are much shorter than the spokes in the Governor Carver chair but otherwise all procedures are the same.

BOSTON ROCKER

The main characteristic of the Boston rocker is the high back piece and the decorative fruit motif (see fig. 2–26). Several different types and styles of this rocker go under the general term, Boston rocker.

Material

Cherry, maple, birch, or walnut. The dowels are maple.

Material List

	Part	Number	Size
A	Seat	1	$1^3/8'' \times 1^3/8'' \times ^3/16''$
B	Back	1	$1^5/8'' \times ^3/8'' \times ^3/8''$
C	Primary Spoke	2	$^1/8''$ dia. x $1^3/4''$
D	Secondary Spoke	5	$^1/16''$ dia. x $1^3/4''$
E	Front Leg	2	$^1/8''$ dia. x $1^1/8''$
F	Back Leg	2	$^1/8''$ dia. x $1^1/4''$
G	Stretcher	3	$^1/16''$ dia. x $1^3/8''$
H	Arm Rest Primary Spoke	2	$^1/16''$ dia. x $^3/4''$
I	Arm Rest Secondary Spoke	4	$^1/16''$ dia. x $^3/4''$
J	Arm Rest	2	$^3/16'' \times ^7/8'' \times ^3/16''$
K	Rockers	2	$^1/16'' \times 2^1/4'' \times ^3/16''$

Construction

1. Lay out and cut the seat (A) and the back (B). Hollow out the seat area as shown in figure 2–32 (see "Construction Notes"). Drill the spoke mortise holes required.

2. Lathe-turn the back support spokes (C and D) to suggested shape and length, creating tenons on both ends. Glue the bottom tenons on the back support spokes into the mortise holes in the seat. Glue the top tenons into the mortise holes in the back.

3. Lathe-turn the legs and stretchers (E, F, and G) to shape and length, creating the required tenons on each end. Drill leg-mounting holes into the seat bottom (see splay angles in fig. 2–32).

Glue the stretcher tenons into the leg mortise holes as you glue the leg tops into the mortise holes in the bottom of the seat.

4. Make the two rockers (K). Place them under the leg assembly and mark the mortise holes. Drill these mortise holes and glue the leg bottom tenons into the rocker mortise holes.

5. Lathe-turn the armrest spokes (H and I) to suggested shapes and lengths, creating a tenon on each end. Cut the armrests (J) to the suggested shape and size. Drill the required matching holes into the seat and the armrests. Glue the bottoms of the armrest spokes (H and I) into the seat (A) and armrests (J).

Finish

Sand the entire reproduction smooth removing all traces of glue. Stain or paint to a color of choice. Paint the fruit design on the back. Cover with several coats of lacquer or similar finish.

SPOON RACK

Just about every Early American household had a spoon rack in the kitchen or dining room. The rack held the pewter spoons in vertical display and the small drawer contained broken spoon parts awaiting the next trip of the tinker, who would melt down the parts and recast new, shiny spoons. Each household thus had several different spoon designs and styles.

Material

Cherry, maple, birch, or basswood.

Material List

	Part	Number	Size
A	Back	1	$1^1/2'' \times 2^1/2'' \times ^1/16''$
B	Side	2	$^7/8'' \times ^3/4'' \times ^1/16''$
C	Shelf	2	$^3/4'' \times 1^3/16'' \times ^1/16''$
D	Spoon Holder	2	$^1/8'' \times 1^1/8'' \times ^1/16''$
E	Drawer Front	1	$^3/8'' \times 1^1/8'' \times ^1/16''$
F	Drawer Back	1	$^3/8'' \times 1^1/8'' \times ^1/16''$
G	Drawer Side	2	$^3/8'' \times ^5/8'' \times ^1/16''$
H	Drawer Bottom	1	$^5/8'' \times 1'' \times ^1/16''$

Construction

1. Lay out and cut the back (A) to shape and size. Take extreme care in cutting in the design at the top.

2. Lay out and cut the sides (B) and the shelves (C). Glue the sides to the notches cut

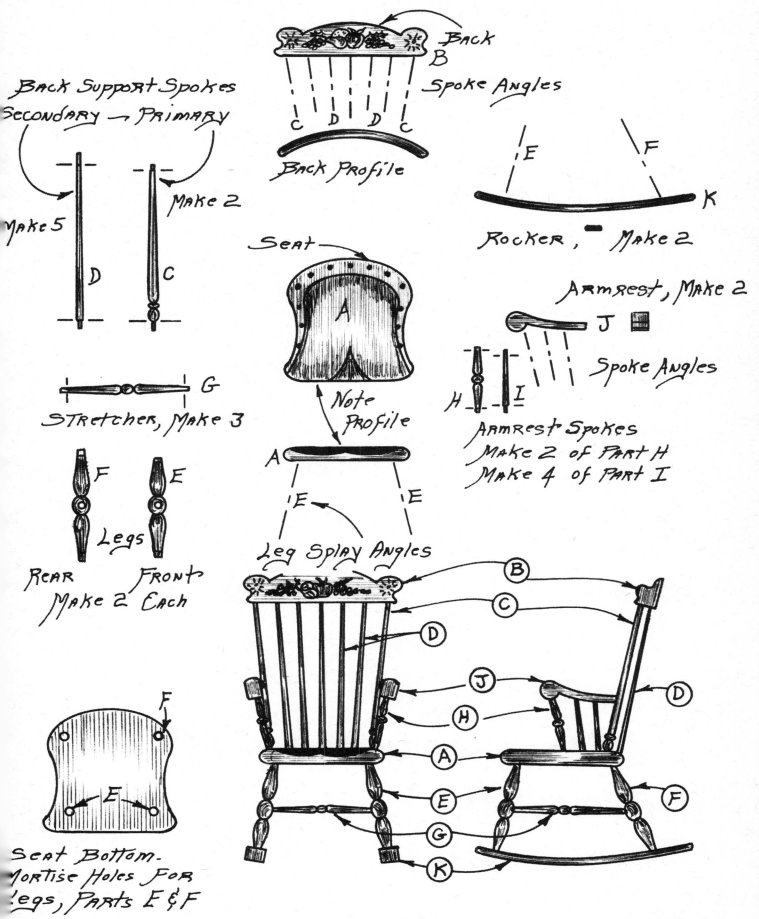

Back Support Spokes
Secondary → Primary

Make 5   Make 2

D   C

Back
B

Spoke Angles

Back Profile
C D D C

E   F
K

Rocker, ▬ Make 2

Seat

A

Armrest, Make 2
J ▣

Spoke Angles

H   I

Armrest Spokes
Make 2 of Part H
Make 4 of Part I

Stretcher, Make 3
G

Note Profile

F   E
Legs

Rear   Front
Make 2 Each

A

E   E

Leg Splay Angles

B
C
D

J
H

A

D

E
F

G

K

Seat Bottom.
Mortise Holes For
Legs, Parts E & F
F
E

93

Fig. 2–32. Boston rocker pattern

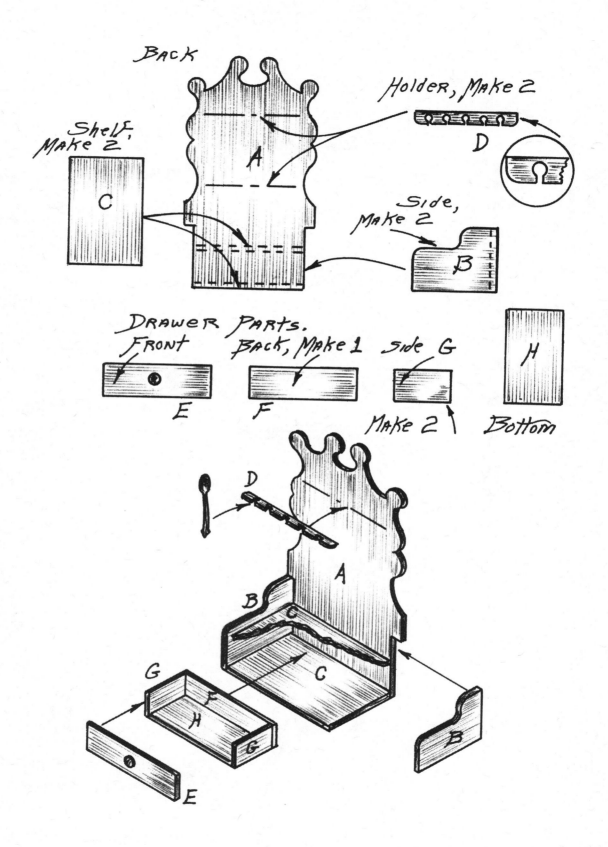

BACK

Holder, Make 2

D

Shelf, Make 2

C

A

Side, Make 2

B

DRAWER PARTS.
FRONT   BACK, Make 1   side G   H

E   F   Make 2   Bottom

D

A

B

G   C

F
H   B
G

E

Fig. 2–33. Spoon rack

into the back (A). Glue the shelves (C) between the sides (B) and to the back (A).

3. Lay out and cut the spoon holder (D) to shape and length. Drill $1/8$-inch-diameter holes as marked in figure 2–33. With a knife file, cut slots into the holes to make the spoon holders.

4. Make a small drawer unit to fit between the two sides. Sand fit the drawer in place.

Finish

Sand the entire reproduction smooth removing all traces of glue. Stain to a color of choice. Cover with several coats of lacquer or similar finish. Suspend scale-size spoons in the slots.

ROCKPORT CUPBOARD

The first cupboard was little more than a board shelf nailed to a house wall. In time, as skills increased, so too did the styling of household furnishings. Cupboards were made in all shapes, sizes, and designs.

The following reproduction (circa 1750) is reproduced from full-sized patterns courtesy of *Early American Life*. This cupboard is offered in two different styles, the original open front design and the classical glass door enclosed design.

Material

Cherry, oak, maple, birch, basswood, or pine. Cherry is preferred.

Material List

	Part	Number	Size
A	Side	2	$1^{1/4}'' \times 6^{1/2}'' \times 1/8''$
B	Back	1	$3'' \times 6^{1/2}'' \times 1/16''$
C	Lower Shelf	2	$2^{3/4}'' \times 1^{3/16}'' \times 1/16''$
D	Upper Shelf	3	$2^{3/4}'' \times 1^{11/16}'' \times 1/16''$
E	Top	1	$3'' \times 7/8'' \times 1/16''$
F	Upper Frame	1	$3'' \times 3^{7/8}'' \times 1/16''$
G	Lower Frame	3	$2'' \times 3/16'' \times 1/16''$
		2	$3'' \times 3/16'' \times 1/16''$
H	Crown Mold	1	$3^{3/4}'' \times 3/16'' \times 3/16''$
		2	$1^{1/4}'' \times 3/16'' \times 3/16''$
I	Drawer Front	2	$3/8'' \times 1^{1/4}'' \times 1/16''$
J	Drawer Back	2	$3/8'' \times 1^{1/4}'' \times 1/16''$
K	Drawer Side	4	$3/8'' \times 1'' \times 1/16''$
L	Drawer Bottom	2	$1^{1/16}'' \times 1'' \times 1/16''$
M	Door	2	$1^{1/4}'' \times 1^{1/2}'' \times 1/8''$

Construction

1. Lay out and cut the sides (A), back (B), lower shelf (C), and upper shelf (D). Cut a $1/16$-by-$1/16$-inch rabbet on the rear inside edges of the sides (A). Glue the back (B) into the rabbets on the sides. Glue the shelves (C and D) between the sides and the back (see fig. 2–34).

2. Lay out and cut the top (E) and upper frame (F) to shape and length. Glue the top (E) to the tops of the sides (A) and the back (B).

3. Lay out and cut the counter top (CT). Glue it to the sides and back. Glue the upper frame (F) to the front edges of the sides.

4. Lay out and cut the parts for the lower frame (G). (See "Construction Notes" for assembly suggestions.) Make the lower frame (G) as a single unit and glue the finished frame to the cupboard as follows: the skirtboard to the bottom shelf (C); the end stiles to the sides (A); and the top rail to the under side of the counter (CT).

5. Make two drawer units from I, J, K, and L. Sand fit the drawer units to the openings. The drawer guides can be made from scrap stock.

6. Make two raised-panel doors (M) to fit the available opening (see "Construction Notes" for details). Hinge the finished doors to the lower frame stiles.

7. Cut crown molding to fit under the top board (E) using 45-degree-miter corner joints. Glue the crown molding to the sides (A), top fascia (F), and top (E).

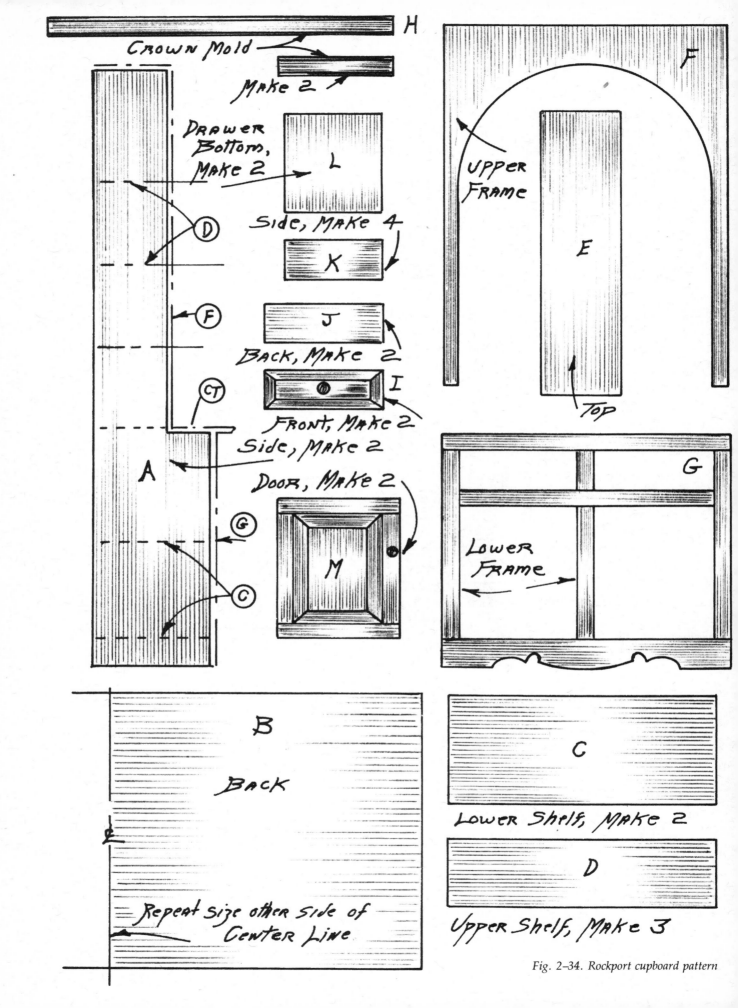

Fig. 2–34. Rockport cupboard pattern

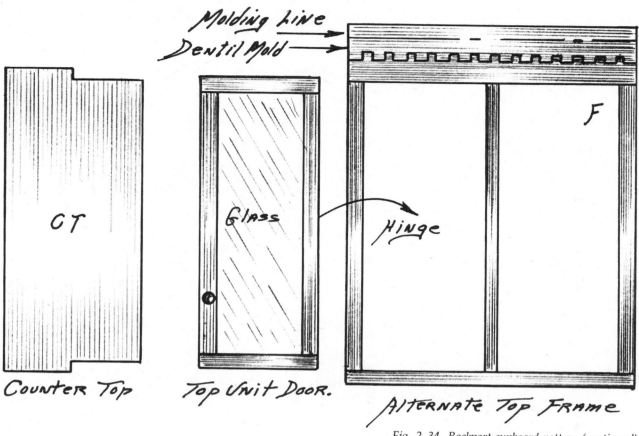

Fig. 2–34. Rockport cupboard pattern (continued)

Alternate Construction

Material List

	Part	Number	Size
F	Under Frame		
	Top Rail	1	3″ x ⁵/₈″ x ¹/₁₆″
	Stile	3	³/₁₆″ x 3¹/₈″ x ¹/₁₆″
	Bottom Rail	1	³/₁₆″ x 3″ x ¹/₁₆″
	Dentil	1	³/₈″ x 3″ dentil mold
CT	Counter Top	1	3¹/₄″ x 1¹/₂″ x ¹/₁₆″
	Glass Door	2	1¹/₄″ x 3¹/₈″ x ¹/₈″

1. The top unit is enclosed in a frame similar to the lower framing using rails and stiles. Make the top frame as shown in figure 2–36. (See "Construction Notes" or step 4 above.) Glue the finished assembly to the sides (A).

2. Glue the dentil trim to the sides (A), the top (E), and the frame front. Cut and glue crown moldings to the sides (A), the top (E), and the top of the front frame. Note that the top (E) is increased ¹/₄ inch in width so that it overhangs both the dentil and crown moldings.

3. Make two door frames to fit the top openings in the frame. Install ¹/₃₂-inch glass or heavy plastic over the open door frames. Install the doors to the top frame with scale-size hinges.

Finish

Sand the entire reproduction smooth removing any trace of glue. Stain or paint to a color of your choice. Cover with several coats of lacquer or similar finish.

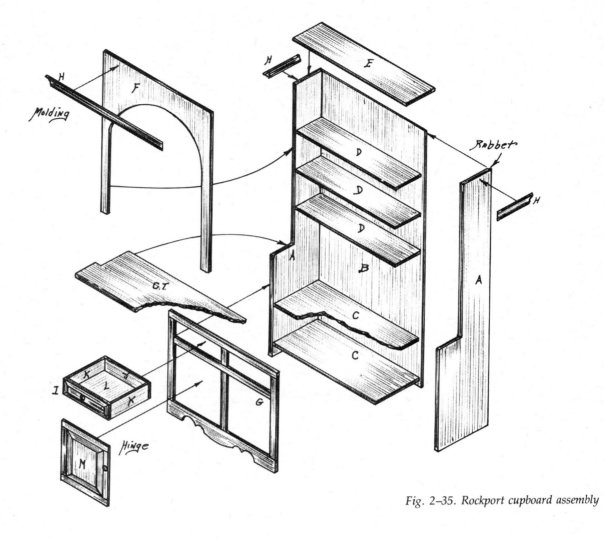

Fig. 2–35. Rockport cupboard assembly

KITCHEN DRESSER

The kitchen dresser was the forefather of modern kitchen cabinets. This reproduction offers a counter-top work space, lower, enclosed storage spaces, and open shelving in a hutch-style top. The original unit was developed full-size for use by *Early American Life* and is reduced and redesigned here with their permission.

Material

Cherry, maple, birch, basswood, or pine. Cherry is preferred.

Material List

	Part	Number	Size
A	Side	2	$1^5/8''$ x $7^1/4''$ x $1/8''$
B	Back	1	$5^1/8''$ x $7^1/4''$ x $1/16''$
C	Base Shelf	2	$1^9/16''$ x $5''$ x $1/16''$
D	Hutch Shelf	3	$1^{11}/16''$ x $5''$ x $1/16''$
E	Counter Top	1	$1^3/4''$ x $5^1/2''$ x $1/16''$
F	Fascia	1	$3/8''$ x $5^1/4''$ x $1/16''$
G	Top	1	$1^1/16''$ x $5^1/2''$ x $1/16''$
H	Frame Skirt	1	$5/16''$ x $5''$ x $1/16''$
	Frame Top Rail	1	$3/16''$ x $5''$ x $1/16''$
	Frame Stiles	5	$3/16''$ x $2''$ x $1/16''$
I	Mold	1	$3/16''$ x $5^3/4''$ Crown (Cove)
		2	$3/16''$ x $1^1/16''$ Crown Mold
J	Door	2	$1^1/8''$ x $2''$ x $1/8''$

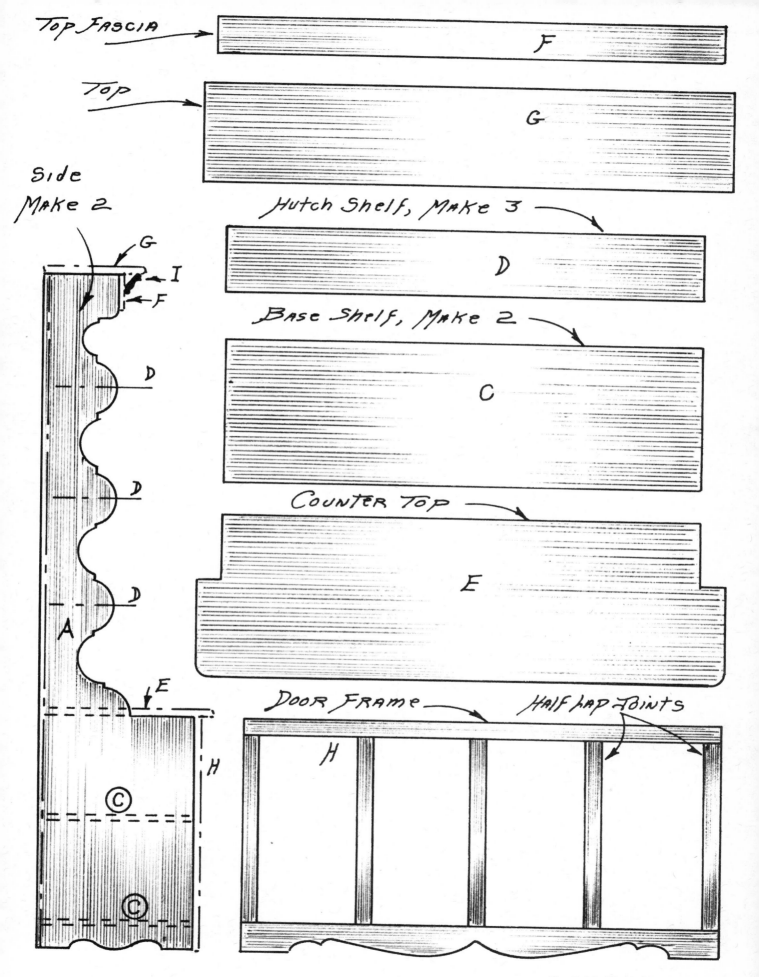

Top Fascia F

Top G

Side
Make 2

G

I

F

D

D

D

A

E

H

©

©

Hutch Shelf, Make 3

D

Base Shelf, Make 2

C

Counter Top

E

Door Frame   Half Lap Joints

H

H

Fig. 2–36. Kitchen dresser pattern

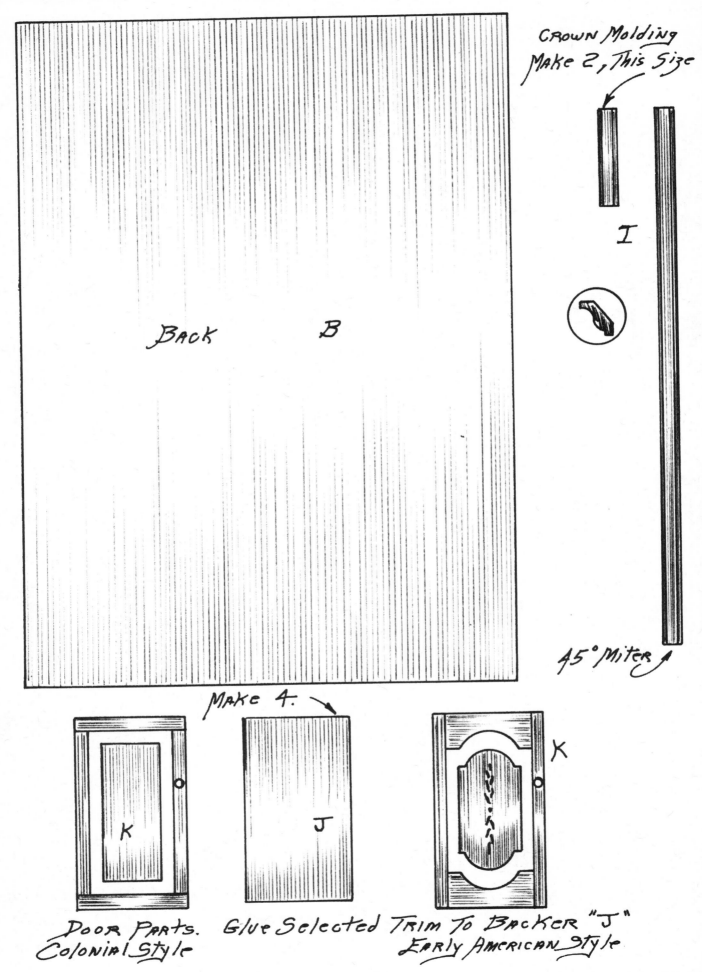

CROWN MOLDING
Make 2, This Size

I

BACK   B

45° Miter

Make 4.

K   J   K

Door Parts.   Glue Selected Trim To Backer "J"
Colonial Style   Early American Style

Fig. 2-36. Kitchen dresser pattern (continued)

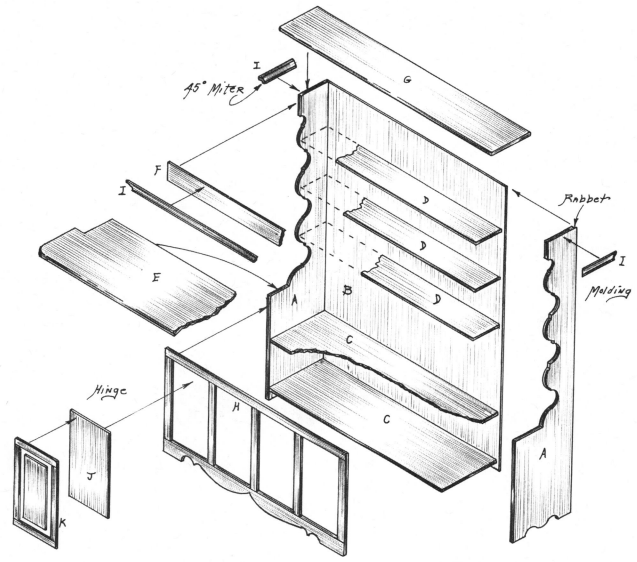

Fig. 2–37. Kitchen dresser assembly

Construction

1. Lay out and cut the side (A) and the back (B). Cut a $^1/_{16}$-by-$^1/_{16}$-inch rabbet on the rear inside edges of the side. Glue the back into these rabbets.

2. Lay out and cut the shelves (C and D). Glue them between the sides (A) and to the back (B) (see fig. 2–36).

3. Lay out and cut the counter top (E), top fascia (F), and top (G) to shape and length. Glue the counter top (E) to the cutouts on the sides (A). Glue the top fascia (F) to the top fronts of the sides (A). Glue the top (G) to the sides (A), back (B), and top fascia (F). Cut 45-degree-angle miters on the molding (I) and glue the molding to the sides (A), top fascia (F),

and top (G).

4. Lay out and cut the lower frame, skirt board, top rail, and five stiles. Make the lower frame as shown in figure 2–36.

5. Make four raised-panel doors (K) to fit the openings in the lower frame (see "Construction Notes") by gluing the selected trim to the backing (J). Attach the finished doors to the frame with scale-sized hinges and pulls.

Finish

Sand the entire reproduction smooth removing any trace of glue. Stain or paint to a color of choice. Cover with several coats of lacquer or similar finish. Stock the open shelves with scale-size chinaware.

6

Dining and Living Room Group

THREE-LEGGED TABLE OR BIBLE STAND

Many stories have developed concerning the three-legged, single stem furniture design. Some authorities claim the three legs symbolize the blessed trinity but in truth the early craftsman realized it was much easier to balance and level three legs than four.

Material

Cherry, maple, birch, walnut, or basswood. Cherry is preferred.

Material List

	Part	Number	Size
A	Stem	1	$^1/_4$" x $^1/_4$" x $2^1/_4$"
B	Leg	3	$1^1/_8$" x $^3/_4$" x $^3/_{32}$"

C–1	Support Block	1	$^3/_8$" x $^1/_2$" x $^3/_{16}$"
C–2	Support Block	1	$^5/_{16}$" dia. x $^1/_{16}$"
D–1	Bible Stand Top	1	$1^1/_2$" x $1^1/_8$" x $^1/_8$"
D–2	Round Top	1	$1^3/_4$" dia. x $^1/_{16}$"
D–3	Drop Leaf Top	1	$^1/_2$" x $1^3/_4$" x $^1/_{16}$"
		1	$1^1/_4$" x $1^1/_4$" x $^1/_{16}$"

Construction

1. Lathe-turn the stem (A) to suggested design and size. Cut three mortise slots 120 degrees apart (see detail fig. 2–38). Lay out and cut the legs (B). Make tenons on each leg top and individually fit the tenons to the stem mortise slots. Glue the legs into the stem.

2. Bible stand or round tabletop. Lay out and cut the support block (C–1 or C–2) and top (D–1 or D–2). Glue the support block to the bottom of the top. Glue the support block to the tenon on top of the stem.

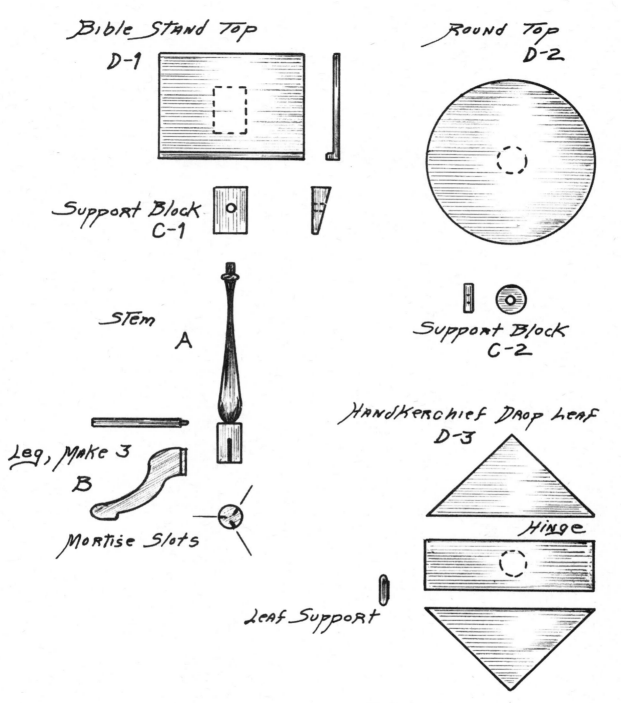

Fig. 2–38. Three-legged table or Bible stand pattern

3. Handkerchief drop-leaf top. Lay out and cut the support block (C–2) and top (D–3). Hinge the two leaves to the center tabletop. Secure the leaf supports to the bottom of the table center so that when they are turned out they will support the leaf. Glue the support block to the table center and to the tenon on the stem.

Finish

Sand the table smooth removing all traces of

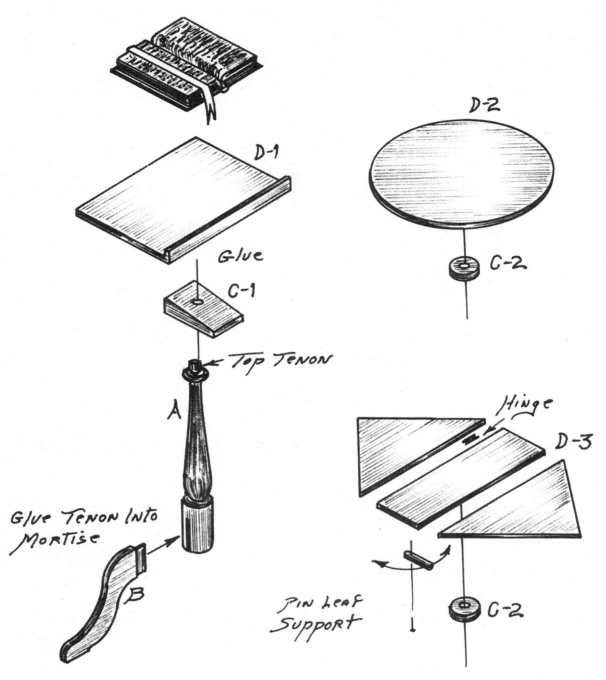

Fig. 2–39. Three-legged table or Bible stand assembly

glue. Stain or paint to a color of choice. Cover with several coats of lacquer or similar finish. Complete with a coat of paste wax.

QUEEN ANNE EXTENSION DINING ROOM TABLE

The formal dining room table was designed with extension leaves to accommodate company. Some tables have several leaves while other models have only one. The basic design is that of a split tabletop that can be extended by adding various width leaves. The following reproduction follows the general design of the Chippendale and Queen Anne periods.

Material

Cherry, maple, birch, walnut, or basswood.

Material List

	Part	Number	Size
A	Stem	2	$3/8''$ dia. x $2\frac{1}{4}''$
B	Leg	6	$1''$ x $1\frac{1}{4}''$ x $1/16''$
C	Cleat	2	$2\frac{3}{4}''$ x $1/2''$ x $1/8''$
D	Tabletop	2	$4''$ x $3\frac{1}{2}''$ x $1/8''$
E	Skirt		18 lineal inches x $1/4''$ x $1/8''$
F	Leaf	1	$2''$ x $4''$ x $1/8''$
			4 lineal inches x $1/8''$ dia. dowel

Construction

1. Lathe-turn the stems (A) to suggested design and size. Make three mortise slots 120 degrees apart (see fig. 2–40). The mortise slots are made by drilling a line of $3/32$-inch-diameter holes and cutting out the stock between the holes.

2. Lay out and cut the six serpentine legs (see "Construction Notes"). Fit each individual leg to a mortise slot by filing a tenon on the leg top. It is expected that each mortise-tenon will be slightly different, therefore, pair matchings will be required. Glue the legs into the stem slots.

3. Lay out and cut the support cleats (C). Drill the required mortise hole as indicated in figure 2–41. Glue the cleats (C) to the top of the stems (A).

4. Lay out and cut thin strips of stock $1/32$ inch thick by $3/8$ inch wide. Make a male/female jig from scrap wood (see detail in fig. 2–41). Laminate three wood strips around the male jig member, gluing each strip as it is applied until a $3/32$-inch thickness is achieved. Make two rounded skirt pieces (E). (The skirt pieces (E) can be solid wood cut to a rounded design if preferred.)

5. Lay out and cut the tabletops (D) and extension leaf (F). A routed molded edge can be added if desired. Glue the finished skirts (E) to the two table rounds and the extension leaf. See detail in figure 2–41.

6. Table lock. One table round and one end of the extension leaf have $1/8$-inch dowel tenons extending out 1 inch. Drill $1/8$-inch holes into the center of the skirt and glue a section of dowel into the holes.

The other table round and end of the extension leaf has a $1/8$-inch-diameter female mortise hole drilled into the skirt board. When the tabletops are used alone the tenon on one round locks into the mortise on the other.

When the extension leaf is used the tenon on the table round fits the mortise hole in the extension, and the leaf tenon fits the mortise hole on the other table round (see detail fig. 2–41).

Finish

Sand the table smooth removing all traces of glue. Stain or paint to a color of choice. Cover with several coats of lacquer or similar finish. Complete with a coat of paste wax.

LOWBOY WITH ALTERNATE TOPS

Almost every Early American household of modest means had a lowboy or a highboy or both. Hundreds of different styles of them appeared all over the country, all based upon the same characteristics. The cabriole legs, the sunburst designs, and the drawer combinations varied only a little from maker to maker. This furnishing, an American classic, is still being produced today. The base or lowboy was used in dining or living rooms as a side table. It is offered here as a single unit or as the base for the three alternate tops—the highboy top, china cupboard, and secretary desk.

Material

Cherry, maple, birch, walnut, or basswood.

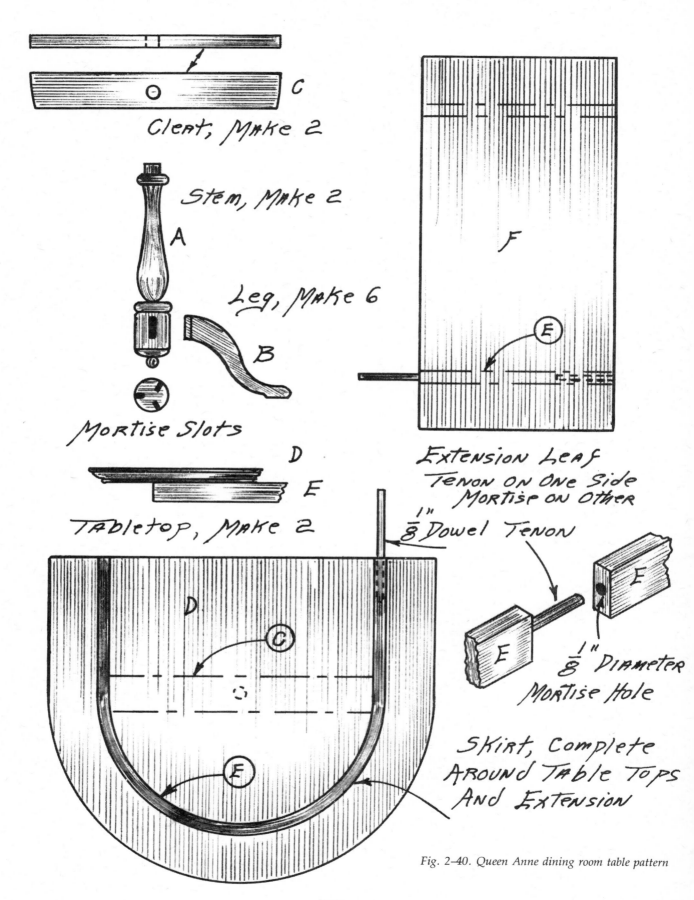

Cleat, Make 2

Stem, Make 2

Leg, Make 6

Mortise Slots

Tabletop, Make 2

Extension Leaf
Tenon on One Side
Mortise on Other

$\frac{1}{8}$" Dowel Tenon

$\frac{1}{8}$" Diameter
Mortise Hole

Skirt, Complete
Around Table Tops
And Extension

Fig. 2-40. Queen Anne dining room table pattern

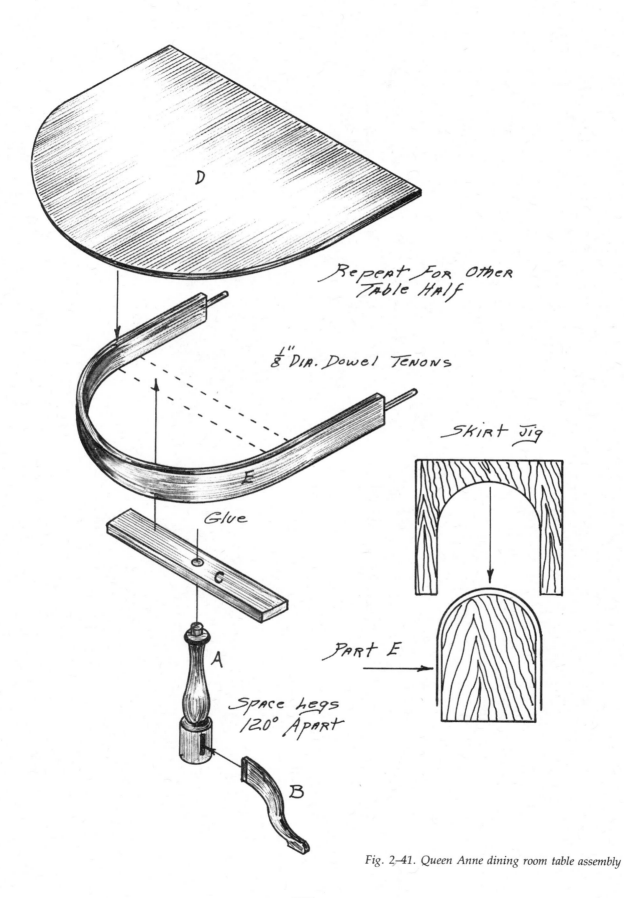

D

Repeat For Other
Table Half

$\frac{1}{8}"$ Dia. Dowel Tenons

E

Skirt Jig

Glue

C

Part E

A

Space Legs
120° Apart

B

Fig. 2-41. Queen Anne dining room table assembly

107

Lowboy Base
With Highboy Top

China Cupboard Top

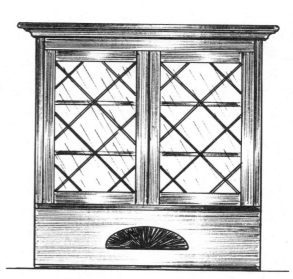

Secretary Desk Top

Alternate Top Designs
Chippendale Style
Circa, Mid 1700s

Fig. 2–42. Lowboy with alternate tops

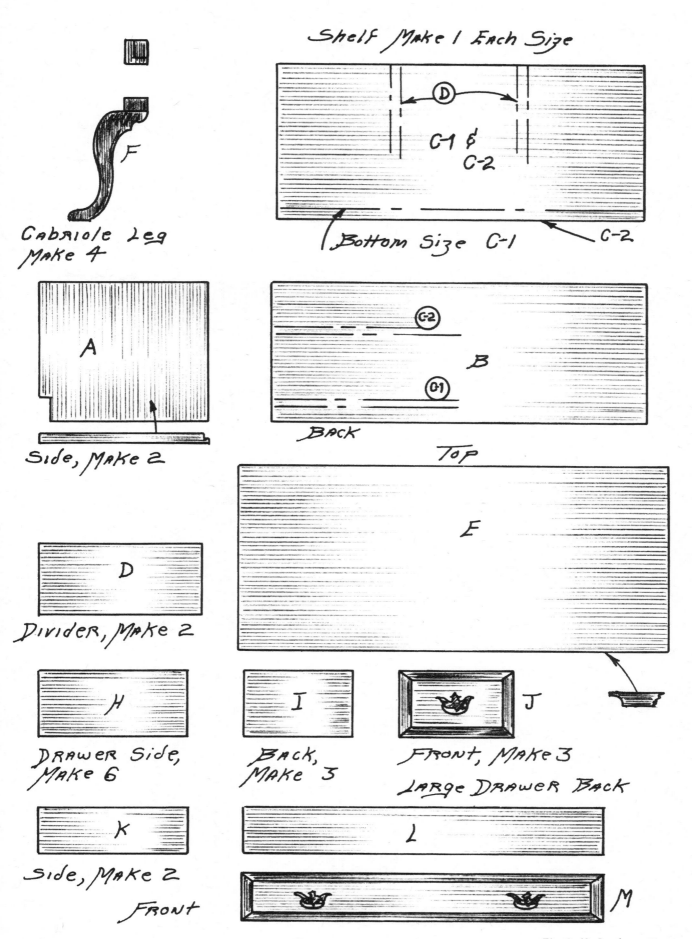

Shelf Make 1 Each Size

D

C-1 &
C-2

Bottom Size C-1   C-2

Cabriole Leg
Make 4

F

A

Side, Make 2

C-2

B

C-1

Back

Top

E

D

Divider, Make 2

H

Drawer Side,
Make 6

I

Back,
Make 3

J

Front, Make 3

Large Drawer Back

K

Side, Make 2

Front

L

M

Fig. 2-43. Lowboy pattern

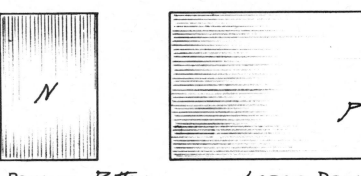

Small Drawer Bottom,
Make 3

Large Drawer Bottom

Front Skirt

G

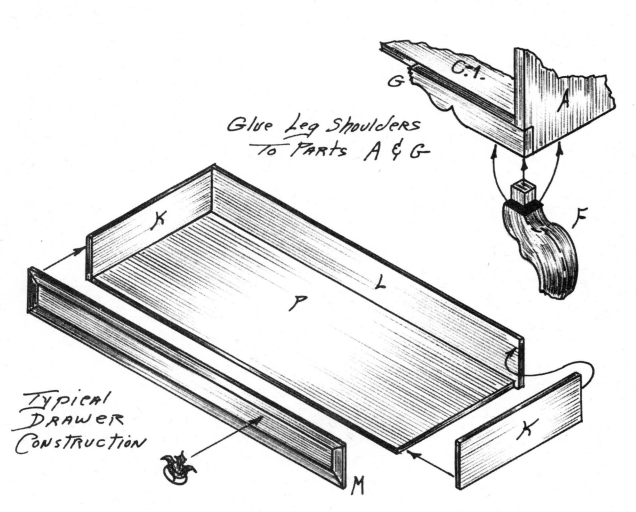

Glue Leg Shoulders
To Parts A & G

Typical
Drawer
Construction

Fig. 2–43. Lowboy pattern (continued)

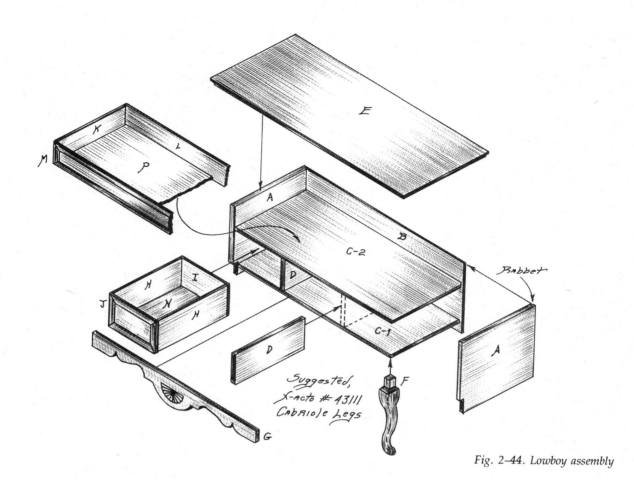

Fig. 2–44. Lowboy assembly

Material List

	Part	Number	Size
A	Side	2	$1^3/4'' \times 1^1/2'' \times 1/8''$
B	Back	1	$4'' \times 1^1/2'' \times 1/16''$
C–1	Shelf	1	$1^9/16'' \times 3^7/8'' \times 1/16''$
C–2	Shelf	1	$1^{11}/16'' \times 3^7/8'' \times 1/16''$
D	Divider	2	$3/4'' \times 1^{11}/16'' \times 1/16''$
E	Top	1	$4^1/2'' \times 2'' \times 1/16''$
F	Leg	4	$7/8'' \times 1^3/8'' \times 1/8''$
G	Skirt	1	$4^1/16'' \times 1/2'' \times 1/16''$
H	Drawer Side	6	$1^1/2'' \times {}^{11}/16'' \times 1/16''$
I	Drawer Back	3	$1^1/8'' \times {}^{11}/16'' \times 1/16''$
J	Drawer Front	3	$1^3/16'' \times {}^{11}/16'' \times 1/16''$
K	Large Drawer Side	2	$1^1/2'' \times 1/2'' \times 1/16''$
L	Large Drawer Back	1	$3^3/4'' \times 1/2'' \times 1/16''$
M	Large Drawer Front	1	$3^3/4'' \times 1/2'' \times 1/16''$
N	Small Drawer Bottom	3	$1'' \times 1^9/16'' \times 1/16''$
P	Large Drawer Bottom	1	$1^9/16'' \times 3^{11}/16'' \times 1/16''$

Construction

1. Lay out and cut the sides (A), back (B), and shelves (C–1 and C–2). Cut a 1/16-by-1/16-inch rabbet on the rear edge of each side (A). (Note the skirt notch in the lower corner of the sides.) Glue the back (B) into the rabbets. Glue the shelves (C–1 and C–2) between the sides (A) and the back (B) (see fig. 2–43).

2. Lay out and cut the divider (D), top (E), and front skirt (G). Glue the top (E) to the sides and back. Glue the divider (D) between the upper shelf (C–2) and the top (E) (see fig. 2–44). Cut the sunburst design into the front skirt. Glue the skirt (G) into the notches in the sides (A).

3. Make the required drawer units (see "Construction Notes" for suggested techniques). Sand fit the drawers into individual openings. Attach scale-size pulls.

4. Glue the four legs to the bottom corners (see detail of leg attachment). The legs will be more secure if they have a tenon glued behind the sides, front skirt, and back.

HIGHBOY TOP

The highboy top combined with the lowboy base creates an excellent piece for Early American bedrooms.

Material List

	Part	Number	Size
A	Side	2	$1^{1/2}$" x $3^{1/2}$" x $^{1/8}$"
B	Back	1	$3^{1/2}$" x $3^{1/2}$" x $^{1/16}$"
C	Shelf	6	$3^{3/8}$" x $1^{3/8}$" x $^{1/16}$"
D	Top	1	$4^{1/2}$" x $1^{1/4}$" x $1^{3/4}$"
E	Top Divider	2	$1^{3/8}$" x $^{3/8}$" x $^{1/16}$"
F	Drawer Side	6	$^{5/8}$" x $1^{3/16}$" x $^{1/16}$"
G	Large Drawer Back	3	$^{5/8}$" x $3^{3/8}$" x $^{1/16}$"
H	Large Drawer Front	3	$^{5/8}$" x $3^{1/2}$" x $^{1/16}$"
I	Large Drawer Bottom	3	$1^{3/16}$" x $3^{1/4}$" x $^{1/16}$"
J	Small Drawer Side	6	$^{3/8}$" x $1^{1/4}$" x $^{1/16}$"
K	Small Drawer Back	2	$^{7/8}$" x $^{3/8}$" x $^{1/16}$"
L	Small Drawer Front	2	$^{15/16}$" x $^{3/8}$" x $^{1/16}$"
M	Small Drawer Bottom	2	$^{13/16}$" x $1^{1/4}$" x $^{1/16}$"
N	Center Drawer Back	1	$1^{3/8}$" x $^{3/8}$" x $^{1/16}$"
P	Center Drawer Front	1	$1^{3/8}$" x $^{3/8}$" x $^{1/16}$"
Q	Drawer Bottom	1	$1^{1/4}$" x $1^{1/4}$" x $^{1/16}$"
R	Drawer Back	1	$3^{3/8}$" x $^{3/8}$" x $^{1/16}$"
S	Drawer Front	1	$3^{3/8}$" x $^{3/8}$" x $^{1/16}$"
T	Molding	1	$^{3/16}$" x $4^{1/4}$" crown or cove
		2	$^{3/16}$" x $1^{1/2}$"

Construction

1. Lay out and cut the sides (A) and back (B). Cut a $^{1/16}$-by-$^{1/16}$-inch rabbet on the back edges of the sides. Glue the back into these rabbets.

2. Lay out and cut the drawer dividers (C) and the top dividers (E). Glue the drawer dividers (C) between the sides as shown in figure 2–45. Glue the top dividers (E) between the two top drawer dividers (C).

3. Make the broken bonnet top (D) (see "Construction Notes"). Glue the finished bonnet to the top divider (C). Lathe-turn a finial and glue it to the center of the bonnet top. Cut the molding (T) making 45-degree-angle miter joints as suggested. Glue the molding to the sides (A) and bottom divider (C).

4. Make the required drawer units. Sand fit each drawer to an individual opening. Attach scale-size maple leaf drawer pulls.

CHINA CUPBOARD TOP

This top was designed to fit the lowboy base to offer an enclosed china cupboard for kitchen or dining room.

Material List

	Part	Number	Size
A	Side	2	$1^{1/4}$" x 4" x $^{1/8}$"
B	Back	1	$3^{3/4}$" x 4" x $^{1/16}$"
C	Shelf	4	$3^{5/8}$" x $1^{1/8}$" x $^{1/16}$"
D	Base	1	$3^{5/8}$" x $^{1/4}$" x $^{1/16}$"
E	Header	1	$3^{5/8}$" x $^{5/16}$" x $^{1/16}$"
F	Top	1	$4^{3/8}$" x $1^{3/4}$" x $^{1/16}$"
G	Molding	1	$^{3/16}$" x $4^{1/4}$" cove or crown
		2	$^{3/16}$" x $1^{1/2}$" cove or crown
H	Door	2	$1^{13/16}$" x $3^{7/16}$" x $^{1/8}$"

Construction

1. Lay out and cut the sides (A) and back (B). Cut a $^{1/16}$-by-$^{1/16}$-inch rabbet on the rear edge of each side. Glue the back into these rabbets.

2. Lay out and cut the shelves (C), base (D), header (E), and top (F). Glue the shelves (C) between the sides (A) as shown in figure 2–47. Glue the header (E) to the tops of the sides (A), and glue the base (D) to the bottom of the sides.
   Glue the top (F) to the tops of the sides and

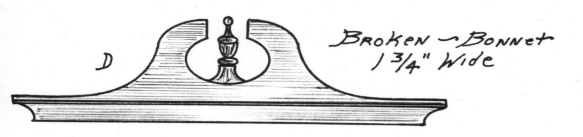

D

Broken~Bonnet 1¾" Wide

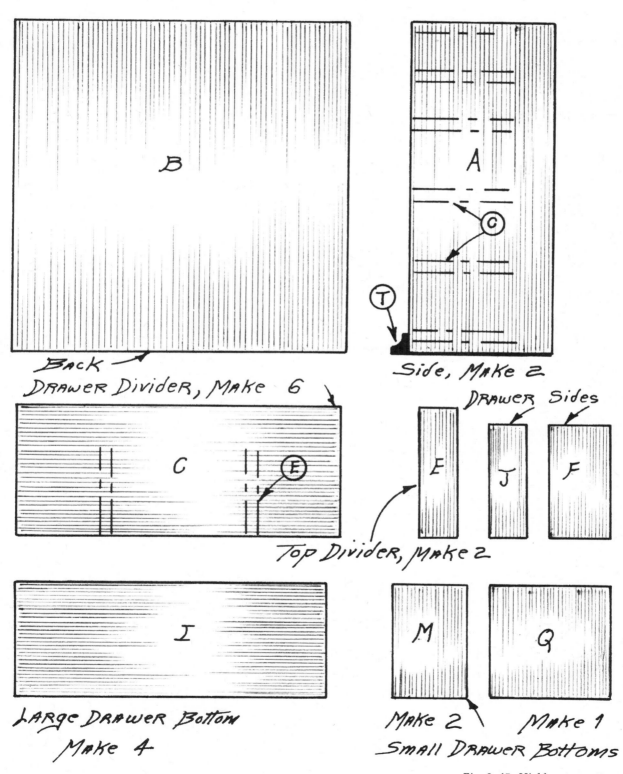

B

Back

Drawer Divider, Make 6

A

C

T

Side, Make 2

C

E

Top Divider, Make 2

Drawer Sides

E

J

F

I

Large Drawer Bottom Make 4

M

Q

Make 2

Make 1

Small Drawer Bottoms

113

Fig. 2–45. Highboy top pattern

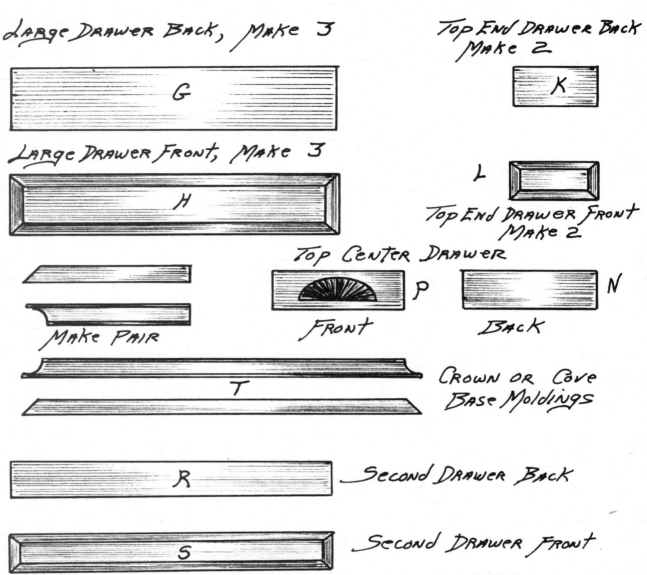

LARGE DRAWER BACK, MAKE 3

G

LARGE DRAWER FRONT, MAKE 3

H

MAKE PAIR

T

R

S

TOP END DRAWER BACK
MAKE 2

K

L

TOP END DRAWER FRONT
MAKE 2

TOP CENTER DRAWER

P   FRONT

N   BACK

CROWN OR COVE
BASE MOLDINGS

SECOND DRAWER BACK

SECOND DRAWER FRONT

Fig. 2–45. Highboy top pattern (continued)

back. Cut the moldings (G) with miter joints and glue to the sides (A), header (E), and top (F).

3. Make two door frames (H) (see "Construction Notes" for suggestions). Glue 1/32-inch glass or heavy gauge plastic to these frames. Attach the doors to the sides (A) with scale-size hinges or pins. Attach two door pulls.

SECRETARY DESK TOP

The desk top combined with the lowboy base is a perfect example of Early American styling for use in the dining or living room areas.

Material List

	Part	Number	Size
A	Side	2	1³/4" × 4¹/4" × ¹/8"
B	Back	1	3³/4" × 4¹/4" × ¹/16"

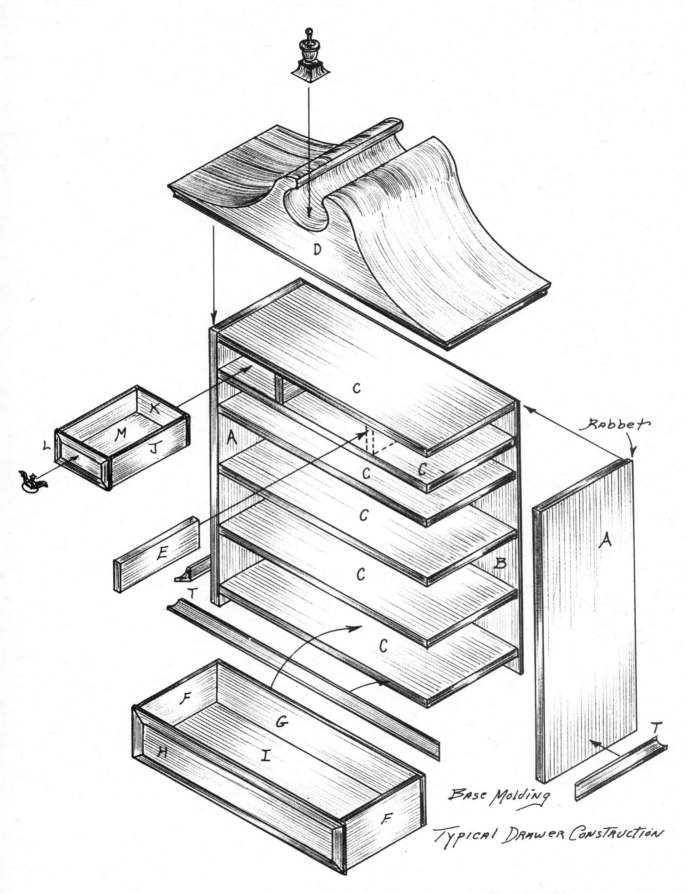

D

L

M K

J

A

C

C

C

C

C

C

C

E

T

F

G

H

I

F

F

Rabbet

A

B

T

Base Molding

Typical Drawer Construction

Fig. 2–46. Highboy top assembly

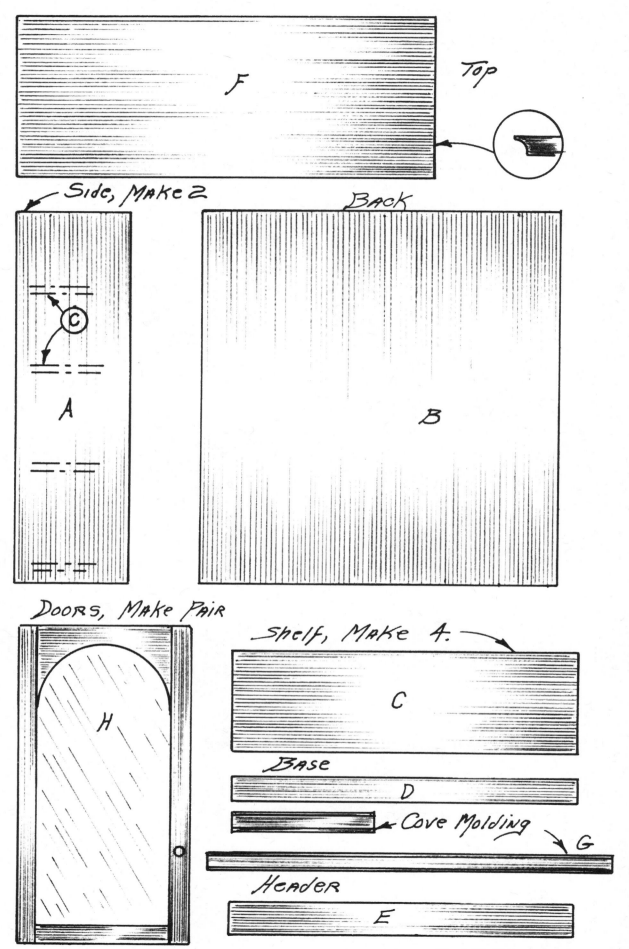

Top

F

Side, Make 2

A

©C

Back

B

Doors, Make Pair

H

Shelf, Make 4.

C

Base

D

Cove Molding

G

Header

E

Fig. 2-47. China cupboard top pattern

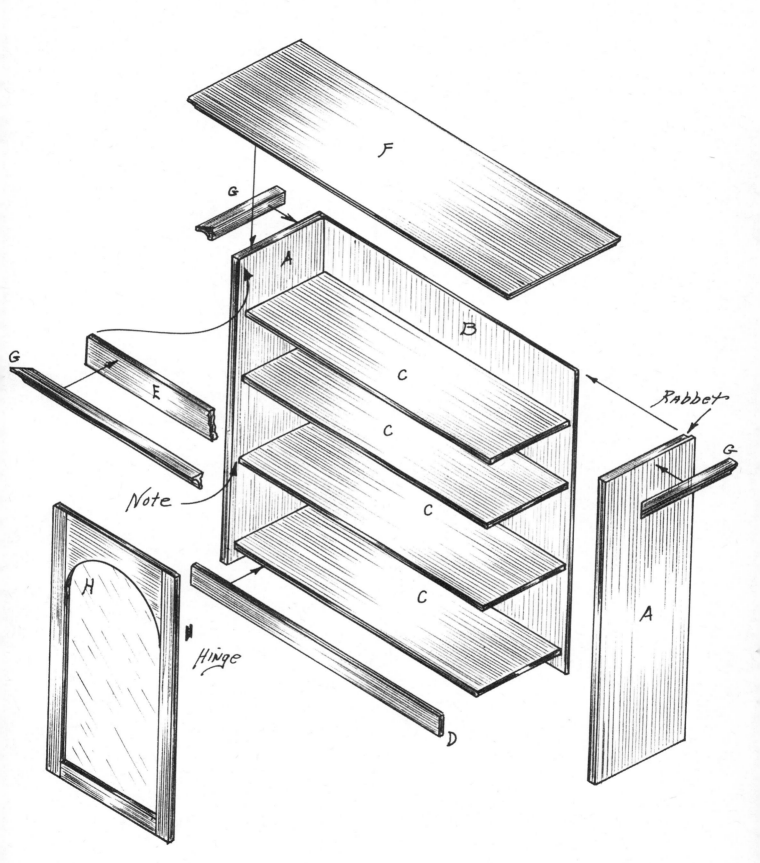

Fig. 2–48. China cupboard top assembly

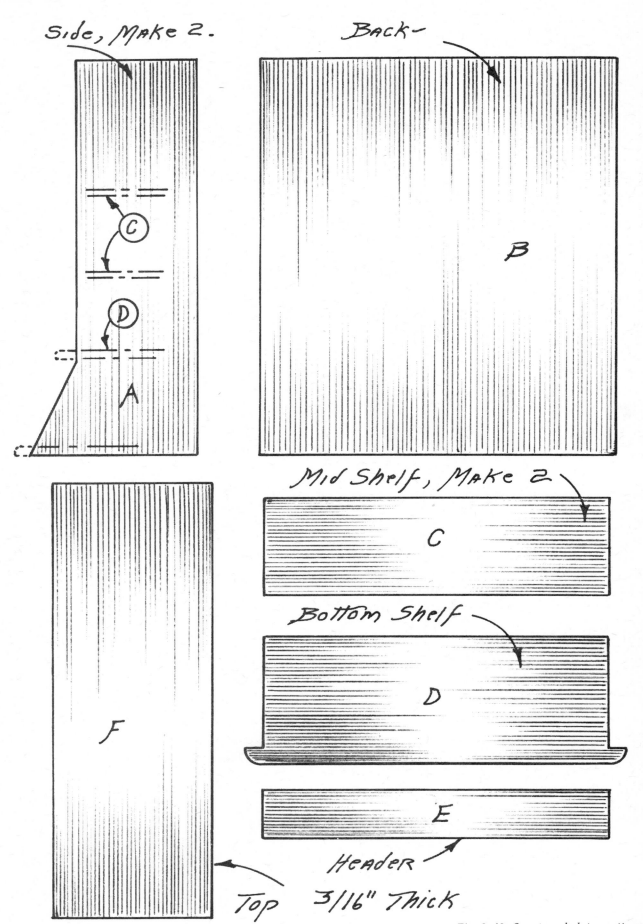

Side, Make 2.

Back

B

Side labels: C, D, A

Mid Shelf, Make 2

C

Bottom Shelf

D

F

E

Top

Header
3/16" Thick

Fig. 2–49. Secretary desk top pattern

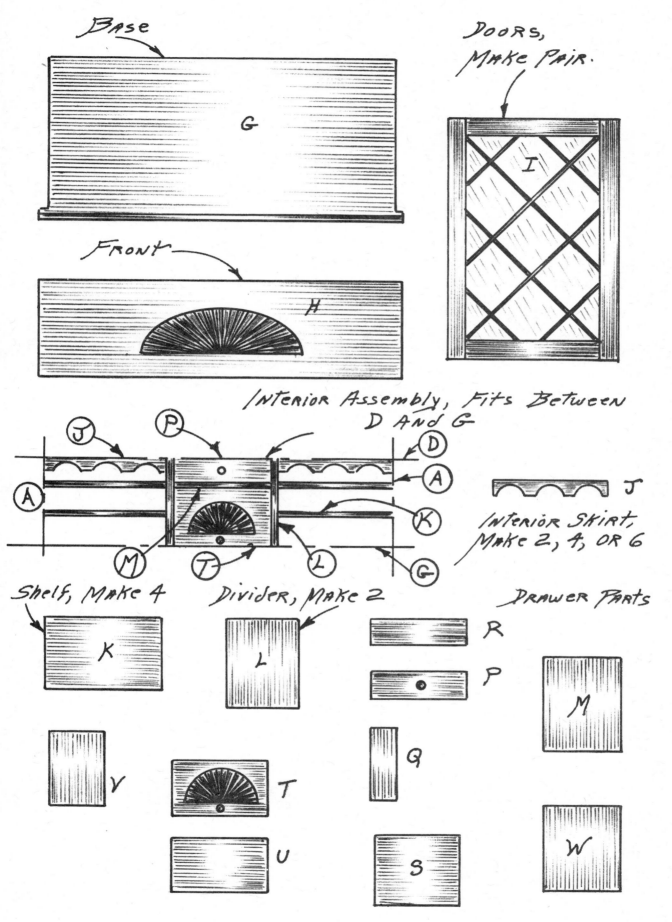

Base

G

Doors, Make Pair.

I

Front

H

Interior Assembly, Fits Between D And G

J   P   D

A   A

M   T   L   G   K

J

Interior Skirt, Make 2, 4, or 6

Shelf, Make 4

K

Divider, Make 2

L

Drawer Parts

R

P

M

V

T

Q

U

S

W

119   *Fig. 2–49. Secretary desk top pattern (continued)*

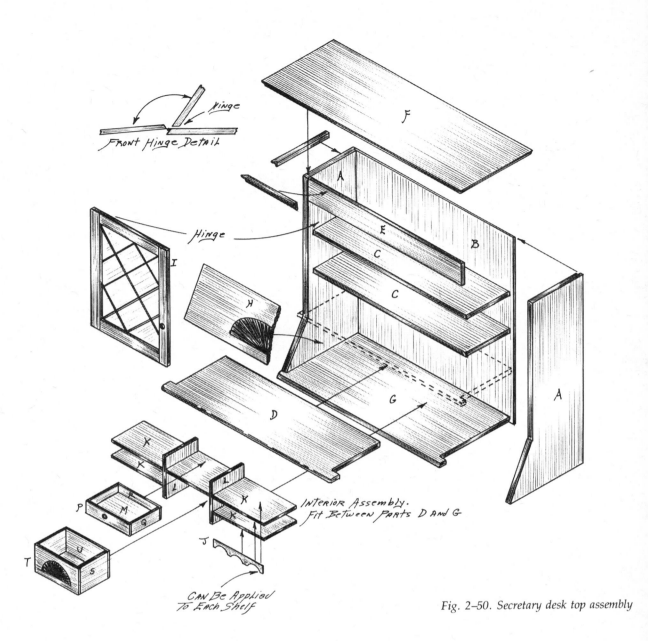

Front Hinge Detail

Hinge

Hinge

H

Interior Assembly.
Fit Between Parts D And G

Can Be Applied
To Each Shelf

Fig. 2–50. Secretary desk top assembly

C	Mid Shelf	2	$3^5/8''$ x $1^1/16''$ x $^1/16''$
D	Bottom Shelf	1	$4''$ x $1^3/8''$ x $^1/16''$
E	Header	1	$3^5/8''$ x $^1/2''$ x $^1/16''$
F	Top	1	$4^3/4''$ x $1^5/8''$ x $^1/16''$
G	Base	1	$3^7/8''$ x $1^3/4''$ x $^1/16''$
H	Front	1	$3^7/8''$ x $1^1/16''$ x $^1/16''$
I	Door	2	$1^3/4''$ x $2^3/8''$ x $^1/16''$
J	Skirt	6	$1^1/4''$ x $^3/16''$ x $^1/32''$
K	Shelf	4	$1^1/4''$ x $^3/4''$ x $^1/16''$
L	Divider	2	$^3/4''$ x $^15/16''$ x $^1/16''$
M	Drawer Bottom	1	$^13/16''$ x $1''$ x $^1/16''$
P	Drawer Front	1	$1''$ x $^1/4''$ x $^1/16''$
Q	Drawer Side	1	$^3/4''$ x $^1/4''$ x $^1/16''$
R	Drawer Back	1	$1''$ x $^1/4''$ x $^1/16''$
S	Drawer Bottom	1	$^7/8''$ x $^3/4''$ x $^1/16''$
T	Drawer Front	1	$^9/16''$ x $1''$ x $^1/16''$
U	Drawer Back	1	$^9/16''$ x $1''$ x $^1/16''$
V	Drawer Side	1	$^9/16''$ x $^3/4''$ x $^1/16''$
W	Drawer Bottom	1	$1''$ x $^3/4''$ x $^1/16''$

Construction

1. Lay out and cut the sides (A) and the back (B). Cut a $^1/16$-by-$^1/16$-inch rabbet on the rear edges of the sides. Glue the back into these rabbets.

2. Lay out and cut the shelves (C and D), header (E), top (F), and base (G). Glue the mid shelf (C) and bottom shelf (D) between the sides as noted in figure 2–50. Glue the header

(E) between the tops of the sides. Glue the top (F) to the sides, back, and header. Cut the molding using miter joints and glue to the sides, header, and top.

Note that the base (G) has the same front angle as found on the bottom of the sides (A) (see detail fig. 2–50). Glue the base (G) between the sides and to the back.

3. Lay out and cut the interior pigeonhole bin area (J, K, and L). Make the pigeonhole assembly as shown in figure 2–49. Glue this assembly between the base (G) and bottom shelf (D). (J can be applied to each K and D if desired.)

Make two small drawer units as shown in figure 2–50. Cut the sunburst design into T. Sand fit the drawer units to their openings.

4. Lay out and cut the front (H). Cut the large sunburst design into this part. (A purchased medallion may be used here if preferred.) Hinge the front to the base (G). The front (H) should close up to just clear the bottom shelf (C). When open it will lay down and rest upon the top of the lowboy.

5. Make two door frames to fit between the bottom shelf (D) and header (E) (see "Construction Notes" for suggested techniques). Glue 1/32-inch glass or heavy gauge plastic to the back of each door frame. Make the diamond muntins from 1/32-inch-square stock and attach to each frame. Attach the doors to the sides with hinges.

Finish

Sand the reproduction smooth removing all traces of glue. Stain or paint to a color of choice. Cover with several coats of lacquer or similar finish. Complete with a coat of paste wax.

The china cupboard can be stocked with scale-size china on the shelves. The desk can have miniature books stacked on the shelves.

QUEEN ANNE TEA TABLE

This reproduction is the forefather of the modern coffee table. It was designed to be placed in front of a chair or settee, therefore the legs are short. This table can be made with longer legs and used as a side table if preferred. Both length legs are offered here. The end extensions are used to hold candle sconces.

Material

Cherry, maple, walnut, or basswood. Cherry is preferred.

Material List

	Part	Number	Size
A	Side	2	2½" x 3/8" x 1/8"
B	End	2	1¼" x 3/8" x 1/8"
C	Leaf Guide	1	1" x 2¼" x 3/16"
D	Top Guide	1	2¼" x 1/8" x 1/8"
E	Tea Table Leg	4	½" x 1⅛" x 1/8"
E	Side Table Leg	4	5/8" x 1⅞" x 1/8"
F	Leaf	2	1" x 3/4" x 3/32"
G	Top	1	3" x 1½" x 1/16"

Construction

1. Lay out and cut the sides (A) and ends (B). Cut the 1/8-inch-wide seats into the ends. Make 45-degree miter joints at the corners. Glue the sides and ends together to form a rectangle.

2. Lay out and cut the leaf guide (C) and top guide (D). Glue the leaf guide between the sides and ends so that the center section of the leaf guide is even with the slot bottoms in the ends. Glue the top guide between the end's center, so that the bottom of the top guide (D) is even with the slot tops in the ends (B).

3. Lay out and cut the legs (E). Drill 1/8-inch-diameter holes into the leg tops. Glue a section of 1/8-inch dowel into these holes allowing 1/4 inch tenon extensions. Drill 1/8 inch mounting holes into the bottom of the leaf guide (C). Glue the leg tenon into these holes setting the legs at a 45 degree angle.

4. Lay out and cut the extension leaves (F). Glue a face to each and sand-fit them so they slide easily in and out of the seats in the ends (B).

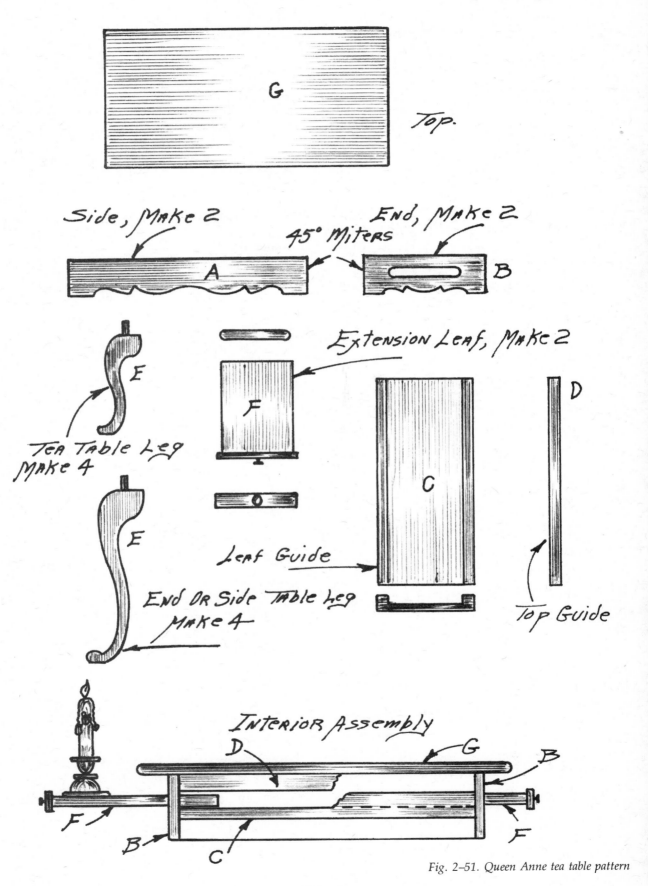

G

Top.

Side, Make 2   End, Make 2

45° Miters

A   B

E

Tea Table Leg
Make 4

Extension Leaf, Make 2

F   C   D

Leaf Guide

Top Guide

E

End Or Side Table Leg
Make 4

Interior Assembly

D   G   B

F

B   C   F

Fig. 2–51. Queen Anne tea table pattern

122

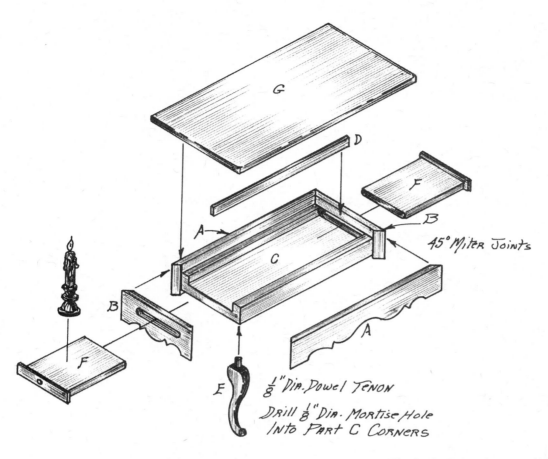

Fig. 2–52. Queen Anne tea table assembly

5. Lay out and cut the top (G). Round over all the edges and glue it to the sides, ends, and top guide.

Finish

Sand the table smooth removing all traces of glue. Stain or paint to a color of choice. Cover with several coats of lacquer or similar finish. Complete with a coat of paste wax.

QUEEN ANNE SIDEBOARD

The sideboard was employed in several rooms in the Early American era. It was always available to hold the punch bowl during the holiday season, the rack of lamb at social dinners, or display gleaming silver service. The following reproduction can be used in any period setting from the 1700s up to the early 1900s.

Material

Cherry, walnut, maple, or basswood. Cherry or walnut is preferred.

Material List

	Part	Number	Size
A	Side	2	$1^{1}/_{4}$" x 1" x $^{3}/_{16}$"
B	Back	1	$2^{3}/_{4}$" x 1" x $^{1}/_{16}$"
C	Rail	1	$2^{5}/_{8}$" x $^{1}/_{8}$" x $^{1}/_{16}$"
D	Skirt	1	$2^{5}/_{8}$" x $^{9}/_{16}$" x $^{1}/_{16}$"
E	Bottom	1	$2^{5}/_{8}$" x 1" x $^{1}/_{16}$"
F	Top	1	$1^{5}/_{8}$" x $3^{1}/_{2}$" x $^{1}/_{16}$"
G	Leg	4	$^{3}/_{4}$" x $1^{5}/_{8}$" x $^{1}/_{8}$"
H	Drawer Bottom	1	$2^{1}/_{2}$" x $1^{1}/_{8}$" x $^{1}/_{16}$"
I	Drawer Back	1	$2^{5}/_{8}$" x $^{3}/_{8}$" x $^{1}/_{16}$"
J	Drawer Side	2	$1^{1}/_{8}$" x $^{3}/_{8}$" x $^{1}/_{16}$"
K	Drawer Front	1	$2^{3}/_{4}$" x $^{3}/_{8}$" x $^{1}/_{16}$"

Construction

1. Lay out and cut the sides (A), back (B), top front rail (C), front skirt (D), and bottom (E).

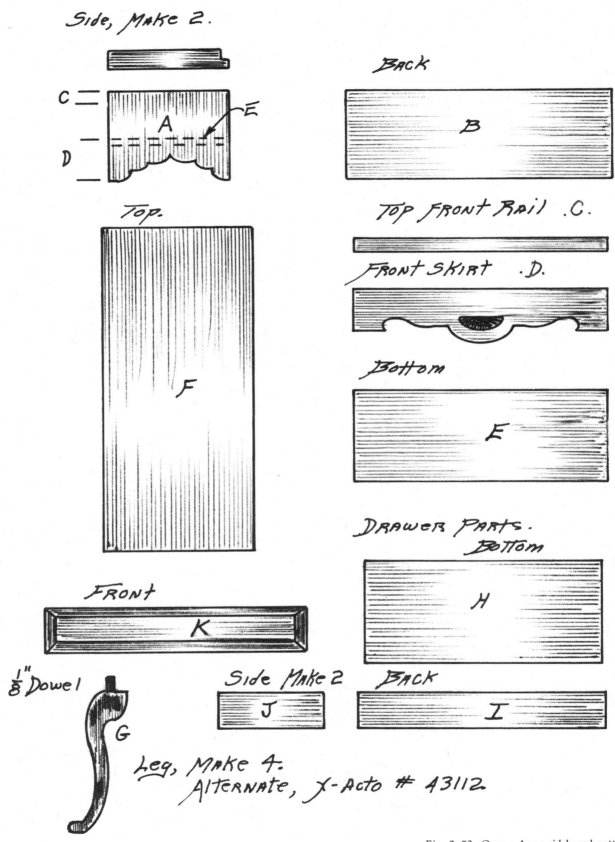

Side, Make 2.

Back

C
A
E
D

B

Top.

Top Front Rail .C.

Front Skirt .D.

F

Bottom

E

Drawer Parts.
Bottom

Front

H

K

⅛" Dowel

Side Make 2

Back

J

I

G

Leg, Make 4.
Alternate, X-Acto # 43112.

Fig. 2–53. Queen Anne sideboard pattern

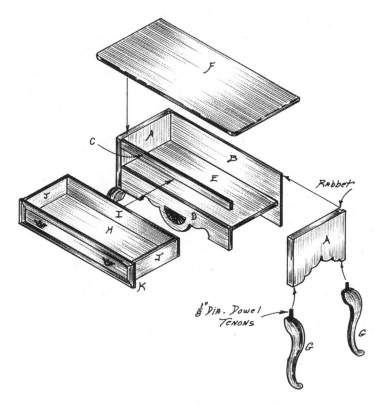

Fig. 2–54. Queen Anne sideboard assembly

Cut a ¹/₁₆-by-¹/₁₆-inch rabbet on the rear edge of the sides. Glue the back into these rabbets. Cut out the design on the front skirt (D). Glue the top front rail (C) and the front skirt (D) to the front edges of the sides. Glue the bottom (E) between the sides and to the back and front skirt.

2. Lay out and cut the top (F). Sand the edges round and glue it to the sides, back, and top front rail.

3. Make a drawer unit from H, I, J, and K. Sand fit the finished drawer into the opening.

4. Lay out and cut the legs (G). (X-ACTO #43112 legs can be used if preferred.) Drill a ¹/₈-inch-diameter hole into the leg tops. Glue a section of ¹/₈-inch dowel into the holes allowing ¹/₄-inch tenon extensions. Drill ¹/₈-inch mounting holes into the corners of the sides. Glue the leg tenon into these holes setting the legs at a 45 degree angle.

Finish

Sand the reproduction smooth removing all traces of glue. Stain or paint to a color of choice. Cover with several coats of lacquer or similar finish. Complete with a coat of paste wax.

COATTAIL SIDE CHAIR

This style chair has endured over generations despite the fact that gentlemen stopped wearing coattails. Some authorities claim the chair was designed so the coattail could be extended to drop over the back when a gentleman sat down. The seat was originally plank, rush, or cane; but in later periods appeared with an upholstered cushion. The following reproduction has a rush seat and fits in well with the Early American period.

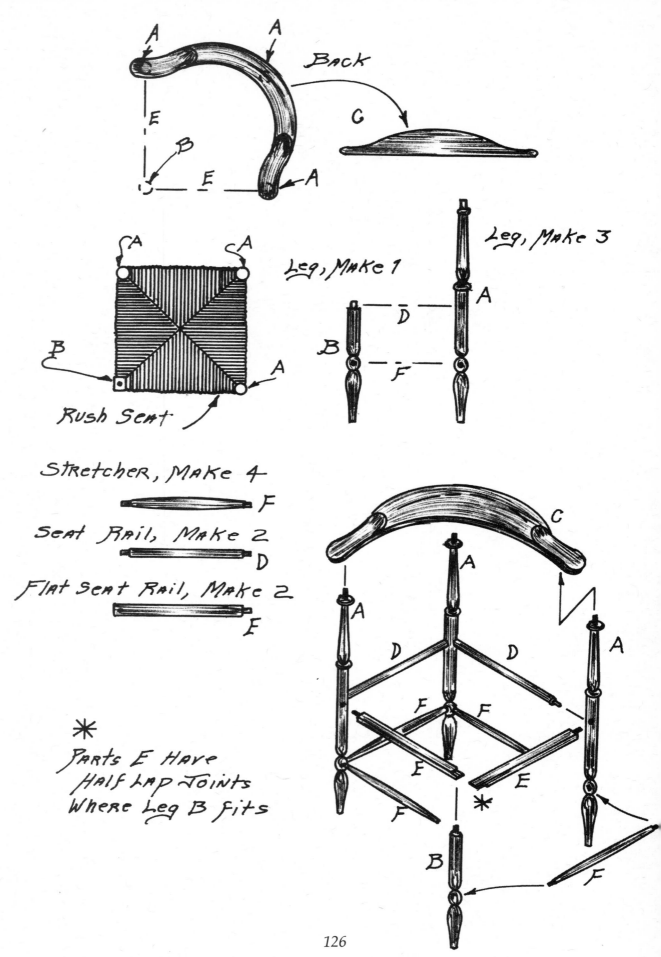

A *A*

Back

C

E

B

E

A

A *A*

Leg, Make 3

Leg, Make 1

B *D* *A*

F

B

Rush Seat

A

Stretcher, Make 4

F

Seat Rail, Make 2

D

Flat Seat Rail, Make 2

E

✳

*Parts E Have
Half Lap Joints
Where Leg B Fits*

C

A

A *A*

D *D*

F *F*

E

E

F

✳

B

F

126

Fig. 2–55. Coattail side chair pattern

Material

All turnings are made from maple dowels.

Material List

	Part	Number	Size
A	Leg	3	$1/8''$ dia. x $2^1/2''$
B	Leg	1	$1/8''$ dia. x $1^1/4''$
C	Back	1	$2^1/4''$ x $1^1/8''$ x $5/16''$
D	Seat Rail	2	$1/8''$ dia. x $1^1/4''$
E	Flat Rail	2	$1^1/2''$ x $1/8''$ x $1/16''$
F	Stretcher	4	$1/8''$ dia. x $1^3/8''$

Construction

1. Lay out and cut the back (C) to suggested shape and size. Extreme care is required because the wood grain will be thin and fragile at certain points.

2. Lathe-turn the legs (A and B), the seat rails (D), and the stretchers (F). (Note that A and B have top tenons.) Drill $1/16$-inch-diameter mortise holes into the legs as noted in figure 2–55. Select legs (A) and glue the seat rails (D) and stretchers (F) into the mortise holes. Glue the stretchers (F) to the legs (A) assembly and into the mortise holes in leg (B).

Lay out and cut the flat seat rails (E). Make a half-lap joint where these rails (E) form a right angle, and make a $1/16$-inch-round tenon on the other ends. Drill a $1/16$-inch-diameter mortise hole through the half-lap joints. Glue the tenons into the mortise holes on the legs (A) and glue the top tenon into the hole in the half-lap joint.

3. Lay the back (C) on top of the legs (A) and mark out for mounting holes. Drill these holes and glue the leg (A) top tenons into the holes in the back.

Finish

Sand the chair smooth removing all traces of glue. Stain or paint to a color of choice. Cover with several coats of lacquer or similar finish. Complete with a coat of paste wax. Apply the rush seat (see "Construction Notes" for instructions).

PLANK SEAT, BOOTJACK-BACK CHAIR

Chairs have been designed in hundreds of different shapes, styles, and designs. One area that adds itself best to artistic expression is the chair back. The following dining room chair was reproduced as a mate to the Early American dining room table. However, single chairs were used throughout the household.

Material

Cherry, maple, birch, or basswood. Legs, stretchers, and spokes are maple dowels.

Material List

	Part	Number	Size
A	Seat	1	$1^3/8''$ x $1^3/8''$ x $1/4''$
B	Back	1	$1^5/8''$ x $3/8''$ x $1/8''$
C	Slat	1	$1/2''$ x $1^5/8''$ x $1/16''$
D	Spindle	2	$1/16''$ dia. x $1^1/2''$
E	Leg	4	$1/8''$ dia. x $1^1/2''$
F	Side Stretcher	2	$1/8''$ dia. x $1^1/2''$
G	Center Stretcher	1	$1/16''$ dia. x $1^1/2''$

Construction

1. Lay out and cut the seat (A), back (B), and bootjack slat (C). Cut the profile into the seat (see side view fig. 2–56). Drill the mortise holes and cut the mortise slots into the seat. Drill the top mortise spoke holes and the mortise slots into the back (B). File the tenons on the bootjack slat (C) to fit the mortise slots.

2. Lathe-turn the spindles (D) to suggested shape and size. Make tenons on each end. Glue the bottom tenons of the bootjack slat (C) and the spindle (D) into the mortise slots in the seat. Glue the top tenons of the bootjack slat (C) and spindles (D) into the back (B).

3. Lathe-turn the legs (E), side stretchers (F), and center stretcher (G) to suggested shape and length. Drill $1/16$-inch-diameter blind mortise holes into the legs (E) for the stretcher tenons. Drill a $1/16$-inch-diameter blind mortise hole into the center of the side stretchers (F) for

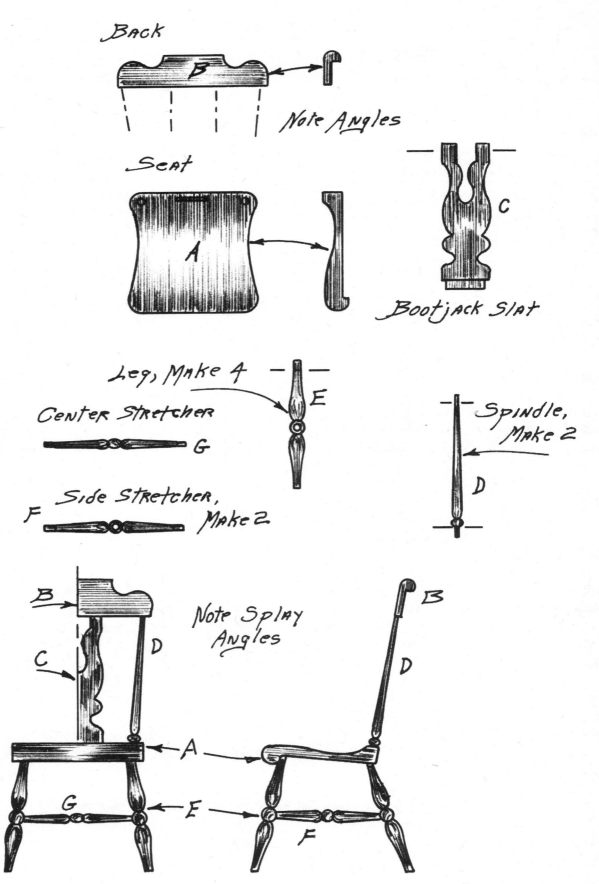

Back

Note Angles

Seat

Bootjack Slat

A

C

Leg, Make 4

Center Stretcher

G

E

Spindle,
Make 2

D

Side Stretcher,
Make 2

F

Note Splay
Angles

B

C

D

A

G

E

B

D

A

E

F

Fig. 2–56. Plank seat, bootjack back chair pattern

the center stretcher (G) tenons. Drill the leg mounting holes into the bottom of the chair seat (note splay angles in fig. 2–56).

4. Glue the side stretchers into the legs while you glue the tenon on the legs into the mounting holes in the seat. Glue the center stretcher into the mortise holes in the side stretchers.

Finish

Sand the chair smooth removing all traces of glue. Stain or paint to a color of choice. Cover with several coats of lacquer or similar finish. Complete with a coat of paste wax.

EIGHTEENTH CENTURY BOOKCASE

There has always been a need for certain period style bookcases. The following miniature was developed along lines found in Early American pieces. The basic length given is six inches but, if the reader prefers, any size bookcase can be made by adding or subtracting in multiples of two inches.

Material

Cherry, maple, mahogany, or basswood. Cherry is preferred.

Material List

	Part	Number	Size
A	Side	2	$1^{1}/_{4}"$ x 7" x $^{1}/_{8}"$
B	Back	1	$6^{1}/_{8}"$ x 7" x $^{1}/_{16}"$
C	Small Shelf	4	6" x $^{3}/_{4}"$ x $^{1}/_{16}"$
D	Large Shelf	2	6" x $1^{3}/_{16}"$ x $^{1}/_{16}"$
E	Counter	1	$6^{1}/_{4}"$ x $1^{3}/_{8}"$ x $^{1}/_{16}"$
F	Top	1	$1^{1}/_{4}"$ x 7" x $^{1}/_{16}"$
G	Top Cornice	1	$6^{1}/_{4}"$ x $^{5}/_{8}"$ x $^{1}/_{16}"$
H	Mold	1	7" x $^{3}/_{16}"$ cove or crown
		2	$1^{1}/_{4}"$ x $^{3}/_{16}"$ cove or crown
I	Lower Top Rail	1	$6^{1}/_{4}"$ x $^{1}/_{4}"$ x $^{1}/_{16}"$
J	Skirt	1	$6^{1}/_{4}"$ x $^{3}/_{8}"$ x $^{1}/_{16}"$
K	Lower Stile	5	$1^{3}/_{4}"$ x $^{3}/_{16}"$ x $^{1}/_{16}"$
L	Top Stile	1	4" x $^{1}/_{4}"$ x $^{1}/_{16}"$
M	Door	6	1" x $1^{7}/_{8}"$ x $^{1}/_{8}"$
N	Bible Shelf	1	$1^{1}/_{4}"$ x $1^{1}/_{4}"$ x $^{1}/_{16}"$
P	Shelf Guide	1	$1^{1}/_{2}"$ x $1^{3}/_{16}"$ x $^{1}/_{4}"$

Construction

1. Lay out and cut the sides (A) and back (B). Cut a $^{1}/_{16}$-by-$^{1}/_{16}$-inch rabbet on the rear edges of the sides. Glue the back into these rabbets.

2. Lay out and cut the shelves (C and D) to lengths and widths. Glue them between the sides and to the back (see in fig. 2–57).

3. Lay out and cut the counter top (E), top (F), and top cornice (G). Glue the counter top (E) to the sides (A) and back (B). Glue the top cornice boards (G) to the sides. Glue the top (F) to the sides (A) and top cornice (G). Cut the moldings (H) to size with 45-degree miter corner joints. Glue cove molding (H) to the sides, top, and top cornice.

4. Lay out and cut the lower top rail (I), skirt (J), and lower stile (K) to shape and lengths. (The notch in the end molding is for the Bible shelf.) Glue the lower top rail to the sides just under the counter top. Glue the skirt (J) to the bottom of the sides. Glue the stiles (K) between the lower top rail and the skirt.

5. Lay out and cut the top stiles (L). Glue them to the counter top (E) and top cornice (G).

6. Make three pairs of raised-panel doors (M) to fit the openings. Hinge the finished doors to the sides and lower stile. Lay out and cut the shelf guide (P). Glue the shelf guide between the lower top rail (I) and the back (B) so the slide area is even with the bottom of the notches cut into the lower top rail. Make the shelf (N). Sand fit the Bible shelf to fit the notch opening in the lower top rail. When the shelf is pulled out, it provides a place for a Bible or dictionary.

Finish

Sand the bookcase smooth removing all traces of glue. Stain or paint to a color of choice.

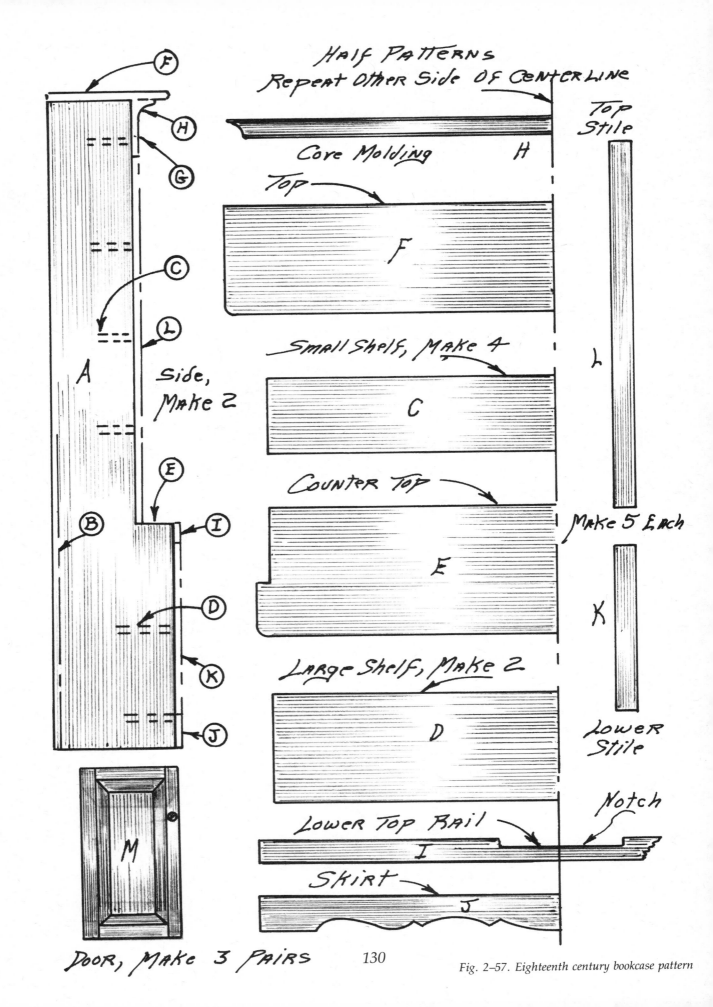

Half Patterns
Repeat Other Side Of Centerline

Top Stile

Core Molding   H

Top

F

L

Small Shelf, Make 4

C

Side, Make 2

A

Counter Top

E

Make 5 Each

K

Lower Stile

Large Shelf, Make 2

D

B

Notch

Lower Top Rail

I

Skirt

J

M

Door, Make 3 Pairs   130

Fig. 2-57. Eighteenth century bookcase pattern

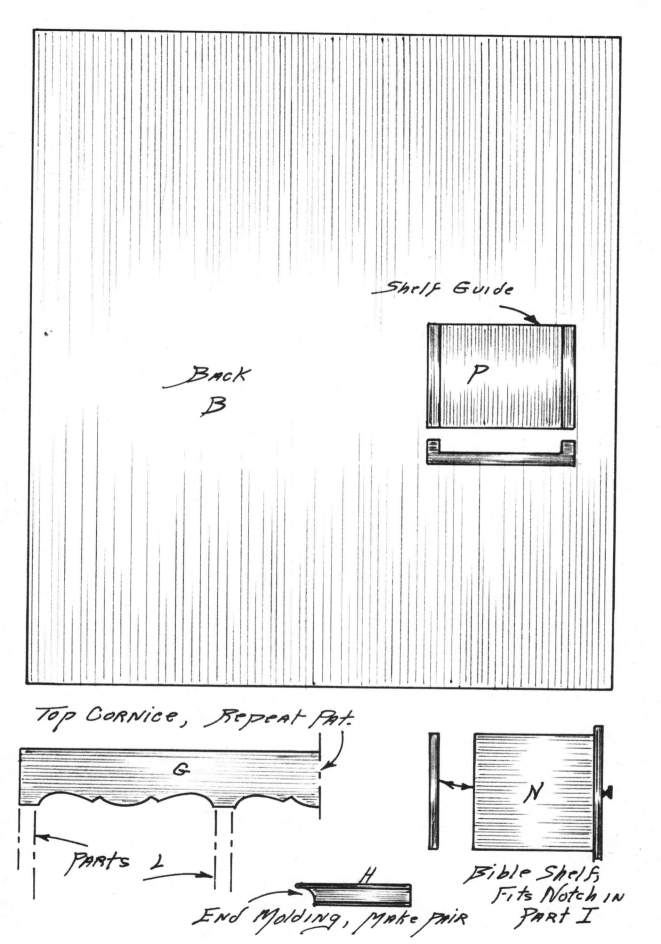

Shelf Guide

Back
B

P

Top Cornice, Repeat Pat.

G

Parts L

H

End Molding, Make Pair

N

Bible Shelf,
Fits Notch in
Part I

Fig. 2–57. Eighteenth century bookcase pattern (continued)

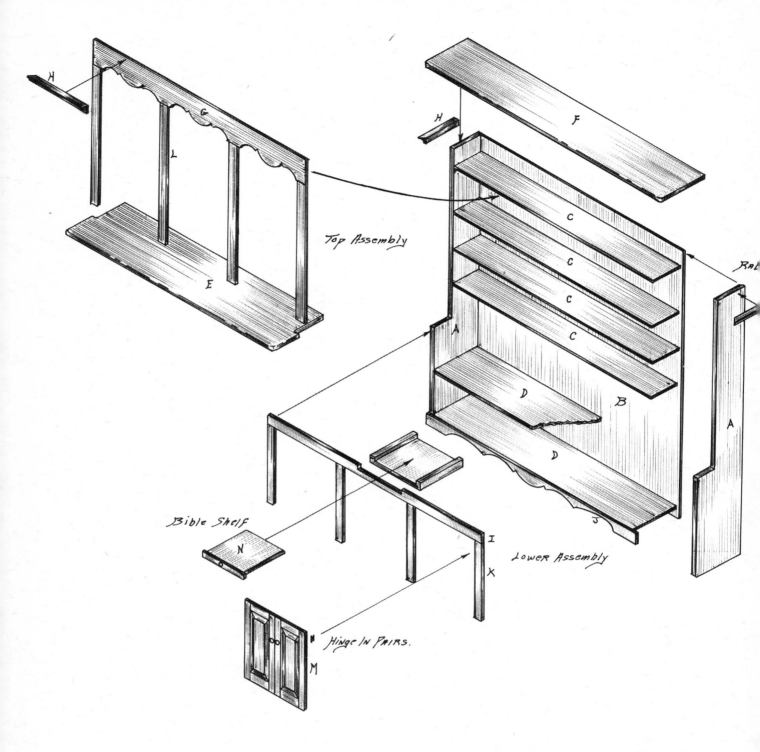

Top Assembly

Bible Shelf

Lower Assembly

Hinge In Pairs.

Fig. 2–58. Eighteenth century bookcase assembly

Cover with several coats of lacquer or similar finish. Complete with a coat of paste wax.

Miniature-size books or objets d'art can be purchased to stock the shelves.

SECTION THREE

Pennsylvania Dutch Furnishings

The main difference between Early American furnishings and Pennsylvania Dutch furniture is the use of color and decoration. The basic lines, shapes, and configurations are almost identical with only subtle deviations. Top cornice moldings, cyma curve skirts, or raised-panel doors seemed to be used universally throughout the period from mid 1700 to mid 1800, therefore Pennsylvania Dutch furnishings were just as at home in Boston, Salem, or Raleigh as in Lancaster.

Craftsmanship progressed in the Pennsylvania Dutch regions at the same rate as it did in the other sections of the country. Skirt boards gave way to lathe-turned legs, and square raised panels became more provincial, employing half- or quarter-circles or arcs and compound molded edges.

One of the major factors that contributed to the Pennsylvania Dutch influence was the increasing use of color and design. Normal household furnishings, once stained or left their natural color, were now painted red, blue, green, or yellow. Bright, bold color burst upon an otherwise drab nineteenth century home. The Pennsylvania Dutch craftsman carried this use of color one step further and decorated furnishings with flowers, birds, and geometric designs. Such motifs were not confined only to furniture, but also danced across glassware, china, birth and wedding certificates, and outbuildings. The decorations were not haphazard, each had a special meaning and symbolism.

Many motifs held religious meanings while others held an expression of family or romantic

Fig. 3–1. Pennsylvania Dutch millback kitchen (Courtesy the Philadelphia Museum of Art, A. J. Wyatt, staff photographer)

love. Nowhere is such meaning better expressed than in the bride's chest or the daughter's blanket chest. Each chest, made by a father for his daughter, was unique and reflected the family unit as "your heart and my heart are as one."

The full meaning of Pennsylvania Dutch furnishings cannot be found in the subtle differences in line or construction but in the "music the colors make on the eye." The Pennsylvania Dutch had a word for it "For Fancy," meaning that everyday items should be pleasing, attractive, and at times spiritual. They

symbolize a higher being, good luck, health and love, wealth, and a wish for long life—a heritage well worth preserving either in full size or in miniature.

The following Pennsylvania Dutch miniature reproductions were developed from antiques found in Pennsylvania museums and private collections. At times an optional design is offered for the furnishing that differs somewhat from the original piece, but at all times the painted motifs are exact copies of typical nineteenth century Dutch designs. They may sometimes seem over decorated, but the reduc-

Fig. 3–2. Decorative coffee pot (Courtesy the Index of American Design)

Fig. 3–3. Bride's chest (Courtesy the Index of American Design)

tion in overall scale precludes the use of very thin, pencil line design work. In full-size furnishings such a line design enhances the piece, but in 1/12-scale miniatures, such a line becomes almost nonexistent. Therefore, an in-creased usage of the tulip design is substituted. These pieces can be used to furnish a totally Pennsylvania Dutch household or individual pieces can be made and incorporated in Early American miniature settings.

7

Bedroom Group

Close examination will show that the basic construction of the following Pennsylvania Dutch bedroom furnishings closely resembles that of Early American and some early Victorian furniture. What makes these miniatures really different and appealing is the decoration.

PENNSYLVANIA DUTCH FOUR-POST BED

The Pennsylvania Dutch four-post bed represents a slight departure from the Early American tester bed in that the height of the posts is greatly reduced. In addition, the width or thickness was increased in order to perhaps portray permanence.

Material

Cherry, maple, basswood, or mahogany. Cherry is preferred.

Material List

	Part	Number	Size
A	Head Post	2	$5/16''$ x $5/16''$ x $3^1/2''$
B	Foot Post	2	$5/16''$ x $5/16''$ x $2^1/2''$
C	Headboard	1	$4^3/4''$ x $2^3/4''$ x $1/8''$
D	Footboard	1	$4^3/4''$ x $1''$ x $1/8''$
E	Blanket Roll	1	$1/4''$ dia. x $4^3/4''$
F	Side Rail	2	$6''$ x $5/8''$ x $3/16''$
G	Slat	6	$1/8''$ x $1/16''$ x $4^1/2''$

Construction

1. Lay out and lathe-turn the head posts (A), foot posts (B), and blanket roll (E) to suggested

137

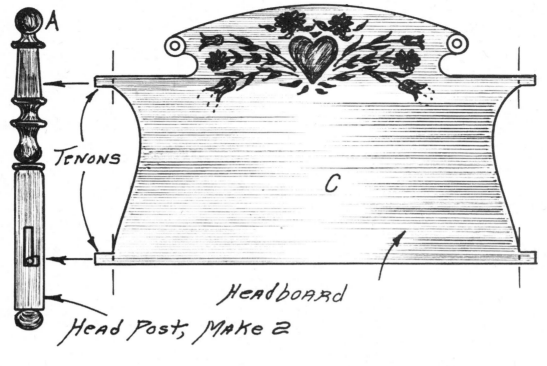

TENONS

A

C

Headboard

Head Post, Make 2

Side Rails, Make 2

F

Dowel Tenon.

Cove Mold

G

Slat, Make 6

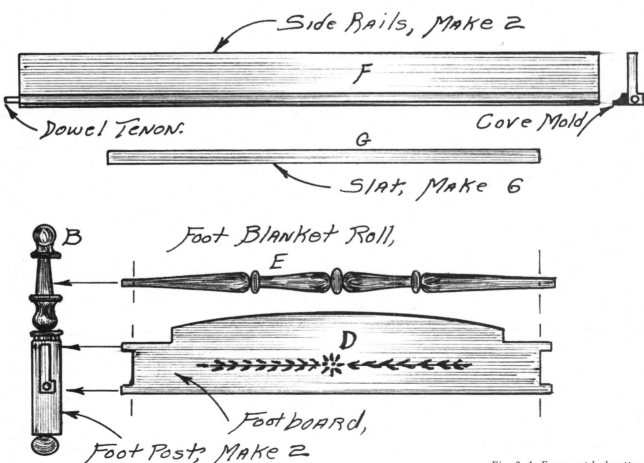

B

Foot Blanket Roll,

E

D

Footboard,

Foot Post, Make 2

Fig. 3–4. Four post bed pattern

138

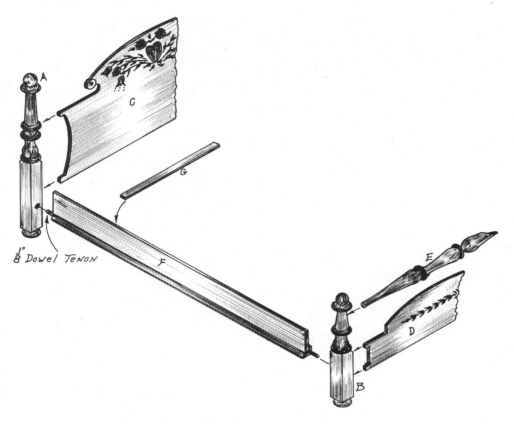

$\frac{1}{8}$" Dowel Tenon

Fig. 3–5. Four post bed assembly

shape and size. Lay out and cut the headboard (C) and footboard (D) (see fig. 3–5). Note the tenons on the headboard and footboard and blanket roll.

2. Drill mortise holes into the finished head posts (A) and foot posts (B) as shown in figure 3–5. Glue the headboard (C) into the head posts (A) and the footboard (D) and blanket roll (E) into the foot posts (B).

3. Lay out and cut the side rails (F) to shape and size. Note the rabbet cut on the inside edges. Drill a $\frac{1}{8}$-inch-diameter hole into the ends of the side rails. Glue a section of $\frac{1}{8}$-inch-diameter dowel into these holes allowing $\frac{1}{4}$ inch to project as a tenon. Line up the side rails to the headboard and footboard assemblies and mark the $\frac{1}{8}$-inch-diameter mortise holes. Dry fit the side rail to the two assemblies.

Finish

It is recommended that the headboard and footboard be finished before assembly.

Stain all the pieces to a color of choice. Hand paint the heart and flower design. Cover with one coat of lacquer or similar covering.

Glue the $\frac{1}{8}$-inch side rail tenons into the headboard and footboard assemblies. Cover with several more coats of lacquer or other finish.

Make the bed slats (G). Drop them on to the rabbet edge made in the side rails. Make a mattress and/or box spring (see "Construction Notes") and install on top of the slats.

SUNBURST MASTER'S BED

The following reproduction clearly displays the integration of furniture styles of the different periods. This miniature bed has overtones of Early American styling with an early Victorian influence. It is possible that such a bed was part of a set and produced in quantity, thereby finding its way into the Pennsylvania Dutch country.

Material

Cherry, walnut, mahogany, and basswood. Cherry is preferred.

Material List

	Part	Number	Size
A	Head Post	2	$1/4''$ x $1/4''$ x $4^3/4''$
B	Headboard	1	$4^1/4''$ x $3^1/2''$ x $1/8''$
C	Foot Post	2	$1/4''$ x $1/4''$ x $2^5/8''$
D	Footboard	1	$4^1/4''$ x $1^5/8''$ x $1/8''$
E	Side Rail	2	$1''$ x $6''$ x $3/16''$
F	Slat	6	$1/8''$ x $1/16''$ x $4^1/4''$

Construction

1. Lay out and lathe-turn the head posts (A) and foot posts (C). Lay out and cut the headboard (B) and footboard (D) to size. Note the stock allowed for tenons on the ends of the footboard and headboard.

Line up the headboard (B) between two head posts and mark the posts for the mortise holes. Drill out these holes and glue the headboard to the head posts. Follow similar construction for the footboard assembly.

2. Lay out and cut the side rails (E). Drill a $1/8$-inch-diameter hole into both ends. Glue a section of $1/8$-inch-diameter dowel into these holes allowing $1/4$-inch tenon extensions. Line up the side rails between the footboard and headboard assemblies and drill the required mortise holes into the head posts and foot posts. Glue the side rails to the head posts and foot posts.

Finish

Sand the entire reproduction smooth removing all traces of glue. Stain if desired.

Cover with several coats of lacquer or similar finish. Make several bed slats. Drop the slats on to the rabbet edge cut into the side rails (E). Install a heavy piece of cardboard over the slats to act as a spring. Make a mattress to fit the opening (see "Construction Notes").

HIGH CHEST (CIRCA 1815)

This miniature is an example of country- or cottage-style furniture construction. This high chest was a homespun version of the more elaborate Queen Anne highboy. The original chest was not decorated but authentic designs are included for optional use.

Material

Basswood, pine, cherry, or maple. Basswood is preferred.

Material List

	Part	Number	Size
A	Side	2	$1^5/8''$ x $4^7/8''$ x $1/8''$
B	Back	1	$3^1/4''$ x $4^7/8''$ x $1/16''$
C	Drawer Divider	7	$3^1/8''$ x $1^9/16''$ x $1/16''$
D	Top/Bottom	2	$3^7/8''$ x $1^{15}/16''$ x $1/16''$
E	Mid-divider	2	$1^9/16''$ x $1/2''$ x $1/16''$
F	Drawer Side	10	$1^3/8''$ x $1/2''$ x $1/16''$
G	Small Drawer Front/Back	6	$1''$ x $1/2''$ x $1/16''$
H	Drawer Bottom	3	$1^3/8''$ x $7/8''$ x $1/16''$
I	Large Drawer Front/Back	6	$3^1/8''$ x $3/4''$ $1/16''$
J	Large Drawer Side	6	$1^3/8''$ x $3/4''$ x $1/16''$
K	Large Drawer Bottom	5	$3''$ x $3/4''$ x $1/16''$
L	Mid-size Drawer Front/Back	4	$3^1/8''$ x $1/2''$ x $1/16''$

Construction

1. Lay out and cut the sides (A) and back (B). Cut a $1/16$-inch-by-$1/16$-inch rabbet on the rear inside edges of the sides (A). Glue the back (B) into these rabbets.

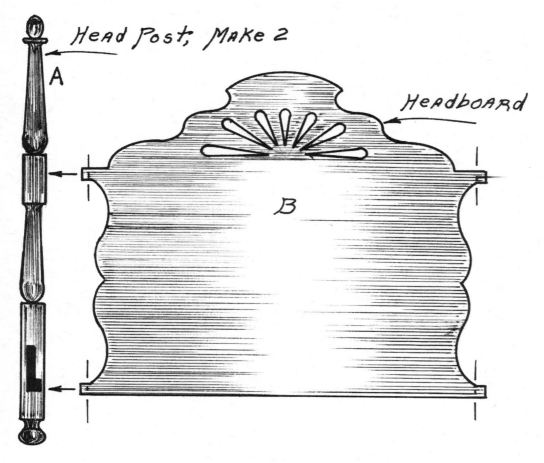

Head Post, Make 2

A

Headboard

B

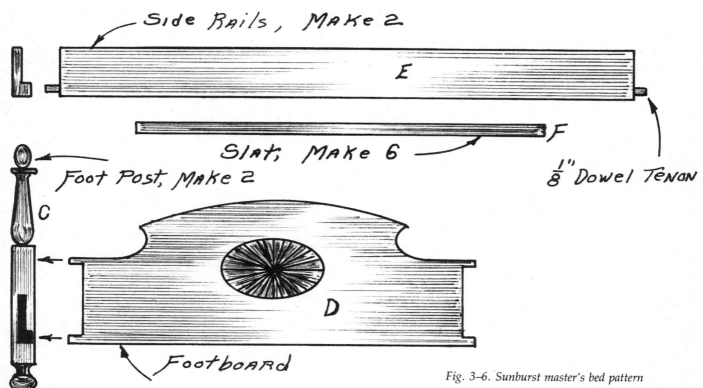

Side Rails, Make 2

E

F

Slat, Make 6

Foot Post, Make 2

C

$\frac{1}{8}$" Dowel Tenon

D

Footboard

Fig. 3–6. Sunburst master's bed pattern

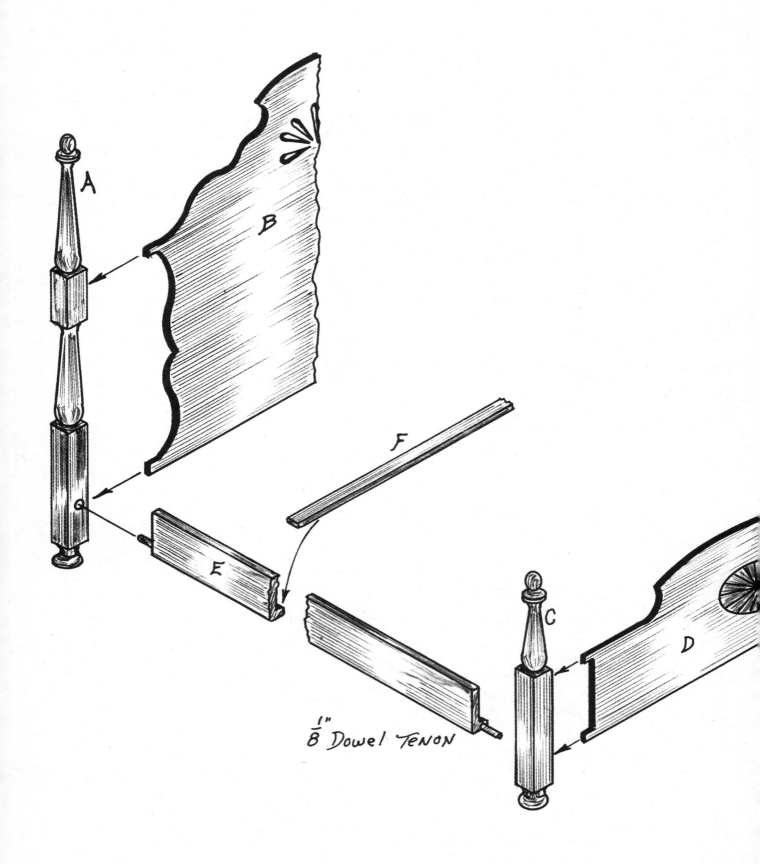

$\frac{1}{8}$" Dowel Tenon

Fig. 3–7. Sunburst master's bed assembly

Fig. 3–8. Pennsylvania Dutch high chest

2. Lay out and cut the drawer dividers (C) and top and bottom (D) to size. Glue a part D to the top and bottom of the sides and back. Glue the drawer dividers between the sides and to the back as noted in figure 3–10. Cut out the top dividers and glue them between the two top drawer dividers (C) (see fig. 3–9). Cut the cove moldings (N) and glue them to the sides (A) and top drawer divider (C) and under the top (D).

3. Make three small drawers to fit the top openings. See typical drawer construction in figure 3–9. Sand fit the drawer units in place. Make five large drawers to fit the lower openings. Sand fit each drawer in place for a tight fit. Make four legs (M) and glue them to the bottom (D).

choice. Hand paint the designs on the drawer fronts and the chest sides. Cover with several coats of lacquer or similar finish. Finish with a coat of paste wax.

Since many chests of this time period used wallpaper as drawer lining, authenticity would be added by papering the interiors of all drawers with scale-size wallpaper.

LOW CHEST

The low chest is a direct offshoot of the previous high chest. This miniature reproduction is the normal dresser height and contains the usual drawers of a bedroom piece.

Finish

Sand the entire miniature smooth removing all traces of glue. Stain or paint to a color of

Material

Basswood, pine, cherry, or maple. Basswood is preferred.

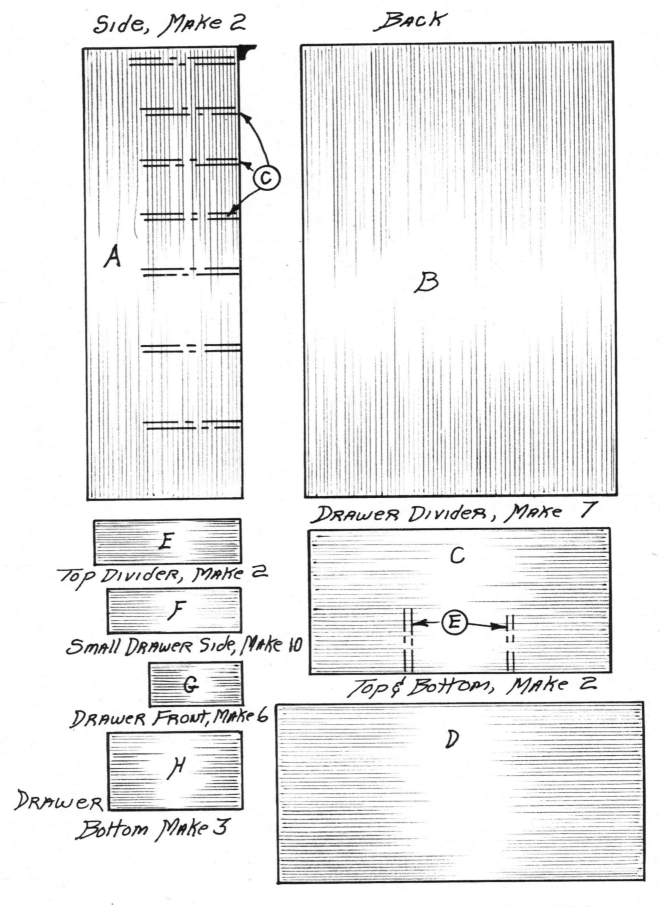

Fig. 3–9. High chest pattern

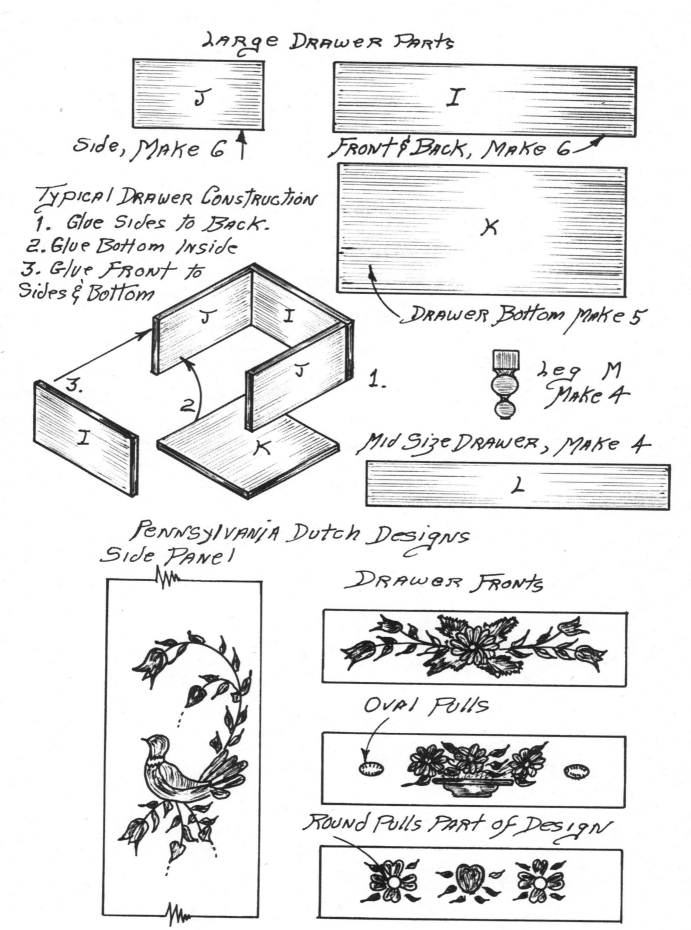

Large Drawer Parts

J

Side, Make 6

I

Front & Back, Make 6

Typical Drawer Construction
1. Glue Sides to Back.
2. Glue Bottom Inside
3. Glue Front to Sides & Bottom

J   I

J

3.   I   2   K

K

Drawer Bottom Make 5

1.

Leg M Make 4

Mid Size Drawer, Make 4

L

Pennsylvania Dutch Designs
Side Panel

Drawer Fronts

Oval Pulls

Round Pulls Part of Design

Fig. 3–9. High chest pattern (continued)

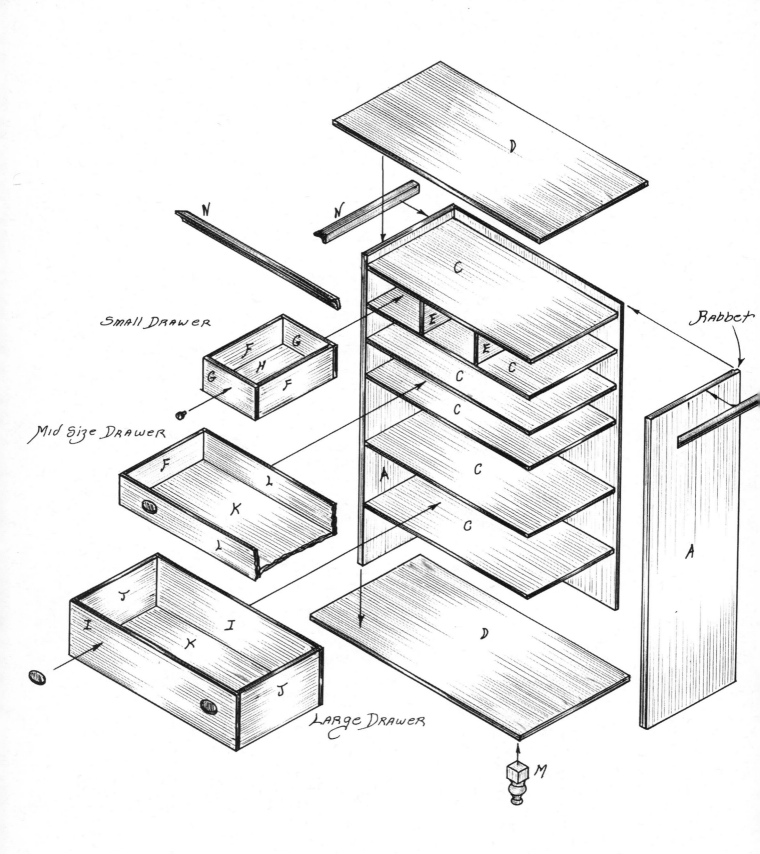

Small Drawer

Mid Size Drawer

Large Drawer

Rabbet

Fig. 3–10. High chest assembly

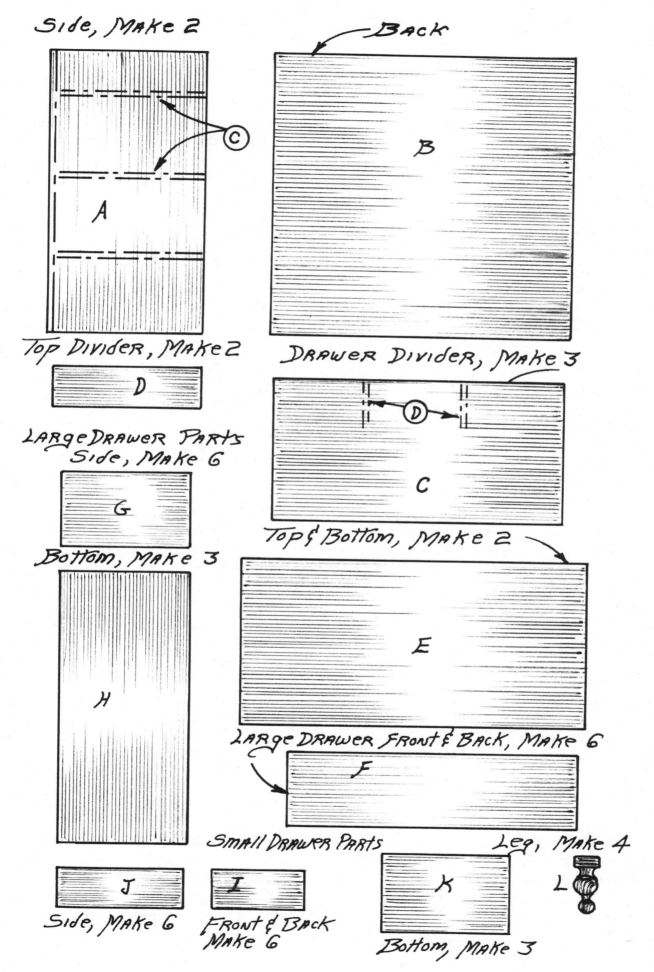

Side, Make 2

C

A

Back

B

Top Divider, Make 2

D

Drawer Divider, Make 3

D

C

Large Drawer Parts
Side, Make 6

G

Bottom, Make 3

H

Top & Bottom, Make 2

E

Large Drawer Front & Back, Make 6

F

Small Drawer Parts

J

Side, Make 6

I

Front & Back
Make 6

Leg, Make 4

L

K

Bottom, Make 3

Fig. 3-11 Low chest pattern

Material List

	Part	Number	Size
A	Side	2	$1^5/8'' \times 3'' \times ^1/8''$
B	Back	1	$3^1/8'' \times 3'' \times ^1/16''$
C	Drawer Divider	3	$3'' \times 1^9/16'' \times ^1/16''$
D	Top Divider	2	$1^1/2'' \times ^7/16'' \times ^1/16''$
E	Top or Bottom	2	$3^5/8'' \times 1^3/4'' \times ^1/16''$
F	Large Drawer Front or Back	6	$3'' \times ^3/4'' \times ^1/16''$
G	Large Drawer Side	6	$1^3/8'' \times ^3/4'' \times ^1/16''$
H	Large Drawer Bottom	3	$2^7/8'' \times 1^3/8'' \times ^1/16''$
I	Small Drawer Front or Back	6	$1'' \times ^7/16'' \times ^1/16''$
J	Small Drawer Side	6	$1^3/8'' \times ^7/16'' \times ^1/16''$
K	Small Drawer Bottom	3	$^7/8'' \times 1^1/4'' \times ^1/16''$
L	Leg	4	$^1/4''$ dia. $\times ^5/8''$

Construction

1. Lay out and cut the sides (A) and the back (B) to shape and size. Cut a $^1/16$-by-$^1/16$-inch rabbet on the rear inside edges of the sides. Glue the back into these rabbets.

Lay out and cut the drawer dividers (C), top dividers (D), and top and bottom (E). Glue parts E to the tops and bottoms of the sides and back (see fig. 3–12). Glue the drawer dividers (C) between the sides and back (see fig. 3–11). Glue the top dividers (D) between the top drawer divider and the top.

2. Make three large and three small drawer units to fit the available spaces. (See "Construction Notes" for suggested techniques.) Sand fit each drawer in place.

Make four legs (L) and glue them to the bottom (E).

Finish

Sand the entire miniature smooth removing all traces of glue. Stain or paint to a color of choice. Hand paint the drawer front design if desired. Cover with several coats of lacquer or similar finish. Finish with a coat of paste wax.

MIRROR CADDY FOR LOW CHEST OF DRAWERS

This miniature mirror stand was designed to go on top of the low chest of drawers. It contains a single, small drawer for grooming articles and a mirror supported between two curved brackets.

Material

The same as the low chest.

Material List

	Part	Number	Size
A	Back	1	$1^1/4'' \times ^3/8'' \times ^1/16''$
B	Side	2	$1'' \times ^3/8'' \times ^1/16''$
C	Bottom	1	$1^1/8'' \times ^{15}/16'' \times ^1/16''$
D	Top	1	$1^3/8'' \times 1^1/8'' \times ^1/16''$
E	Drawer Back	1	$1^3/16'' \times ^5/16'' \times ^1/16''$
F	Drawer Side	2	$^7/8'' \times ^5/16'' \times ^1/16''$
G	Drawer Bottom	1	$1^1/8'' \times ^7/8'' \times ^1/16''$
H	Drawer Front	1	$1^3/8'' \times ^5/16'' \times ^1/16''$
I	Leg	4	$^1/8''$ oval
J	Bracket	2	$^1/2'' \times 1^1/4'' \times ^1/8''$
K	Mirror Backer	1	$1^1/2'' \times 1'' \times ^1/16''$

Construction

1. Lay out and cut frame (parts A, B, C, and D). Glue the back (A) between the sides (B). Glue the bottom (C) between the back and sides. Glue the top (D) on top of the back and sides.

2. Make a small drawer unit from parts E, F, G, and H (see "Construction Notes"). Sand fit the drawer to its opening.

3. Make four small oval legs (I). Glue these legs to the bottom of part C. Make two serpentine mirror brackets (J). Glue these to the top of part D. Make the mirror frame (K).

4. Glue a piece of $^1/32$-inch mirror in the opening or behind the open frame. Suspend the finished frame between the two serpentine brackets and secure with hinge pins.

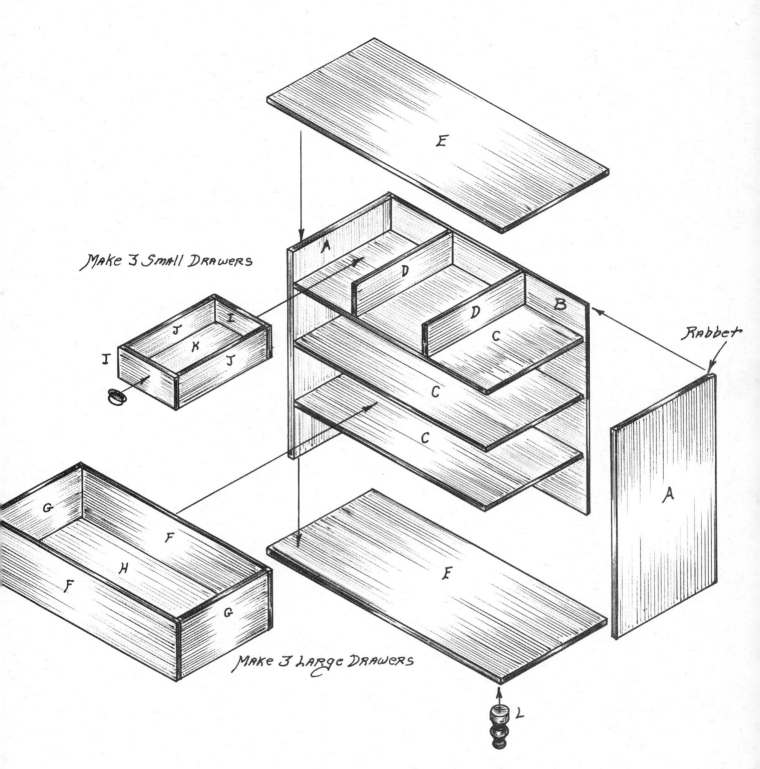

Make 3 Small Drawers

Rabbet

Make 3 Large Drawers

Possible Drawer Designs

Fig. 3–12. Low chest assembly

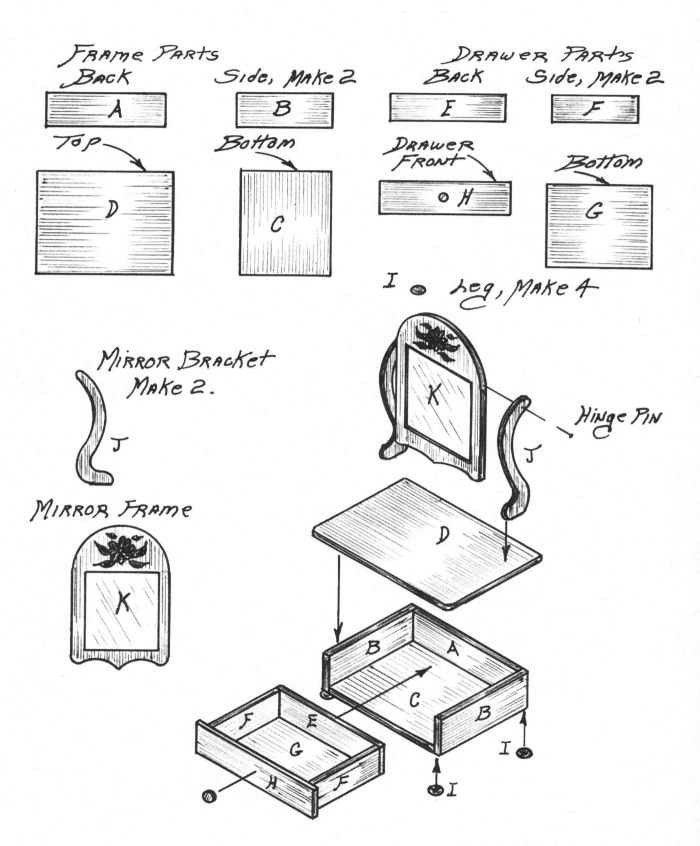

FRAME PARTS
Back

Side, MAKE 2

Top

Bottom

DRAWER PARTS
Back

Side, MAKE 2

DRAWER
FRONT

Bottom

I   Leg, MAKE 4

MIRROR BRACKET
Make 2.

Hinge Pin

MIRROR FRAME

Fig. 3–13. Mirror caddy pattern and assembly

Fig. 3–14. Bride's chest

Finish

Hand paint the floral design on the mirror frame. Stain the entire reproduction to match the low chest. Cover with several coats of lacquer or similar finish.

BRIDE'S CHEST (BLANKET CHEST)

The bride's chests were often made by fathers for their daughters. All through their early lives, young girls would learn the arts of sewing, needlepoint, and embroidery, making items they would use later in their own homes. The bride's chest contained all of the needlework, which represented hours of laborious work.

Because of the close family ties involved with the bride's chest, the decorations often symbolized good fortune or love. These chests were bright cherry red and a delight to behold, almost as if the exterior reflected the contents.

Material

Pine, basswood, cherry, or mahogany. The chest is painted not stained.

Material List

	Part	Number	Size
A	Side	2	$1^1/2$" x $2^3/8$" x $1/16$"
B	Back	1	$3^1/2$" x $2^3/8$" x $1/16$"
C	Divider	2	$3^1/2$" x $1^7/16$" x $1/16$"
D	Spacer	1	$1/2$" x $1^7/16$" x $1/16$"
E	Skirt	1	$3^5/8$" x $3/8$" x $1/16$"
F	Front	1	$3^5/8$" x $1^1/2$" x $1/16$"
G	Top	1	$4^1/8$" x $1^{13}/16$" x $1/16$"
H	Hinge	2	$1/4$" x 1" x $1/16$"
I	Pin	2	$1/8$" dia. x $3/4$"
J	Drawer Front	2	$1^1/2$" x $1/2$" x $1/16$"
K	Drawer Back	2	$1^7/16$" x $1/2$" x $1/16$"
L	Drawer Side	4	$1^5/16$" x $1/2$" x $1/16$"
M	Drawer Bottom	2	$1^5/16$" x $1^1/2$" x $1/16$"

Construction

1. Lay out and cut the sides (A), back (B), dividers (C), and spacer (D). With butt joints, glue the sides (A) to the back (B). Glue the dividers (C) between the sides and to the back (see fig. 3–15). Glue the spacer (D) between the dividers (C) in the center.

2. Lay out and cut the skirt (E) and the front (F) to size and shape. Glue them to the sides and dividers.

3. Lay out and cut the top (G) and hinges (H)

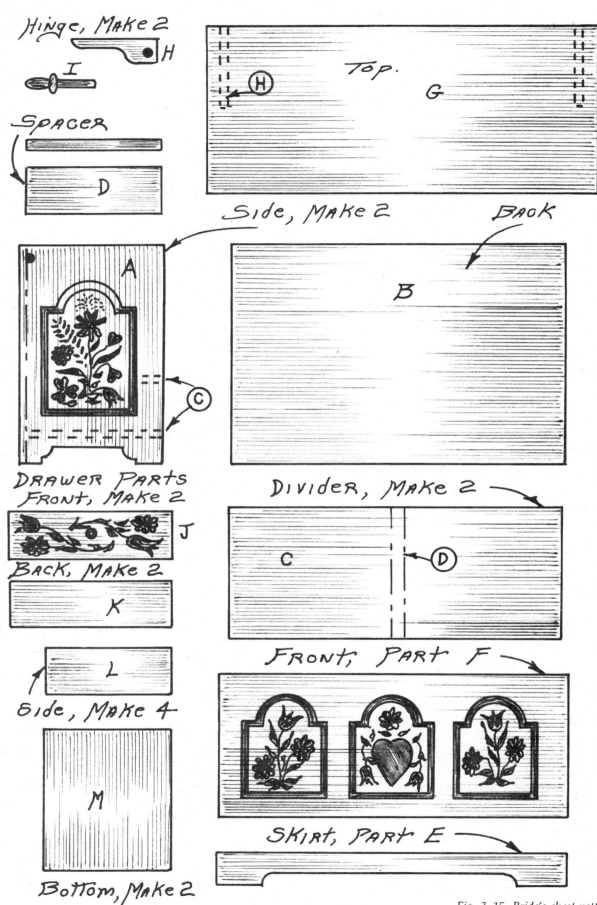

Hinge, Make 2

Spacer

Side, Make 2

Top.

Back

Drawer Parts
Front, Make 2

Back, Make 2

Side, Make 4

Bottom, Make 2

Divider, Make 2

Front, Part F

Skirt, Part E

Fig. 3–15. Bride's chest pattern

to shape and size. Lathe turn the hinge pins (I) to suggested shape. Lay the top (G) on the chest assembly so that the back edge is flush with the rear of the back. Mark on the top the outside edge of each side. Remove the top and glue the hinges (H) on these marks allowing a very slight clearance away from the side mark. Drill a ¹/₈-inch-diameter hole through the hinges as marked. Realign the top back on the chest assembly and mark the hinge holes on the sides. Drill a ³/₁₆-inch-diameter hole on these marks. The hinge pin (I) will fit through the hinges (H) and go into the sides. The pins should be tight in the hinges, but loose in the sides.

4. Make two drawer units to fit the openings. (See "Construction Notes" techniques on drawer making.) Sand fit the drawers to their openings.

Finish

The following suggestions will serve for any painted or decorated finish.

Paint the entire chest with a thinned flat paint; for example blue, green, red, or yellow. After this coat has dried, sand until the wood grain shows slightly through the paint. Cover with a single coat of lacquer or similar finish. Sand lightly. Trace on the preferred floral decorations. With waterproof, colored inks, color in the design. Allow the ink to dry and then cover with another coat of lacquer. After this cover coat has dried, wipe on a glaze coat made up of one-half flat black paint and one-half thinner. Wipe this glaze while it is still wet until the desired aged look is achieved.

After the glaze coat has dried, apply several coats of lacquer or similar finish, sanding between every two coats. When the last coat has

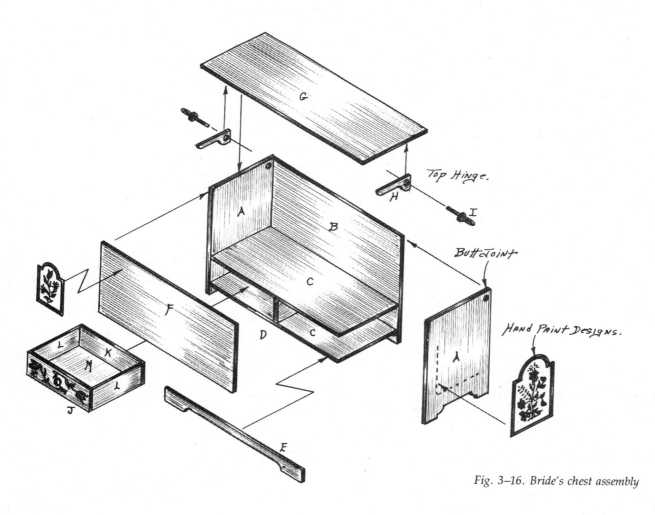

Fig. 3–16. Bride's chest assembly

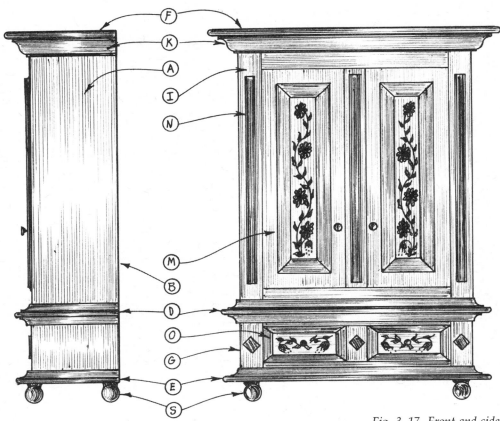

Fig. 3–17. Front and side view of kas

dried, apply paste wax with 0000 steel wool. Buff to a mellow satin sheen.

Optional interior finish. Many old trunks and chests had wallpaper interiors. The inside of the chest area and the drawer interior can be papered in scale-size patterns if desired.

KAS

The kas was a huge chest designed for bedroom storage. Many homes of this time period lacked closets and the kas was the answer to this need. Secondly, the heavy bed covers were carefully stored away in the kas during the warmer months. It was not uncommon for a household to have more than one kas, each decorated for a certain color scheme.

Material

Cherry, maple, basswood, or mahogany. Cherry is preferred.

Material List

	Part	Number	Size
A	Side	2	$1^7/_{16}$″ x $5^7/_8$″ x $^1/_8$″
B	Back	1	$4^1/_8$″ x $5^7/_8$″ x $^1/_{16}$″
C	Shelf	4	4″ x $1^3/_8$″ x $^1/_{16}$″
D	Mid Shelf	1	$4^7/_8$″ x $1^{15}/_{16}$″ x $^1/_{16}$″
E	Bottom	1	$4^7/_8$″ x $1^{15}/_{16}$″ x $^1/_{16}$″
F	Top	1	$4^7/_8$″ x $1^{15}/_{16}$″ x $^1/_{16}$″
G	Frame Rails	2	$4^1/_4$″ x $^1/_4$″ x $^1/_{16}$″
	Frame Stiles	3	$^3/_8$″ x $^9/_{16}$″ x $^1/_{16}$″
H	Medallion	3	$^1/_4$″ x $^1/_4$″ x $^1/_{32}$″
I	Top Frame Stiles	3	$^3/_8$″ x $3^5/_8$″ x $^1/_{16}$″
	Top Rail	1	$^5/_8$″ x $4^1/_4$″ x $^1/_{16}$″
	Bottom Rail	1	$^3/_8$″ x $4^1/_4$″ x $^1/_{16}$″
J	Chair Rail Molding	3	$^1/_8$″ x $3^1/_2$″ x $^1/_{32}$″

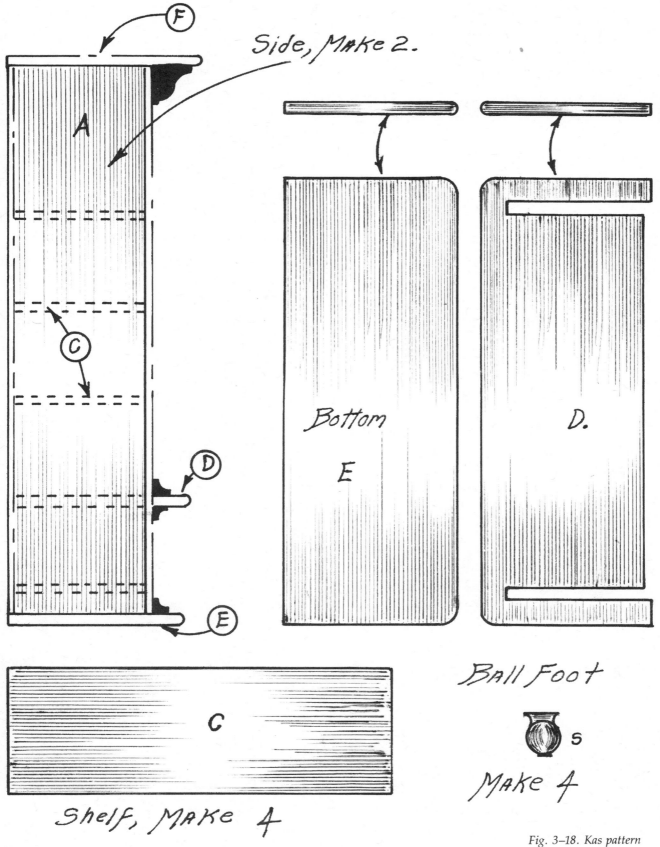

F

Side, Make 2.

A

C

D

Bottom

E

D.

E

Ball Foot

Make 4

C

Shelf, Make 4

Fig. 3–18. Kas pattern

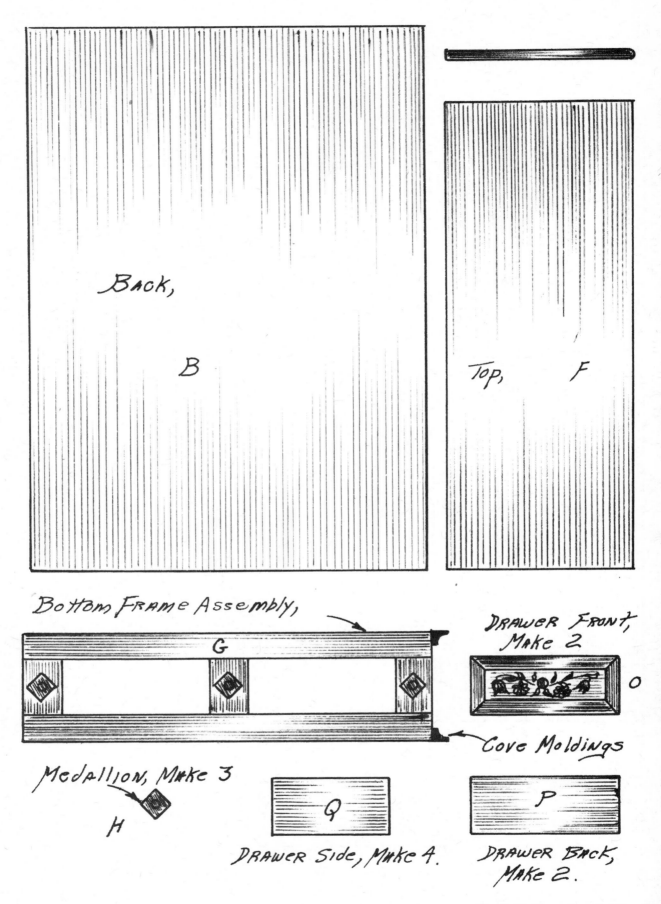

Back,

B

Top,   F

Bottom Frame Assembly,

G

Drawer Front,
Make 2

O

Cove Moldings

Medallion, Make 3

H

Q

Drawer Side, Make 4.

P

Drawer Back,
Make 2.

Fig. 3–18. Kas pattern (continued)

156

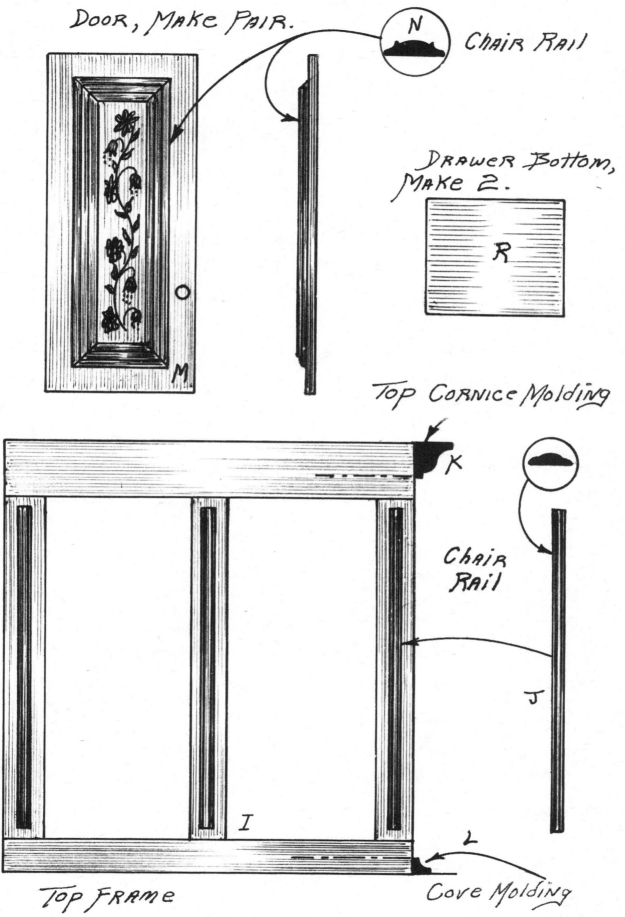

Door, Make Pair.

N — Chair Rail

Drawer Bottom, Make 2.

R

O

M

Top Cornice Molding

K

Chair Rail

J

I

L

Top Frame

Cove Molding

157

Fig. 3–18. Kas pattern (continued)

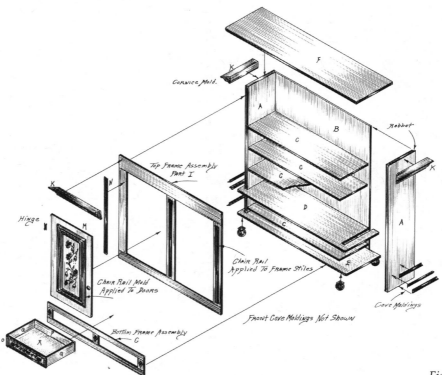

Fig. 3–19. Kas assembly

K	Cornice Molding (crown)		10 linial inches x ³/₈″ x ³/₈″
L	Lower Molding (cove)		10 linial inches x ¹/₄″ x ¹/₄″
M	Door	2	1⁹/₁₆″ x 3⁵/₈″ x ¹/₈″
N	Door Molding	1	18 linial inches x ¹/₄″ x ¹/₁₆″
O	Drawer Front	2	1⁵/₈″ x ⁹/₁₆″ x ¹/₁₆″
P	Drawer Back	2	1⁵/₈″ x ⁹/₁₆″ x ¹/₁₆″
Q	Drawer Side	4	1¹/₄″ x ⁹/₁₆″ x ¹/₁₆″
R	Drawer Bottom	2	1¹/₂″ x 1¹/₄″ x ¹/₁₆″

Construction

1. Lay out and cut the sides (A), the back (B), the shelves (C), shelf (D), and bottom (E). Cut a ³/₃₂-by-³/₃₂-inch rabbet on the rear inside edges of the sides. Glue the back into these rabbets. Glue the shelves (C) between the sides and to the back (see fig. 3–18).

2. Lay out and cut the stock for the top and bottom frames (G and I) (see details in fig. 3–18). Glue the finished frames to the sides and shelves (C). Cut out the small medallions (H) and glue them to the bottom frame stiles.

3. Lay out and cut the top cornice moldings (K) with 45-degree miter joints. Glue top cornice molding to the sides, the top, and top frame. Lay out and cut the side cove moldings with 45-degree miter joints (see part A in fig. 3–18). Lay out and cut the scale-size chair rail molding for the frame stiles. Glue the moldings in place.

4. Make two drawer units to fit the available openings (see "Construction Notes"). Sand fit the drawers in place. Make two plain solid doors (M). With 45-degree miter joints, apply the chair rail moldings to the doors. Apply the doors to the opening with scale-size hinges or by employing the hinge pin concept shown in the "Construction Notes." Make four legs (S). Glue the legs to the bottom.

Finish

Sand the entire reproduction smooth removing all traces of glue. Hand paint (ink) the suggested decorations on the drawers and doors. (See the bride's chest for techniques on finishing.)

8

Kitchen and Dining Room Group

The Pennsylvania Dutch kitchen was a cheerful, happy, brightly furnished room—a family room. Most of the furniture reflected this brightness and was painted or decorated with symbolic flower, bird, or geometric patterns. The Pennsylvania Dutch have been credited with inventing many items and customs, including the rocking chair, apple pie, the Easter bunny, and Santa Claus. Their daily cooking was often considered beyond comparison and included scrapple, beef filling, deep-dish apple crisp, and specialty items for all of the child-centered holidays. Such attention to children, family pleasure, and enjoyable living comes through in their furniture decorations.

DOUGH TROUGH

The dough box or trough was present in almost every Early American or Pennsylvania Dutch household. It was in this trough that the dough was made, allowed to rise, and later shaped into loaves. The trough top became a work area much like modern counter tops. The following miniature shows a more complex dough trough than usual, in that it is free-standing on four turned legs.

Material

Cherry, maple, basswood, or pine. Cherry is preferred.

Fig. 3–20. Pennsylvania Dutch dining room (Courtesy the Philadelphia Museum of Art, A. J. Wyatt, staff photographer)

Material List

	Part	Number	Size
A	Base	1	1³/₈" x 2¹/₄" x ¹/₈"
B	End	2	1⁵/₈" x 1¹/₁₆" x ¹/₁₆"
C	Side	2	2³/₄" x 1¹/₁₆" x ¹/₁₆"
D	Leg	4	³/₁₆" dia. x 1³/₈"
E	Top	1	2" x 3¹/₄" x ¹/₁₆"

Construction

1. Lay out and cut the base (A) and legs (D) to shape and size. Lathe-turn the legs to suggested design with ¹/₈-inch-diameter tenons on the tops. Drill ¹/₈-inch-diameter mounting holes into the bottom of the base. Note the splay angle for the legs in figure 3–21.

2. Lay out and cut the ends (B) and sides (C) to shape and size. Glue the ends (B) between the sides (C). After the glue has dried, rub the assembly on a flat sheet of sandpaper to correct the compatible angles on the top and bottom. Glue the assembly to the base.

3. Make the top (E). The top can have inte-

rior cleats to lock it in place if preferred. Such cleats will have compatible angles to the sides (C). Fit the top over the ends and sides.

Finish

Sand the entire reproduction smooth removing all traces of glue. Stain to a color of choice. Cover with several coats of lacquer or similar finish.

BALLOON-BACK CHAIR

The following miniature was developed from a circa 1815 kitchen chair. It has a plank seat and a decorated back slat and crown. This chair goes well in the average kitchen or in bedrooms, therefore, several can be made and used throughout the miniature setting.

Material

Cherry, maple, mahogany, basswood. Cherry is preferred.

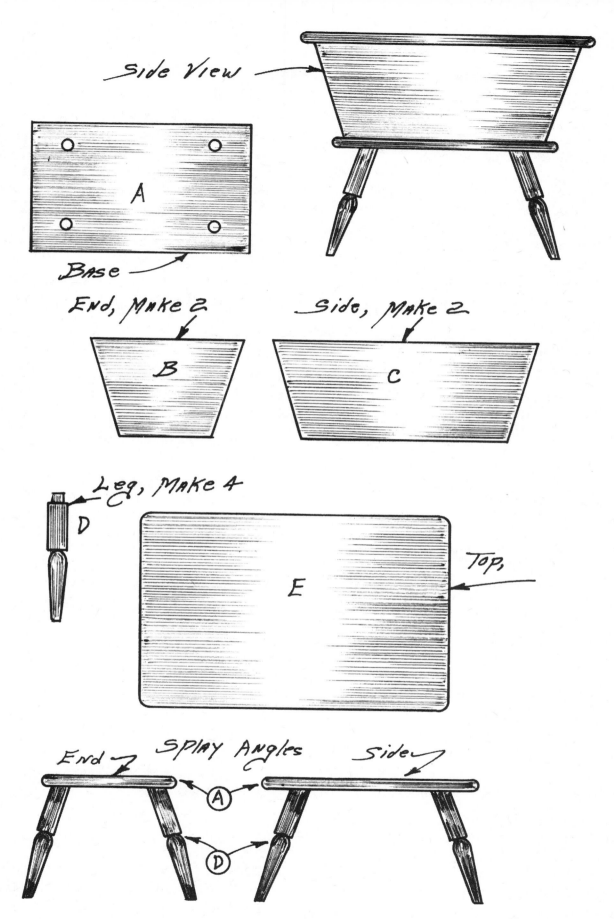

Side View

Base

A

End, Make 2

B

Side, Make 2

C

Leg, Make 4

D

Top,

E

Splay Angles

End Side

Ⓐ

Ⓓ

Fig. 3–21. Dough trough pattern

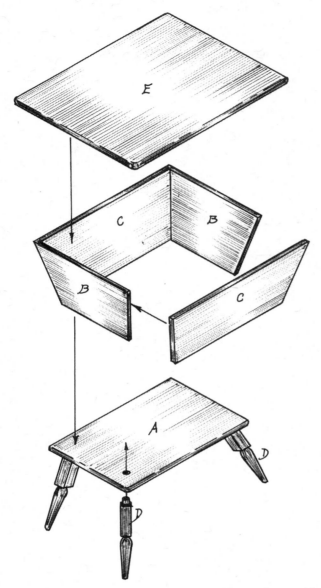

Fig. 3–22. Dough trough assembly

Material List

	Part	Number	Size
A	Seat	1	$1^{1}/4''$ x $1^{3}/8''$ x $^{1}/4''$
B	Leg	4	$^{1}/8''$ dia. x $1^{1}/2''$
C	Stretcher	4	$^{1}/16''$ dia. x $1^{3}/8''$
D	Slat	1	$^{1}/2''$ x $1^{1}/16''$ x $^{1}/16''$
E	Left Post	1	$^{3}/8''$ x $1''$ x $^{1}/16''$
F	Right Post	1	$^{3}/8''$ x $1''$ x $^{1}/16''$
G	Crown	1	$^{1}/2''$ x $1^{1}/2''$ x $^{1}/16''$

Construction

1. Lay out and cut the seat (A) to shape and size (see "Construction Notes" for suggested techniques). Drill $^{1}/16$-inch-diameter leg mounting holes into the bottom of the seat. See splay angles bottom of figure 3–23.

Lathe-turn the legs (B) to suggested shape and size, making a $^{1}/16$-inch-diameter top tenon. Drill $^{3}/64$-inch-diameter holes in the legs for the stretchers (C).

2. Lathe-turn the stretchers (C) to shape and size. Glue one stretcher between two selected legs as the leg tops are glued into the front mounting holes. Glue the two side stretchers into the front legs. Glue the last stretcher between the last two legs. Glue the side stretchers into the rear legs as they are assembled and glued into the seat. This whole operation should be completed at one time in order to gain some flexibility before the glue sets.

3. Make the back assembly by cutting parts D, E, F, and G to suggested shape and size. It is recommended that the back parts be glued together, sanded to shape, and mounted on to the plank seat (A). See tenon allowance on the bottom of Parts D, E, and F. (The back may be made from a single piece of stock if preferred. The thin side rails, however, are very fragile and extreme care must be taken in all operations.)

Finish

Sand the chair smooth removing all traces of glue. Stain or paint to a color of choice. Hand paint the designs. Cover with several coats of lacquer or similar finish. If a painted chair is desired, see instructions given for finishing for the "Bride's Chest."

PLANK-BOTTOM CHAIR

Many chair styles offer a large back area for possible decoration. The New England Hitchcock chair is a good example. The Dutch used

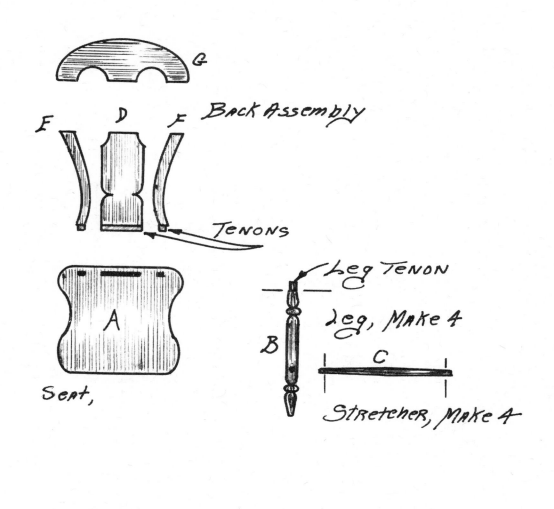

Back Assembly

Tenons

Leg Tenon

Leg, Make 4

Stretcher, Make 4

Seat,

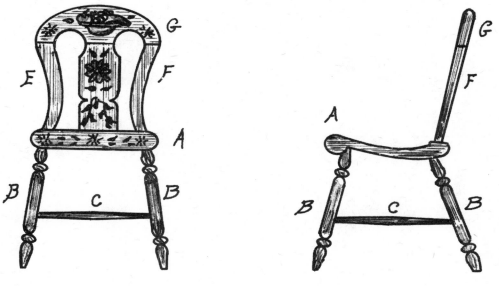

Fig. 3–23. Balloon-back chair pattern

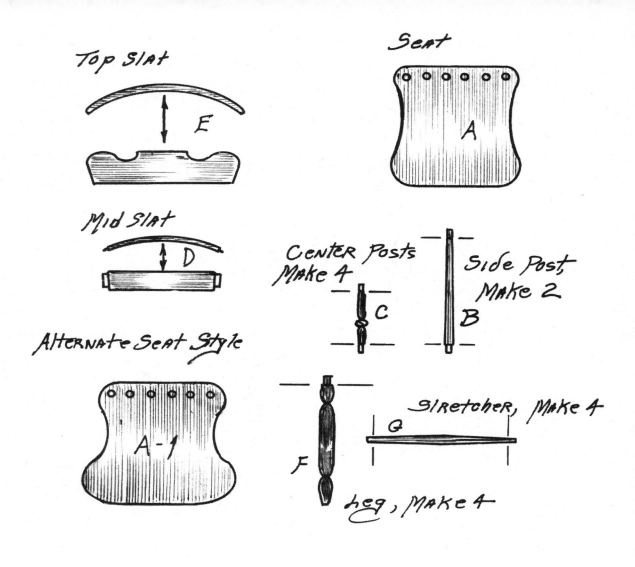

Top Slat

E

Seat

A

Mid Slat

D

Center Posts
Make 4

C

Side Post,
Make 2

B

Alternate Seat Style

A-1

F

G

Stretcher, Make 4

Leg, Make 4

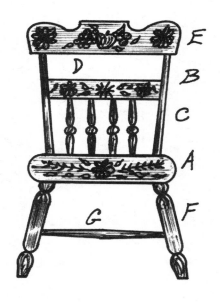

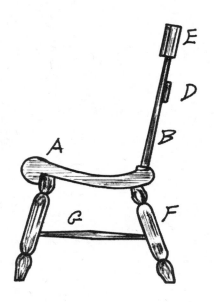

Fig. 3–24. Plank bottom chair pattern

164

Fig. 3–25. Trestle table

the chair back as well as the seat edge for color-ful design. The following miniature incorpo-rates the common center fruit design of the Hitchcock-style chair with Pennsylvania Dutch floral decoration on the crown.

Material

Cherry, maple, mahogany. Cherry is pre-ferred.

Material List

	Part	Number	Size
A	Seat	1	$1^3/_8''$ x $1^1/_4''$ x $1/_4''$
B	Side Post	2	$1/_8''$ dia. x $1^3/_8''$
C	Center Post	4	$1/_{16}''$ dia. x $3/_4''$
D	Mid Slat	1	$1/_4''$ x $1^1/_4''$ x $3/_{16}''$
E	Top Slat	1	$1^5/_8''$ x $3/_8''$ x $3/_8''$
F	Leg	4	$1/_8''$ dia. x $1^1/_2''$
G	Stretcher	4	$1/_{16}''$ dia. x $1^1/_2''$

Construction

1. Two possible seat designs are offered in figure 3–24. Lay out and cut the seat (A) to chosen size and design. Drill the required back post holes and the leg mounting holes. See leg and back splay angles in the bottom of figure 3–24.

2. Lathe-turn the side posts (B) and center posts (C) leaving a $1/_{16}$-inch-diameter tenon on each end. Glue the side posts (B) and center posts (C) into the seat. Make the mid slat (D) and the top crown slat (E) to shape and size. Mark these pieces to receive the tenons from the side and center posts. Glue the mid slat and top crown slat to the center and side posts.

3. Lathe-turn the legs (F) and stretchers (G) to suggested design. Drill the required stretcher mortise holes into the legs.

Select two legs and glue one stretcher be-tween them as you glue the top leg tenons into the front leg holes in the seat. Glue two side stretchers into the front legs. Glue the last stretcher between the other two legs and glue the leg tenons into the rear leg holes in the seat. Glue the side stretchers to the rear legs. The whole leg assembly should be completed as one operation in order to achieve some flexi-bility before the glue sets.

Finish

Sand the chair smooth removing all traces of glue. Stain or paint to a color of choice. Follow the directions given for the "Bride's Chest" for decorations.

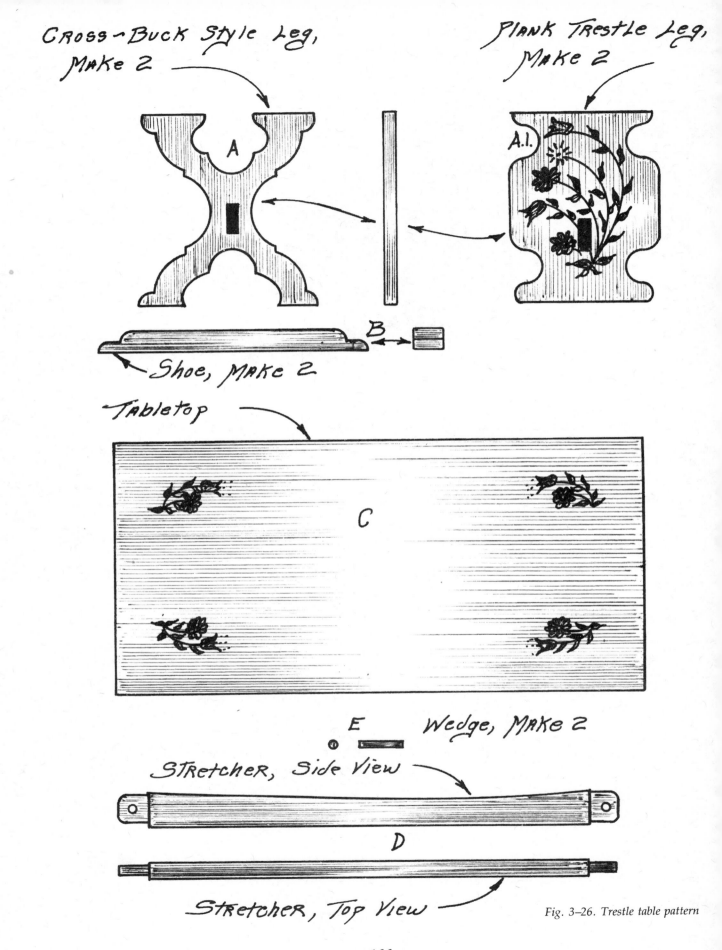

Cross-Buck Style Leg, Make 2

A

A.I.

Plank Trestle Leg, Make 2

B

Shoe, Make 2

Tabletop

C

E   Wedge, Make 2

Stretcher, Side View

D

Stretcher, Top View

Fig. 3–26. Trestle table pattern

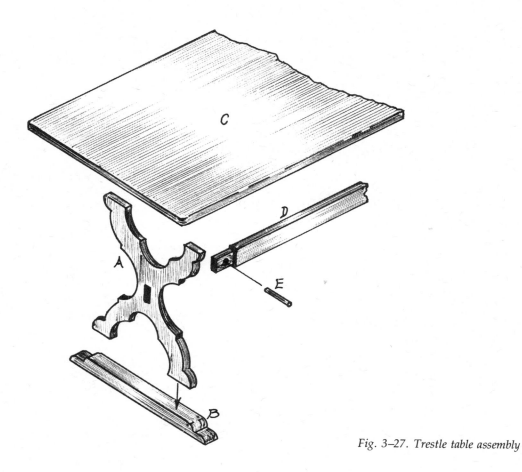

Fig. 3–27. Trestle table assembly

TRESTLE TABLE

The following trestle table is offered with two different style trestle legs, the cross-buck and the plank type. This style table was used throughout the country in several different designs and table sizes.

Material

Basswood, pine, cherry, maple, or mahogany.

Material List

	Part	Number	Size
A	Cross-buck leg	2	2″ x 2⅛″ x ⅛″
A–1	Plank-type leg	2	1⅝″ x 2⅛″ x ⅛″
B	Shoe	2	2½″ x ¼″ x ¼″
C	Top	1	5½″ x 2¾″ x ⅛″
D	Stretcher	1	5¼″ x ½″ x ³⁄₁₆″

Construction

1. Lay out and cut the desired trestle leg design (A or A–1). Cut out the shoes (B). Glue the legs to the shoes. Cut the stretcher slots into the legs.

2. Lay out and cut the stretcher (D) to suggested shape and size. Cut the required tenon shoulders on both ends. Insert the stretcher ends through the slots on the legs and mark the ends as they clear the outside edges of the legs.

Drill ¹⁄₁₆-inch-diameter holes for the stretcher lock pins. These holes should just touch the leg marks. Install the stretcher between the two legs, and lock it in place with the pins.

3. Lay out and cut the tabletop (C) to shape and size. Glue the tops of the legs to the bottom of the tabletop. Small dowel tenons can be

drilled into the tops of the legs with mortise holes drilled into the bottom of the tabletop if preferred.

Finish

Sand the entire table smooth removing all traces of glue. Stain the table to a desired color. Apply the tabletop decorations if preferred. Cover the table with several coats of lacquer or similar finish.

TRESTLE BENCH

This bench was designed to accompany the Pennsylvania Dutch trestle table. Many homes with large families had two such benches with a chair on either end for the parents.

Material

Same as the trestle table.

Material List

	Part	Number	Size
A	Leg	2	$1^{1}/_{4}$" x $1^{1}/_{4}$" x $^{1}/_{8}$"
B	Seat	1	6" x $1^{1}/_{4}$" x $^{1}/_{8}$"
C	Stretcher	1	$4^{3}/_{4}$" x $^{1}/_{4}$" x $^{1}/_{8}$"

Construction

1. Lay out and cut the sides (A) and seat (B) to shape and size. Cut the stretcher mortise slots into the sides. Cut the required splay angle on top of the sides. Lay out and cut the stretcher (C) to shape and size. Cut tenons on both ends to fit the mortise slots in the sides. Drill $^{1}/_{16}$-inch-diameter holes where these tenons clear the sides of parts A.

2. Glue one side to the underside of the seat (see fig. 3–28). Insert the tenon into the free side and as this part is glued to the side, insert the other tenon end into the preglued side (A) mortise slot. Lock the stretcher in place with dowel pins.

Finish

Finish the same as the trestle table.

PIE SAFE

Before the invention of screening, the housewife had a problem keeping insects away from pies and pastry. The answer to this problem was the pie safe. This was a cupboard with a wood frame that contained several pierced tin or copper panels. The piercing was too small for insects to enter yet allowed free air circulation. In the Pennsylvania Dutch region, the tin piercing was installed in geometric or floral designs. The following miniature was developed from several such pie safes.

Material

Cherry, pine, basswood, or mahogany.

Material List

	Part	Number	Size
A	Side Frame	2	$1^{1}/_{4}$" x $^{3}/_{8}$" x $^{1}/_{8}$"
		4	$1^{7}/_{8}$" x $^{1}/_{4}$" x $^{1}/_{8}$"
		2	$1^{1}/_{4}$" x $^{1}/_{4}$" x $^{1}/_{8}$"
A–1	Copper Screen	2	1" x $2^{1}/_{8}$" light sheet stock
B	Back	1	$2^{7}/_{8}$" x $2^{1}/_{2}$" x $^{1}/_{16}$"
C	Shelf	3	$2^{3}/_{4}$" x $1^{3}/_{16}$" x $^{1}/_{16}$"
D	Front Frame Skirt	1	3" x $^{3}/_{8}$" x $^{1}/_{16}$"
	Stile	2	$1^{7}/_{8}$" x $^{1}/_{4}$" x $^{1}/_{16}$"
	Top Rail	1	3" x $^{1}/_{4}$" x $^{1}/_{16}$"
E	Top	1	$3^{3}/_{8}$" x $1^{9}/_{16}$" x $^{1}/_{16}$"
F	Door Frame	4	$1^{9}/_{16}$" x $^{3}/_{16}$" x $^{1}/_{16}$"
		4	$1^{1}/_{2}$" x $^{3}/_{16}$" x $^{1}/_{16}$"
F–1	Door Screen	2	$1^{1}/_{16}$" x $1^{9}/_{16}$" light sheet stock

Construction

1. Cut $^{1}/_{4}$-by-$^{1}/_{8}$-inch wood strips and make two side frames (A) with half-lap joints. Cut a $^{1}/_{16}$-by-$^{1}/_{16}$-inch rabbet on the rear inside edges of both side frames. Glue the back into these rabbets.

2. Lay out and cut the shelves (C) to size.

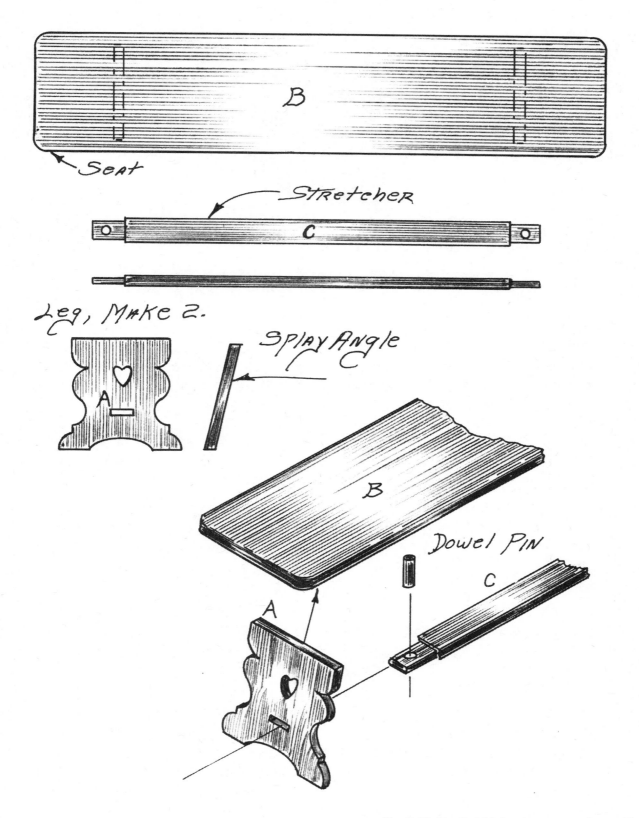

Seat

Stretcher

Leg, Make 2.

Splay Angle

Dowel Pin

Fig. 3–28. Trestle table bench pattern and assembly

169

Fig. 3–29. Pie safe

Make two metal side panels (A–1) (see design in fig. 3–29). Glue the metal side panels to the frame. Glue the shelves between the sides and to the back. The shelves will help lock the metal panels to the side frame. With ¹⁄₁₆-by-¹⁄₄-inch stock, make the front frame (D). Glue the front frame to the sides and shelves. Lay out and cut the top (E). Glue the top to the sides, back, and the top of the front frame.

3. Make two open door frames (F). Make two metal door panels (F–1) (see design pattern in fig. 3–29). Glue the metal panels to the door frames. Install the finished doors to the frame with hinges or pins. (See ''Construction Notes'' for detailing.)

Finish

Sand the entire miniature smooth removing all traces of glue. Paint or stain to a color of choice. Cover wood parts with several coats of lacquer or similar finish.

LANCASTER-STYLE JELLY CUPBOARD

In most early American households, the fruit harvest time was one of week-long activity as jams and jellies were made and preserved for the winter months. A special cupboard like the one that follows was made to store the fruit. This cupboard was developed from an 1840 antique and makes an excellent addition to any kitchen scene.

Material

Cherry, maple, basswood, or mahogany.

Material List

	Part	Number	Size
A	Side	2	1¹⁄₄" x 2¹⁄₂" x ¹⁄₈"
B	Back	1	3" x 2¹⁄₂" x ¹⁄₁₆"
C	Shelf	2	2⁷⁄₈" x 1³⁄₁₆" x ¹⁄₁₆"
D	Top or Bottom	2	3¹⁄₂" x 1¹⁄₂" x ¹⁄₁₆"
E	Frame Rails	3	3¹⁄₈" x ³⁄₁₆" x ¹⁄₁₆"
	Frame Stiles	3	2¹⁄₈" x ³⁄₁₆" x ¹⁄₁₆"
F	Door	2	1³⁄₈" x 1⁹⁄₁₆" x ¹⁄₈"
G	Drawer Side	4	1¹⁄₈" x ¹⁄₂" x ¹⁄₁₆"
H	Drawer Back	2	1³⁄₈" x ¹⁄₂" x ¹⁄₁₆"
	Drawer Front	2	1³⁄₈" x ¹⁄₂" x ¹⁄₁₆"
I	Drawer Bottom	2	1³⁄₁₆" x 1¹⁄₈" x ¹⁄₁₆"
J	End Skirt	2	1" x ¹⁄₄" x ¹⁄₁₆"
K	Back Skirt	1	3¹⁄₄" x ¹⁄₄" x ¹⁄₁₆"
L	Leg	4	⁵⁄₁₆" dia. x ¹⁄₂"

Construction

1. Lay out and cut the sides (A), back (B), shelves (C), and top and bottom (D). Cut a

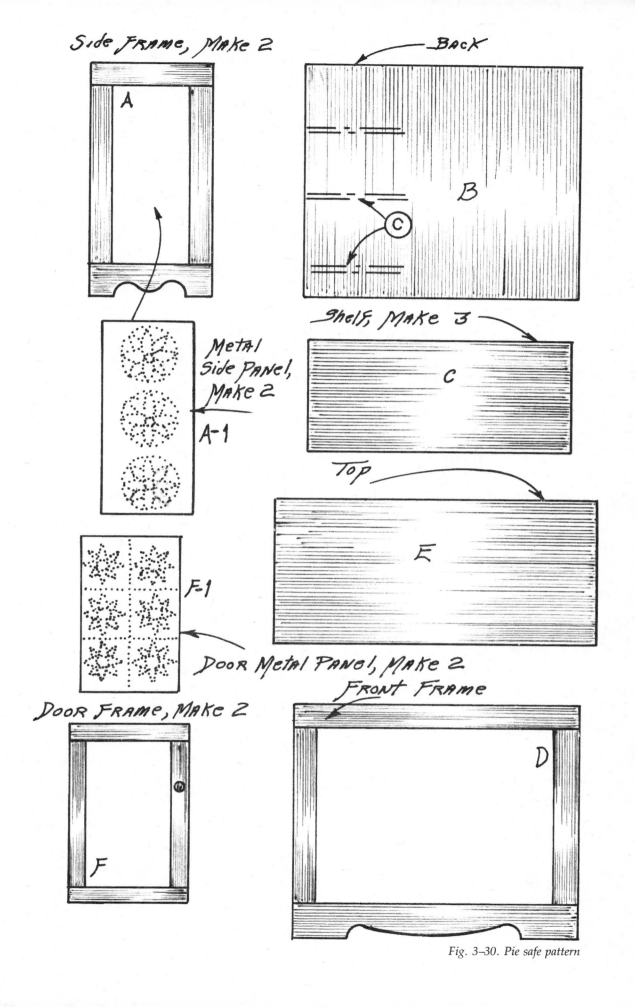

Side Frame, Make 2

A

BACK

B

C

Metal Side Panel, Make 2

A-1

Shelf, Make 3

C

F-1

Top

E

Door Metal Panel, Make 2

Door Frame, Make 2

F

FRONT FRAME

D

Fig. 3–30. Pie safe pattern

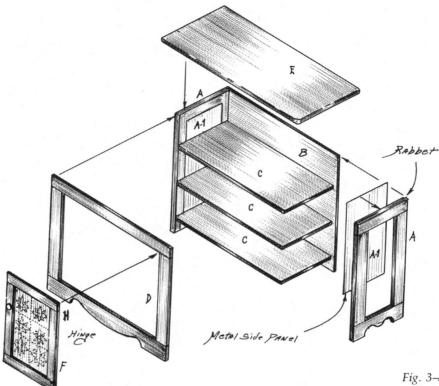

Fig. 3–31. Pie safe assembly

¹/₁₆-by-¹/₁₆-inch rabbet on the rear inside edges of the sides. Glue the back into these rabbets. Glue the shelves between the sides and to the back (see shelf spacing in fig. 3–31). Glue parts D to the top and bottom of the sides and back.

2. Make a cabinet frame (E) with half-lap joints. Glue the frame to the sides, top, and bottom.

Make two drawer units to fit the top opening (see "Construction Notes" for detailing). Note that the drawer fronts have a half-round shape.

Make two raised-panel doors to fit the opening (see "Construction Notes" for suggestions). Hinge the doors to the frame with scale-size hinges or with pin hinges.

3. Lay out and cut the top skirts (J and K). Glue the top skirts to the top.

Finish

Sand the cupboard smooth removing all traces of glue. Paint or stain to a color of choice. The two door panels have an apple and grape design as an option. Hand paint the door designs. Cover with several coats of lacquer or similar finish.

MAHATONGA VALLEY KITCHEN DRESSER

The following miniature china dresser reproduction was developed from several antique examples found in Pennsylvania. Each section of the country had their own designs for china cupboards, and this style seems to have been used mostly in the Pennsylvania Dutch region. This dresser is offered two different ways: as an free standing cupboard or as a corner cupboard. The frontal design and doors are the same for either style.

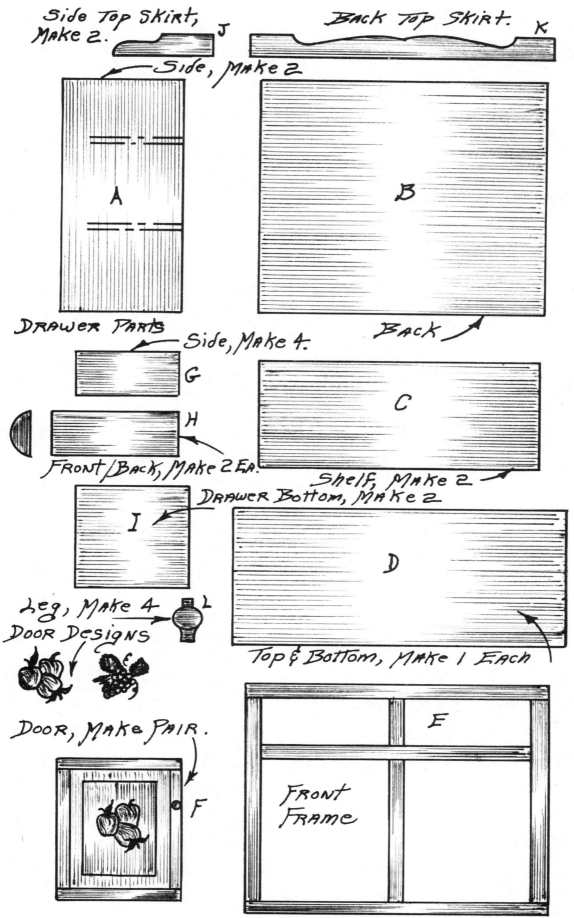

Side Top Skirt, Make 2. J

Back Top Skirt. K

Side, Make 2

A

B

Back

DRAWER PARTS

Side, Make 4. G

H

Front/Back, Make 2 Ea.

C

Shelf, Make 2

I

Drawer Bottom, Make 2

D

Leg, Make 4 L

DOOR Designs

Top & Bottom, Make 1 Each

Door, Make Pair.

F

E

Front Frame

Fig. 3–32. Lancaster-style jelly cupboard pattern

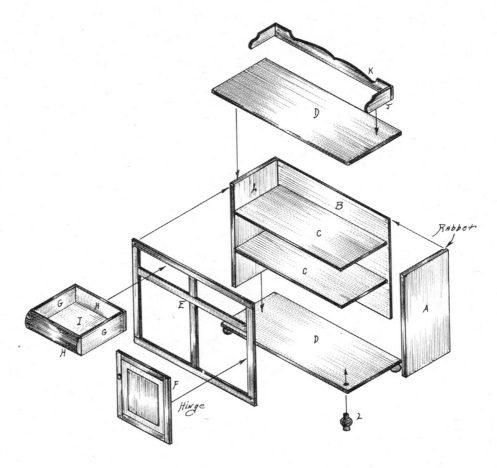

Fig. 3–33. Lancaster-style jelly cupboard assembly

Material

Cherry, basswood, pine, or mahogany.

Material List

	Part	Number	Size
A	Side	2	1½″ x 6½″ x ⅛″
B	Back	1	3¼″ x 6½″ x 1/16″
C	Shelf	5	3⅛″ x 1 7/16″ x 1/16″
D	Frame Stiles	2	¾″ x 5¾″ x 1/16″
	Frame Top Rail	1	¾″ x 3½″ x 1/16″
	Frame Skirt	1	⅜″ x 3½″ x 1/16″
	Frame Mid Rail	1	¼″ x 2¾″ x 1/16″
E	Top	1	4¼″ x 1⅞″ x 1/16″
F	Door	2	1⅜″ x 1 15/16″ x ⅛″
G	Molding	1	3/16″ x 3/16″ x 4″ crown
		2	3/16″ x 3/16″ x ¾″ crown

Construction

1. Lay out and cut the sides (A), back (B), and shelves (C). Cut a 1/16-by-1/16-inch rabbet on the rear inside edges of the sides. Glue the back into these rabbets. Glue the shelves between the sides and to the back (see fig. 3–34).

2. Lay out and make the front frame (D). Glue the finished frame assembly to the sides and shelves. Make the top (E). Glue the top to the tops of the sides and back. Cut the cove molding (G) to size using 45-degree miter joint corners. Glue the cove molding to the sides, the front frame, and the top.

3. Make two raised-panel doors (F) to fit the available opening (see "Construction Notes"). Hinge the finished doors to the frame opening.

CORNER CUPBOARD

Material List

	Part	Number	Size
A	Side	1	2⅜″ x 6½″ x 1/16″
		1	2 5/16″ x 6½″ x 1/16″

B	Shelf	5	1¹¹⁄₁₆″ x 3¹⁄₂″ x ¹⁄₁₆″
C	Front Frame		See material list for "Frame D" for the Mahatonga Valley Kitchen Cupboard
D	Top	1	2¹⁄₈″ x 4³⁄₈″ x ¹⁄₁₆″
E	Molding	1	4″ x ³⁄₁₆″ x ³⁄₁₆″ crown mold

Construction

1. Lay out and cut the sides (A) to suggested size. Note that one side is made the thickness size less than the other side because of the right-angle butt joint construction (see detail and note in fig. 3–36).

Lay out and cut the shelves (B) to size. Glue the sides together at a right angle and glue shelves between them (see shelf location in fig. 3–36).

2. Make the front frame unit (C) (shown as part D in fig. 3–34). Glue the finished frame assembly to the sides and shelves. Make two raised-panel doors (F) (see "Construction Notes"). Hinge the doors to the frame opening.

3. Lay out and cut the top (D) to size. Glue the top to the tops of the sides. Cut the cove molding with 45-degree, angle-end cuts. Glue the molding under the top and to the front frame top.

Finish

The dresser can be painted or stained. Sand the reproduction smooth removing all traces of glue. Paint or stain to a color of choice. Hand paint the floral design if preferred (see finishing instructions for the Bride's Chest for techniques). Cover with several coats of lacquer. Finish with paste wax.

Fig. 3–34. Mahatonga Valley kitchen cupboard

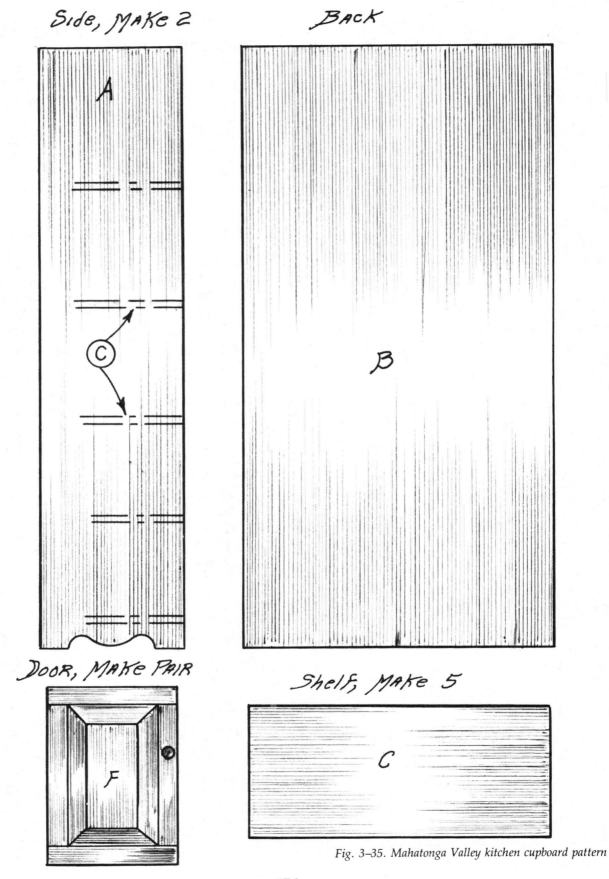

Side, Make 2

A

C

Back

B

Door, Make Pair

F

Shelf, Make 5

C

Fig. 3–35. Mahatonga Valley kitchen cupboard pattern

176

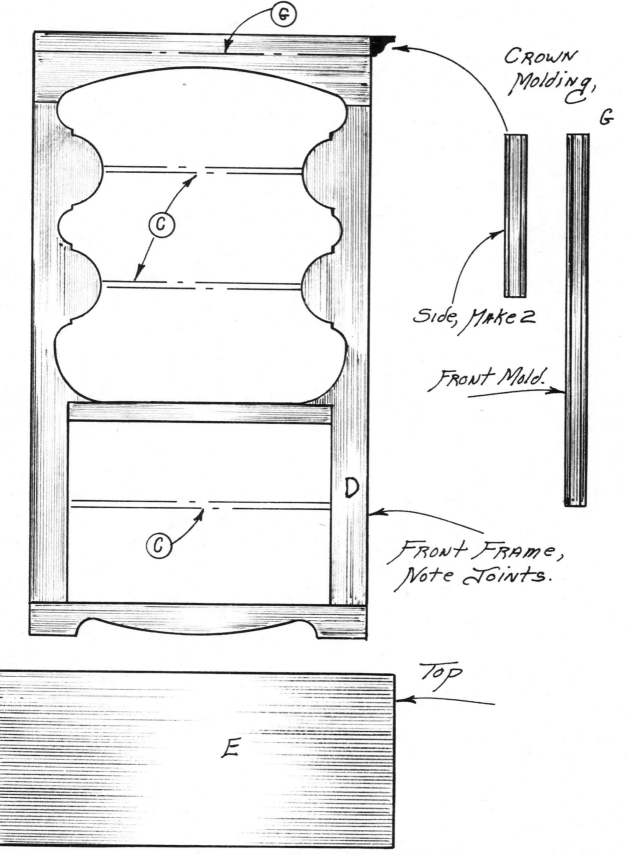

G

CROWN
Molding,
G

Side, Make 2

FRONT Mold.

C

D

C

FRONT FRAME,
Note Joints.

Top

E

Fig. 3–35. Mahatonga Valley kitchen cupboard pattern (continued)

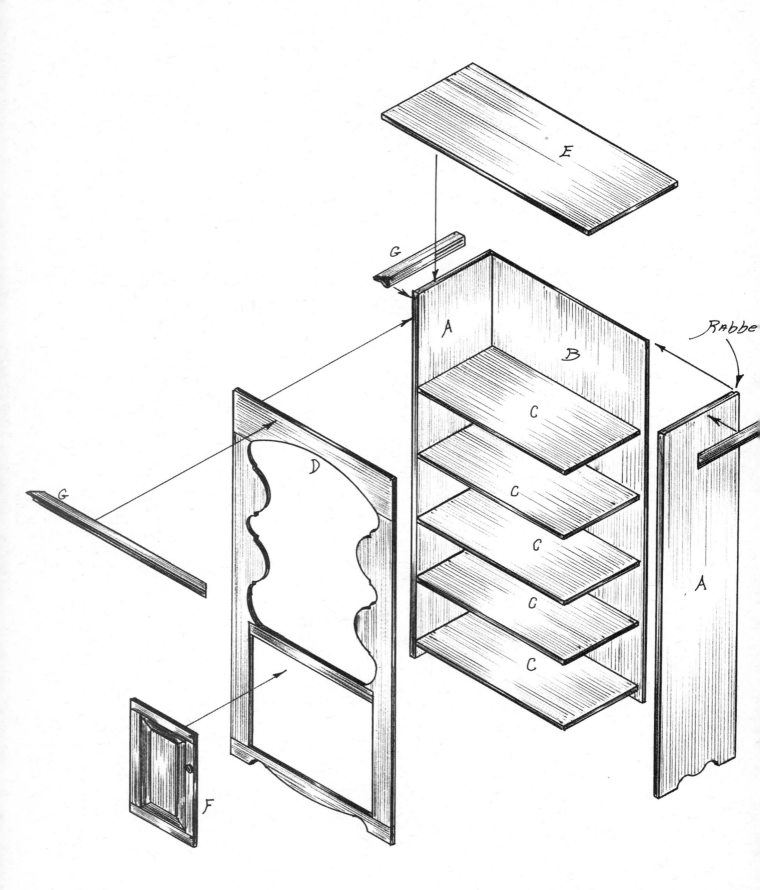

Fig. 3–36. Mahatonga Valley kitchen cupboard assembly

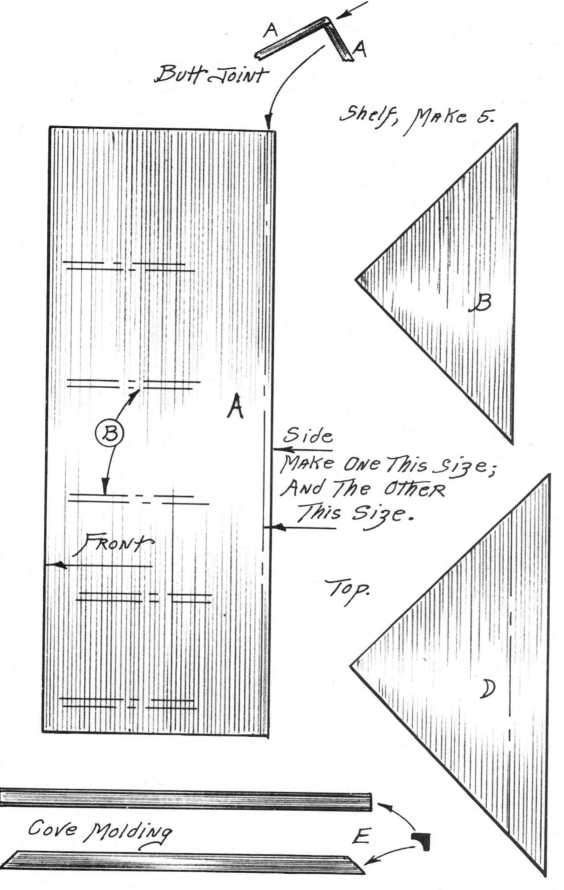

A

Butt Joint

Shelf, Make 5.

B

A

Side
Make One This Size;
And The Other
This Size.

Front

Top.

D

Cove Molding

E

Fig. 3–37. Mahatonga Valley kitchen corner cupboard pattern

179

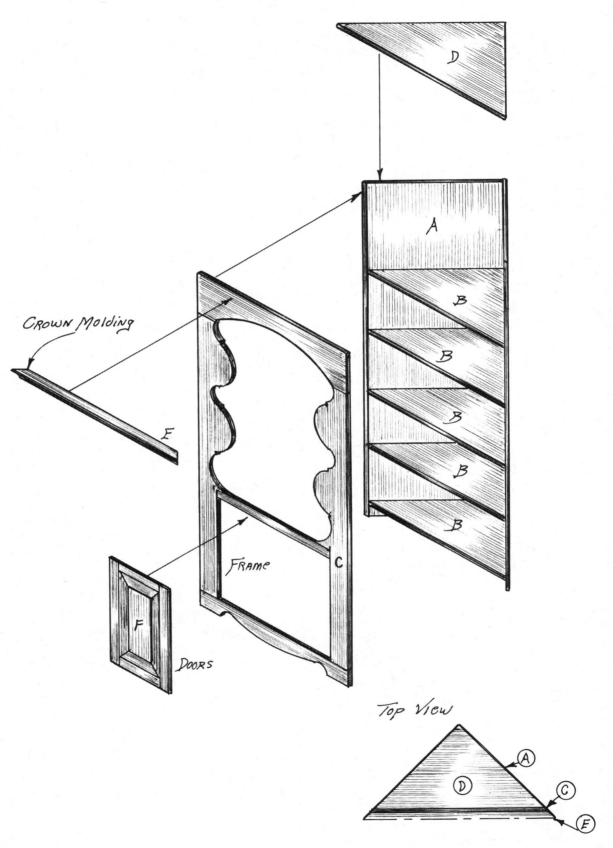

CROWN MOLDING

E

FRAME

C

F

DOORS

A

B

B

B

B

B

D

Top View

D

A

C

E

Fig. 3–38. Mahatonga Valley kitchen corner cupboard assembly

180

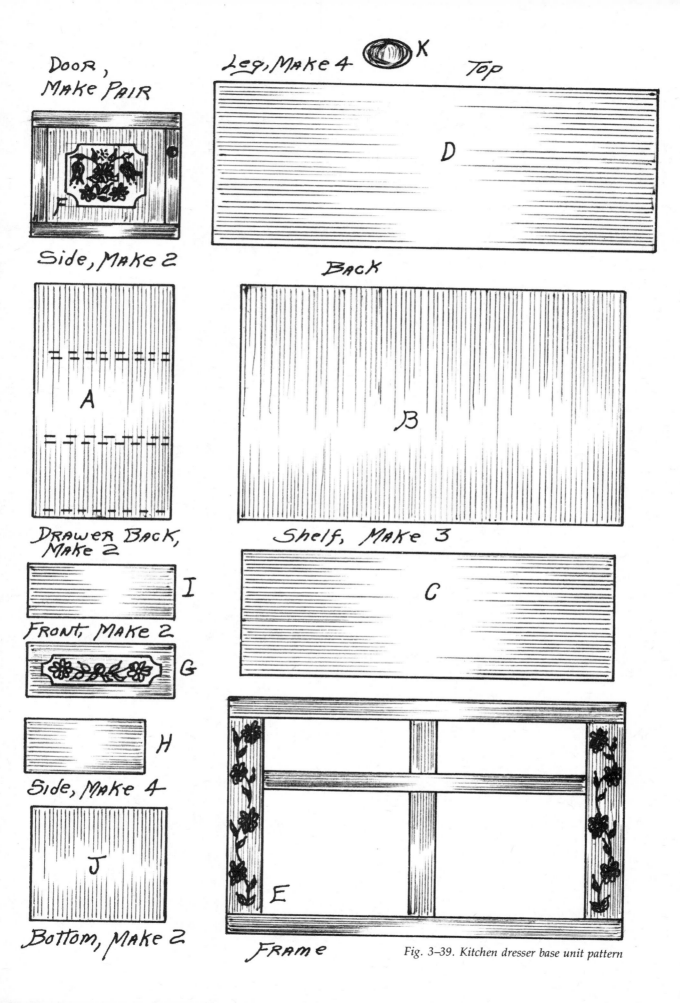

Fig. 3–39. Kitchen dresser base unit pattern

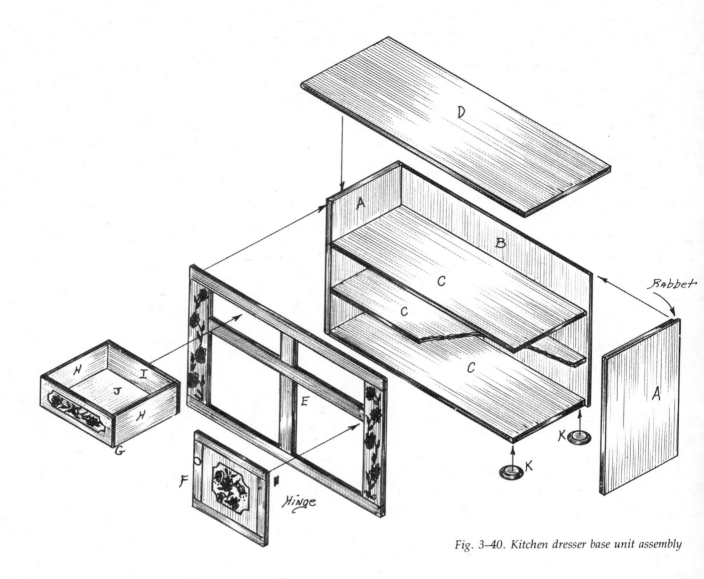

Fig. 3-40. Kitchen dresser base unit assembly

KITCHEN DRESSER BASE UNIT

The kitchen dresser was the grandfather of modern kitchen cabinets. They offered lower storage areas, drawer space, counter work areas and a top china closet; some with glass doors others with solid wood raised panels. The following reproduction was developed from a model in the Philadelphia Museum of Art.

Material

Cherry, maple, basswood, mahogany. Cherry is preferred.

Material List

	Part	Number	Size
A	Side	2	$1^1/2''$ x $2^1/2''$ x $1/8''$
B	Back	1	$4''$ x $2^1/2''$ x $1/16''$
C	Shelf	3	$1^7/16''$ x $3^7/8''$ x $1/16''$
D	Top	1	$4^5/8''$ x $1^3/4''$ x $1/16''$
E	Frame Rails	3	$4^1/8''$ x $3/16''$ x $1/16''$
	Frame End Stiles	2	$2^1/8''$ x $3/8''$ x $1/16''$
	Frame Mid Stile	1	$2^1/8''$ x $1/4''$ x $1/16''$
F	Door	2	$1^9/16''$ x $1^3/8''$ x $1/8''$
G	Drawer Front	2	$1^9/16''$ x $9/16''$ x $1/16''$
H	Drawer Side	4	$1^1/4''$ x $9/16''$ x $1/16''$
I	Drawer Back	2	$1^9/16''$ x $9/16''$ x $1/16''$
J	Drawer Bottom	2	$1^7/16''$ x $1^3/16''$ x $1/16''$
K	Leg	4	$1/2''$ oval, $1/4''$ high

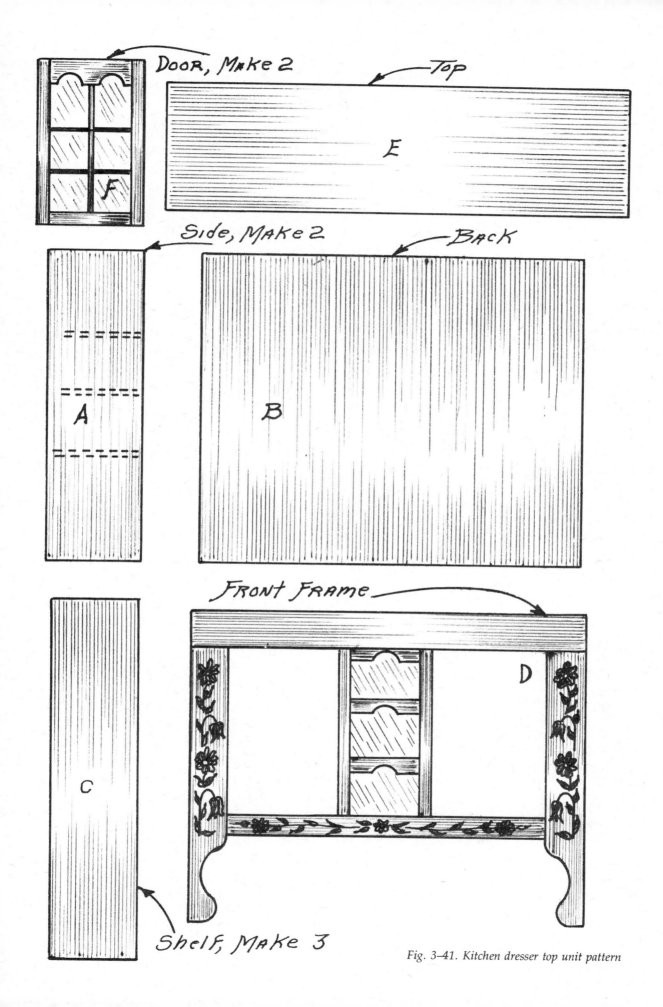

Door, Make 2

Top

E

Side, Make 2

Back

A

B

Front Frame

D

C

Shelf, Make 3

Fig. 3-41. Kitchen dresser top unit pattern

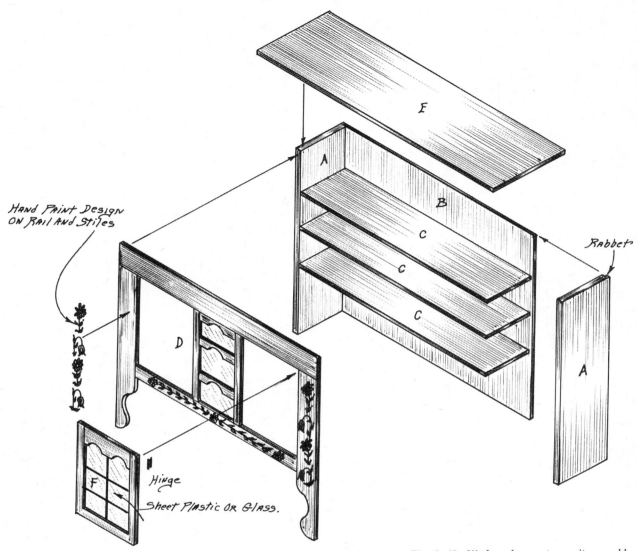

Hand Paint Design
On Rail And Stiles

Rabbet

Hinge

Sheet Plastic or Glass.

Fig. 3–42. Kitchen dresser top unit assembly

Construction

1. Lay out and cut the sides (A) and back (B). Cut a 1/16-by-1/16-inch rabbet on the rear inside edges of the sides. Glue the back into these rabbets.

2. Lay out and cut the shelves (C) and top (D) to size. Glue the shelves between the sides and to the back (see fig. 3–39). Glue the top on top of the sides and back. Make a front frame (E). Note the end stiles are wider than normal.

3. Make two drawer units to fit the openings (see "Construction Notes" for construction de-

tailing). Sand fit the drawers in place. Drawer guides can be made from scrap stock.

Make two raised-panel doors to fit the available spacing (see "Construction Notes" for suggestions for door construction). Apply the finished doors (F) to the frame with hinge pins or scale-size hinges.

TOP UNIT

The following top unit was designed to fit on top of the preceding base unit. However, it can be hung on a wall as a separate fixture.

Material

Same as base unit.

Material List

	Part	Number	Size
A	Side	2	$1'' \times 3^3/_8'' \times {}^1/_8''$
B	Back	1	$4'' \times 3^3/_8'' \times {}^1/_{16}''$
C	Shelf	3	$3^7/_8'' \times {}^{15}/_{16}'' \times {}^1/_{16}''$
D	Frame End Stile	2	${}^3/_8'' \times 3'' \times {}^1/_{16}''$
	Frame Top Rail	1	$4^1/_8'' \times {}^3/_8'' \times {}^1/_{16}''$
	Frame Bottom Rail	1	$3^5/_{16}'' \times {}^1/_4'' \times {}^1/_{16}''$
	Frame Mid Stiles	2	$1^3/_4'' \times {}^1/_8'' \times {}^1/_{16}''$
	Frame Mid Rails	3	${}^3/_4'' \times {}^3/_{16}'' \times {}^1/_{16}''$
E	Top	1	$4^7/_8'' \times 1^3/_8'' \times {}^1/_{16}''$
F	Door	2	$1^1/_8'' \times 1^3/_4'' \times {}^1/_{16}''$

Construction

1. Lay out and cut the sides (A) and back (B) to size. Cut a $^1/_{16}$-by-$^1/_{16}$-inch rabbet on the rear inside edges of the sides. Glue the back into these rabbets.

Lay out and cut the shelves to size. Glue the shelves between the sides and to the back (see location in fig. 3–41).

2. Lay out and make the front frame (D). Glue a section of glass or plastic behind the center frame area (see fig. 3–41 for location). Glue the finished frame to the sides and shelves. Lay out and cut the top (E) to size. Glue the top on top of the sides and back.

3. Make two open door frames to fit the openings. Make and glue in the window muntins. Glue sheet plastic or $^1/_{32}$-inch glass in the opening or behind the door frame. Secure the finished doors to the frames with pins or scale-size hinges.

Finish

Sand the reproduction smooth removing all traces of glue. Stain or paint to a color of choice. In the case of painting, after the paint has dried, sand smooth allowing some wood grain to show through. Cover the stain or paint with one coat of lacquer. Hand paint the offered decorations with ink or paints, and allow to dry. Cover with another coat of lacquer or similar finish. Sand lightly after drying. Wipe on a glaze coat of half flat black paint and half thinner, if desired, for aged look. Sand lightly. Cover this with several coats of lacquer or similar finish. Finish with a coat of paste wax applied with 000 steel wool.

9

Keeping Room Group

The average late eighteenth century living room was an austere setting. Wooden chairs, settees, or rockers comprised most of the comfortable furniture. At times, cushions or pillows were made for the hard seats, adding a bit of color, folk art, and personal comfort.

The usual Pennsylvania Dutch keeping room very often had a large table, several chairs or benches, wall or freestanding cupboards, and several lighting devices. This living area also doubled as a leisure-time workroom. Wives and daughters worked on their sewing, while the boys carved clothespins or the household supply of "lucifers" or matches.

The following miniature reproductions were selected from several museums in Pennsylvania. They represent a good selection for single room settings or for a full scale-size house. They can be mixed and matched with Early American furnishings for different period or regional house settings.

FLY-BRACKET DROP-LEAF TABLE

This drop-leaf table uses fly-bracket supports to hold up the two side leaves. This bracket can be part of the top side apron or added just under the extended tabletop edge. The bracket swings around a center screw so that it fits tight to the apron when not in use, or swings out to support the leaf when the extension is desired.

Material

Cherry, maple, basswood, or mahogany.

Fig. 3–43. *Pennsylvania Dutch keeping room*

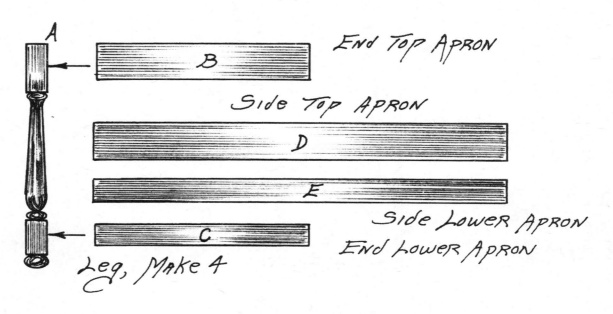

A

End Top Apron

B

Side Top Apron

D

E

Side Lower Apron
End Lower Apron

C

Leg, Make 4

Top

F

Drop Leaf, Make 2.

G

Fig. 3–44. Fly-bracket drop-leaf table pattern

	Part	Number	Size
A	Leg	4	$1/4''$ x $1/4''$ x $2^1/2''$
B	End Top Apron	2	$2^1/4''$ x $3/8''$ x $1/16''$
C	End Lower Apron	2	$2^1/4''$ x $3/16''$ x $1/16''$
D	Side Top Apron	2	$4^5/16''$ x $3/8''$ x $1/16''$
E	Side Lower Apron	2	$4^5/16''$ x $3/16''$ x $1/16''$
F	Top	1	$3^1/2''$ x $6^1/2''$ x $1/16''$
G	Leaf	2	$1''$ x $6^1/2''$ x $1/16''$

Construction

1. Lathe-turn the legs (A) to suggested shape and size. Lay out and cut the end top apron (B), end lower apron (C), side top apron (D), and side lower apron (E). Glue the end top apron (B) and end lower apron (C) to the sides and make two end assemblies. Glue the side top apron (D) and side lower apron (E) to the two end assemblies to complete the rectangle.

2. Lay out and cut the top (F) and leaves (G). Round off the edges on all parts. Glue the top to the leg assembly tops. Turn the table over, top down. With scale-size H hinges, secure the two leaves to the top. Make the two fly brackets from scrap stock and secure these brackets to the top with a screw. Check the swing operation of this bracket so that in the closed position it does not interfere with the drop leaf action (see bottom fig. 3–45).

Finish

Sand the entire table smooth removing all traces of glue. Stain to a color of choice. Cover with several coats lacquer or similar finish.

OLD COUNTRY CHILD'S CHAIR

The peasant's or child's chair made the move across the Atlantic with the Pennsylvania Dutch settlers. It offers design areas in its functional layout in the shape of cyma scrolls and turns, plus it becomes a perfect vehicle for symbolic paintings. Perhaps the aim was that the bright decoration would compensate for the lack of seating comfort.

Material

Cherry, maple, mahogany, or basswood.

Material List

	Part	Number	Size
A	Back	1	$1''$ x $3^1/8''$ x $1/8''$
B	Leg	1	$1''$ x $1^3/16''$ x $1/8''$
C	Seat	1	$1^3/16''$ x $1''$ x $1/8''$

Construction

1. Lay out and cut the back (A), leg (B), and seat (C) to size and design. Sand or break (round over) all the edges. Glue the leg to the seat, and glue the seat to the back.

Finish

Sand smooth, removing all traces of glue. Stain or paint to a color of choice. Cover with one coat of lacquer or similar finish. Paint on the decorations. Cover with another coat of selected finish. Wipe on an age glaze of half flat black paint and half thinner. Cover with several coats of finish.

DEACON'S BENCH

The following bench has been made in every section of the country in many different styles and shapes. The main differences between the Pennsylvania Dutch style and some of the others are the solid decorated back, the plank trestle-type legs, and the solid armrests. This miniature was styled after a piece in the Philadelphia Museum of Art.

Material

Cherry, basswood, maple, or mahogany.

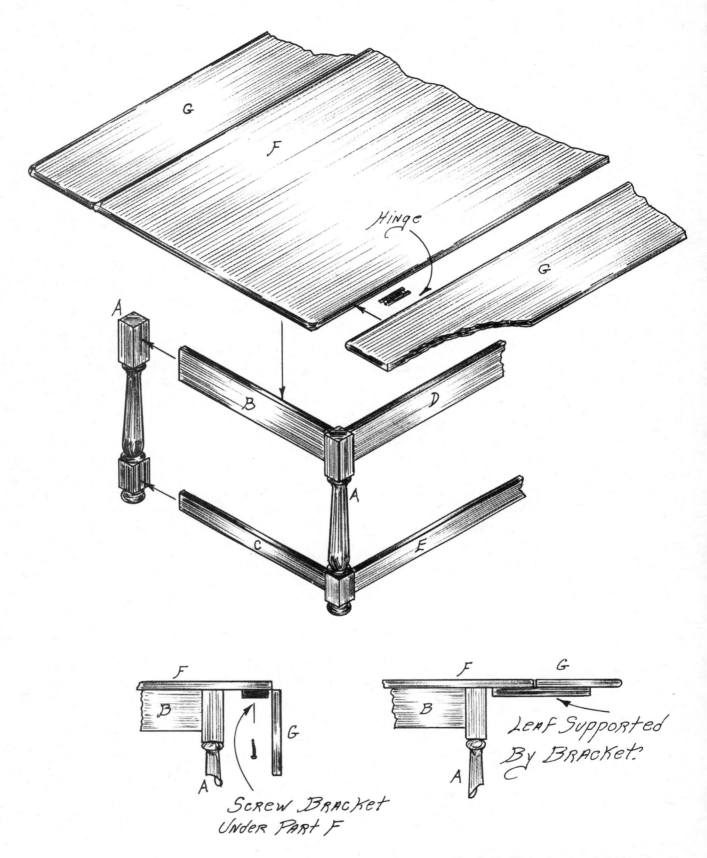

Hinge

Screw Bracket
Under Part F

Leaf Supported
By Bracket.

Fig. 3-45. Fly-bracket drop-leaf table assembly

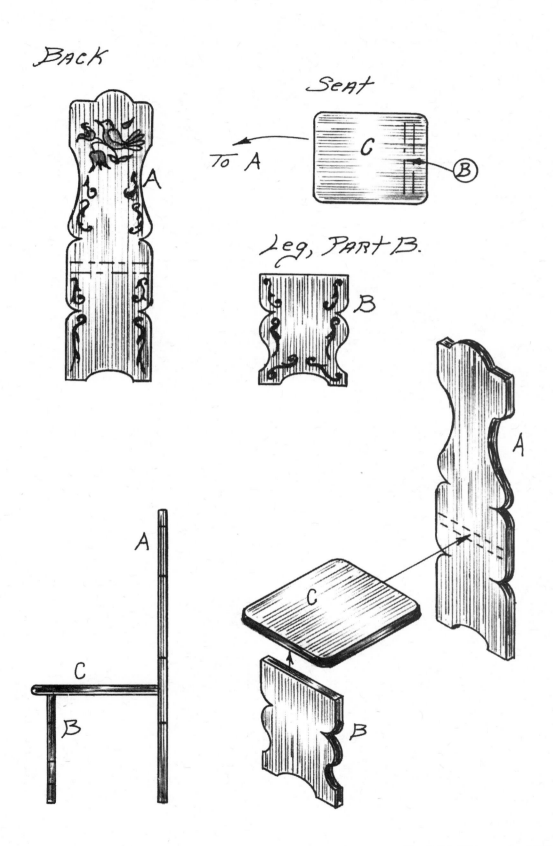

BACK

Seat

TO A

Leg, Part B.

Fig. 3–46. Old country child's chair

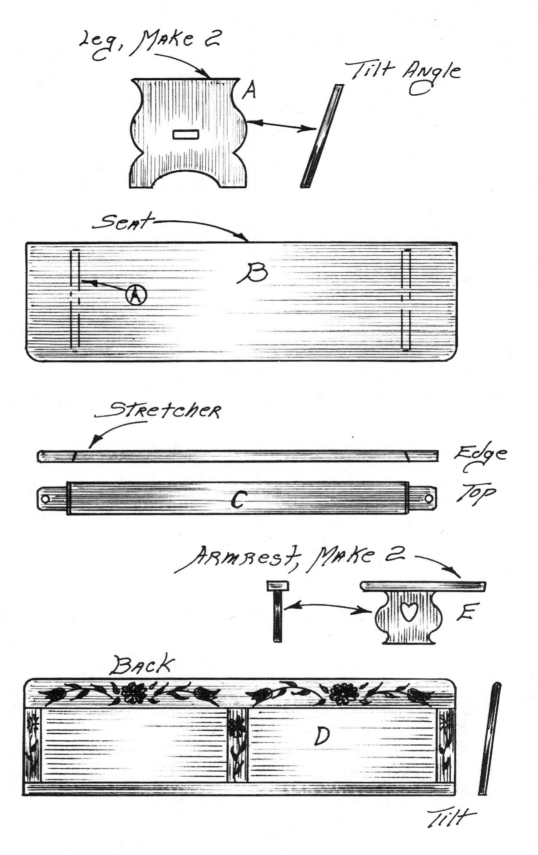

Fig. 3–47. Deacon's bench pattern

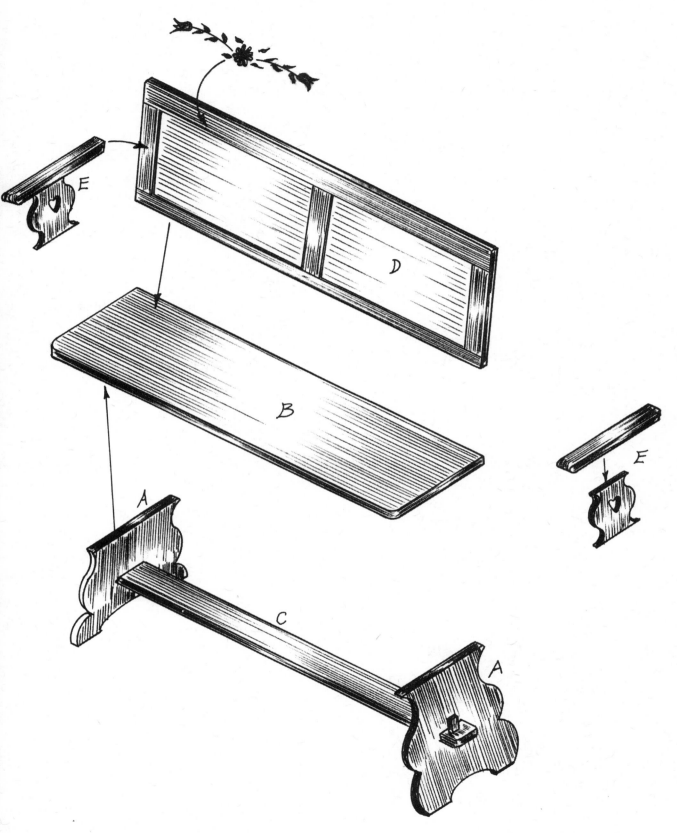

Fig. 3-48. Deacon's bench assembly

Material List

	Part	Number	Size
A	Leg	2	1¼" x 1¼" x 3/32"
B	Seat	1	4½" x 1¼" x 3/32"
C	Stretcher	1	4½" x 5/16" x 1/8"
D	Back	1	4½" x 1¼" x 1/16"
E	Armrest	2	1¼" x 3/16" x 1/16"
		2	¾" x 9/16" x 1/16"

Construction

1. Lay out and cut the legs (A), seat (B), and stretchers (C) to shape and size. Cut the stretcher mortise slots into the legs. Cut the top and bottom angles on the legs (see fig. 3–47 for splay angle). Make the required tenons on the stretchers. Dry fit the stretcher tenons to the leg mortise slots.

2. Glue one leg to the seat. Insert the stretcher tenon into the other leg, and as this leg is glued to the seat bottom, insert the other tenon end into the preglued leg. Drill a 1/16-inch-diameter hole through the stretcher ten-

ons as they extend through the exterior of the legs, and insert a dowel pin through the holes.

3. Lay out and cut the solid stock for the back (D). Laminate the 1/16-inch-thick frame stock to the solid backer to make a panel effect (see "Construction Notes"). Cut the mounting angles on the bottom of the back assembly, and glue the back to the legs (see tilt angle in fig. 3–47).

4. Lay out and cut the armrests (E). Glue the armrests to the back and stretchers.

Finish

This bench can be painted or stained. Follow the directions given for the "Old Country Child's Chair" or the "Bride's Chest."

BALLOON-BACK ROCKER

It's difficult to say if the balloon-style back was developed so that designs could be painted on it, or if the designs required a large surface and the balloon-back was the perfect answer. Regardless, this style rocker was used extensively in the Pennsylvania Dutch region, both painted and stained but always symbolically decorated with flowers, unicorns, or birds.

Material

Cherry, maple, or mahogany.

Fig. 3–49. Balloon-back rocker

Material List

	Part	Number	Size
A	Seat	1	1¼" x 1½" x ¼"
B	Back	1	2" x 1⅝" x 1/8"
C	Armrest	2	1" x 3/16" x 3/32"
D	Primary Support	2	1/16" dia. x 5/8"
E	Secondary Support	2	1/16" dia. x 5/8"
F	Leg	4	1/8" dia. x 1½"
G	Stretcher	4	1/16" dia. x 1⅝"
H	Rocker	2	2½" x ¼" x 1/16"

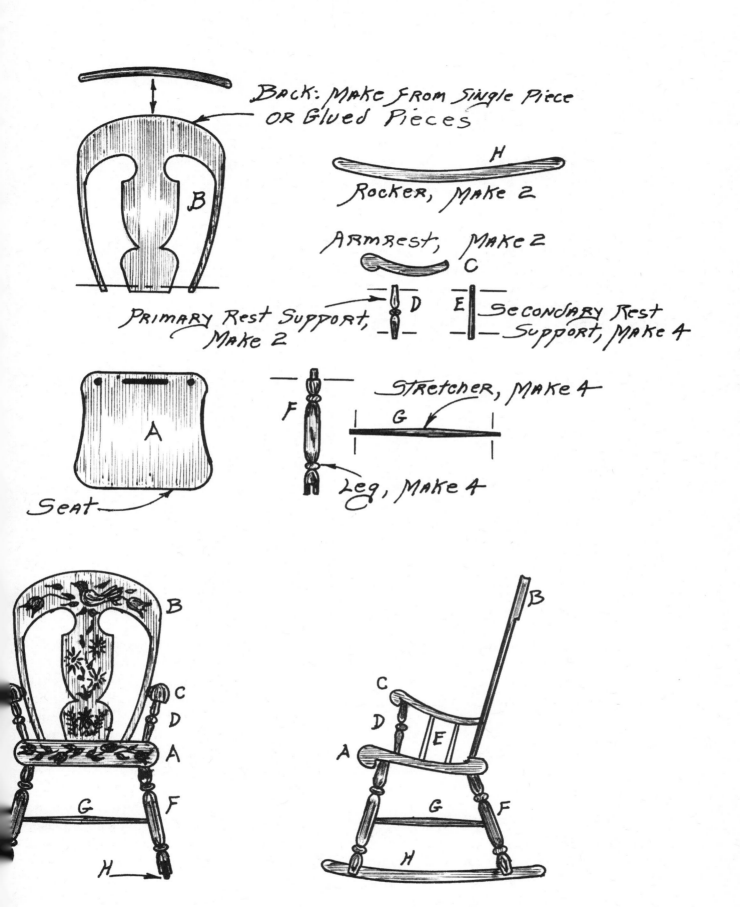

BACK: MAKE FROM SINGLE PIECE OR GLUED PIECES

B

ROCKER, MAKE 2 H

ARMREST, MAKE 2 C

PRIMARY REST SUPPORT, MAKE 2 D

E SECONDARY REST SUPPORT, MAKE 4

Seat A

F STRETCHER, MAKE 4 G

Leg, MAKE 4

Fig. 3–50. Balloon-backer rocker pattern and assembly

Construction

1. Lay out and cut the seat (A) and back (B) to suggested shape and size. It is best to cut the back from a solid block of wood; shape it, and then cut it loose from the holding stock.

Note the tenons on the bottom of the back. Cut matching mortise holes (slots) into the seat. Glue the back into the seat.

2. Lathe-turn the legs (F) and stretchers (G) to shape and length. Note the tenons on top of the legs, and the rocker slots cut on the bottoms. Drill $3/64$-inch stretcher mounting holes into the legs. Drill leg mounting holes into the bottom of the seat (see splay angles in fig. 3–50). Glue two legs into the front leg holes in the seat. At the same time glue in the front stretcher (G). Glue the two side stretchers into the front leg mortise holes. Glue the rear stretcher between the last two legs and as these leg tenons are glued into the rear mounting holes on the seat, glue the side stretcher tenons into the rear leg mortise holes. The whole leg and stretcher assembly should be completed in one operation before the glue has time to set.

3. Allow the leg assembly to dry. Make the rockers (H) and fit them to the slots cut into the legs. Glue the rockers into place. Check the rocking action. Adjustments can be made by sanding.

4. Lathe-turn the armrest supports (D, E) to shape. Lay out and cut the armrest to suggested design. Drill matching mounting holes into the armrest and the seat. Glue the armrest supports into the seat. Glue the armrest supports into the armrest, and glue the armrest to the back.

Finish

Sand the entire rocker smooth removing all traces of glue. Stain or paint to a color of choice. Follow the directions given for the "Bride's Chest" or the "Old Country Child's Chair" for decorative painting and finish.

HANGING WALL CUPBOARD

The average Pennsylvania Dutch household had several hanging wall cupboards. The following example has a glass door, perhaps in order to display special china or other prized possessions.

Material

Cherry, basswood, or mahogany.

Material List

	Part	Number	Size
A	Side	2	$1/2''$ x $2^5/8''$ x $1/16''$
B	Back	1	$1^1/2''$ x $2^5/8''$ x $1/16''$
C	Shelf	3	$7/16''$ x $1^1/2''$ x $1/16''$
D	Top	1	$2^1/4''$ x $3/4''$ x $1/16''$
E	Frame Stiles	2	$3/16''$ x $2^1/16''$ x $1/16''$
	Frame Bottom Rail	1	$1^{11}/16''$ x $3/16''$ x $1/16''$
	Frame Top Rail	1	$1^{11}/16''$ x $3/8''$ x $1/16''$
F	Molding	1	$2^1/4''$ x $3/16''$ x $3/16''$ crown
		2	$1''$ x $3/16''$ x $3/16''$ crown
G	Door	1	$1^5/16''$ x $2^1/8''$ x $1/16''$

Construction

1. Lay out and cut the sides (A), back (B), and shelves (C). Cut a $1/16$-by-$1/16$-inch rabbet on the rear inside edges of the sides. Glue the back into these rabbets. Glue the shelves between the sides the back (see location in fig. 3–51).

2. Lay out and cut the top (D). Glue the top on top of the sides and back. Make the front frame (E), with half-lap joints. Glue the frame to the sides, shelves, and top. Cut the cove moldings (F) with 45-degree miter corners. Glue the moldings to the sides, shelves, and front frame.

3. Make the open door frame (G). Make and install the muntins. Glue heavy gauge plastic or $1/32$-inch glass into the door opening. Install the finished door to the front frame with hinges. Figure 3–51 offers patterns for a butterfly rat-tail hinge.

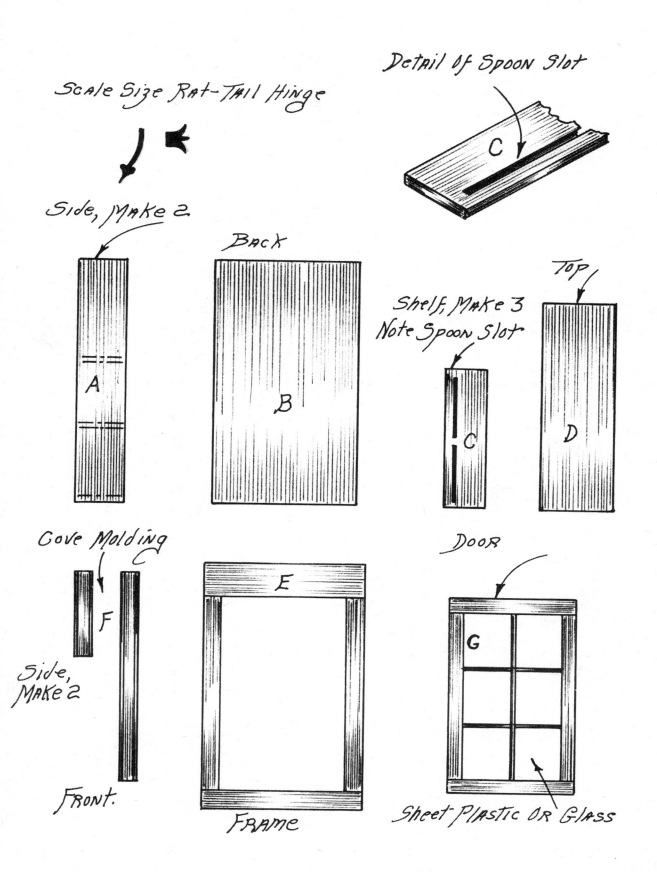

Detail of Spoon Slot

Scale Size Rat-Tail Hinge

Side, Make 2

A

Back

B

Shelf, Make 3
Note Spoon Slot

C

Top

D

Cove Molding

F

Side,
Make 2

Front.

E

Frame

Door

G

Sheet Plastic or Glass

Fig. 3–51. Hanging wall cupboard pattern

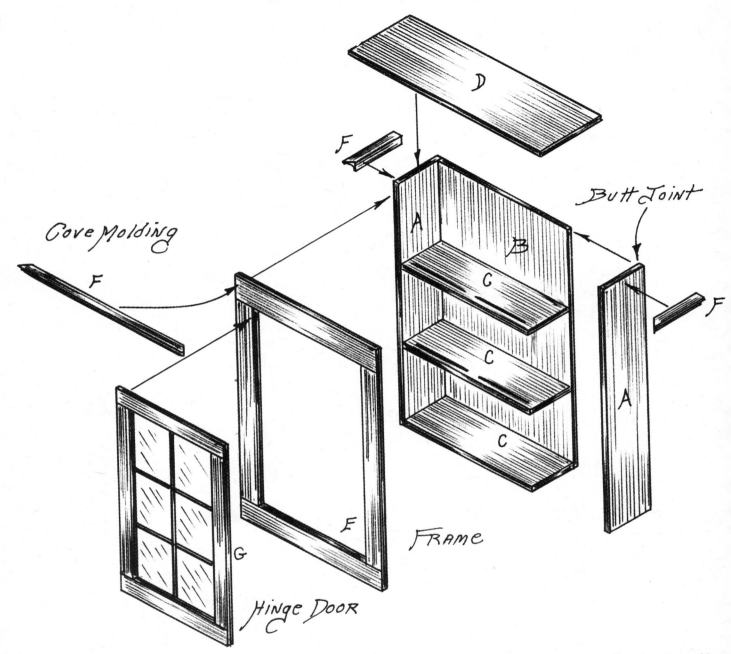

Cove Molding

F

Butt Joint

A

B

C

C

C

D

F

F

A

Frame

F

Hinge Door

G

Fig. 3–52. Hanging wall cupboard assembly

Finish

Sand the entire cupboard smooth removing all traces of glue. Stain or paint to a color of choice. Cover with several coats of lacquer or similar finish.

SCALLOP-SIDED CORNER CUPBOARD

The following miniature was adapted from an antique model on display in the Philadelphia Museum of Art. The Shelburne Museum

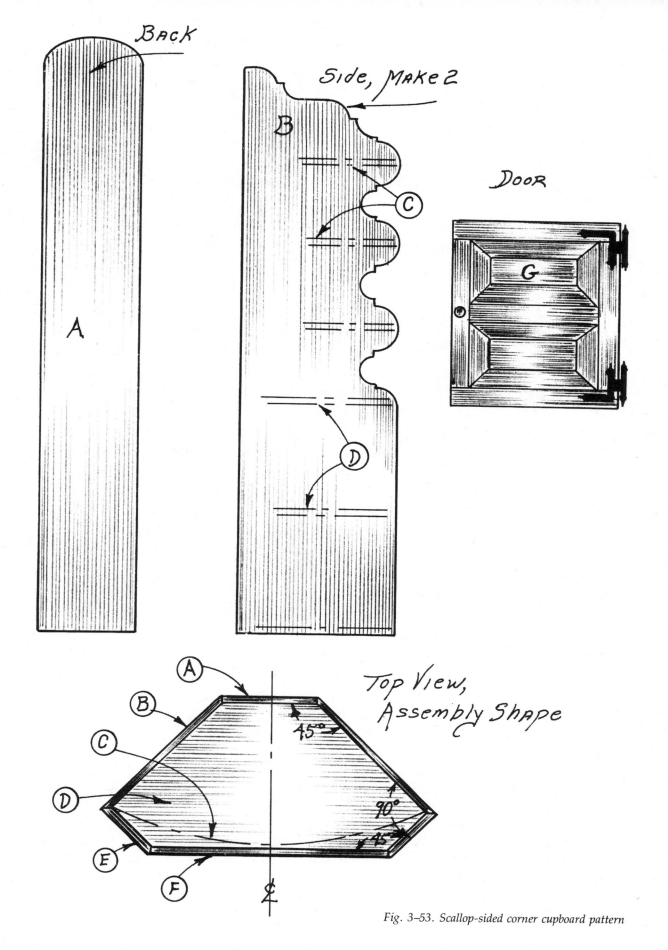

Fig. 3–53. Scallop-sided corner cupboard pattern

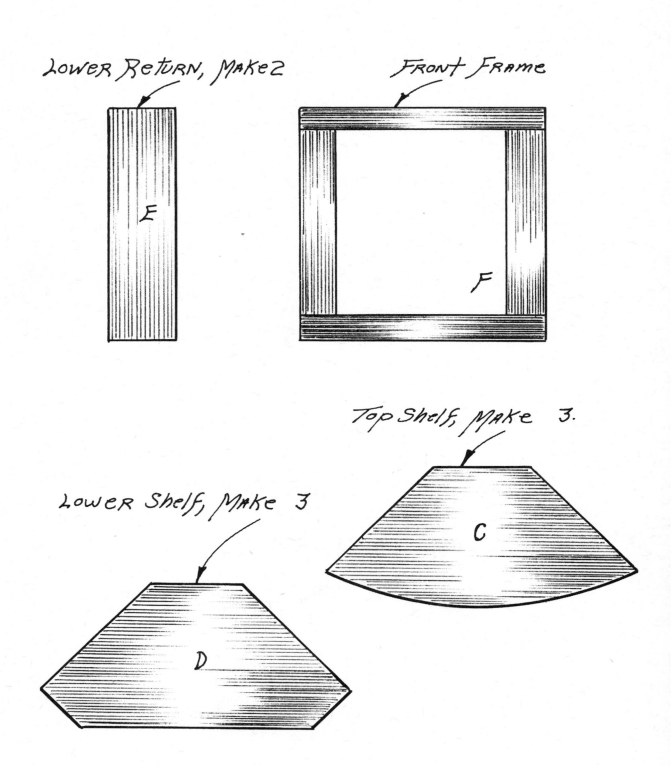

Fig. 3-53. Scallop-sided corner cupboard pattern (continued)

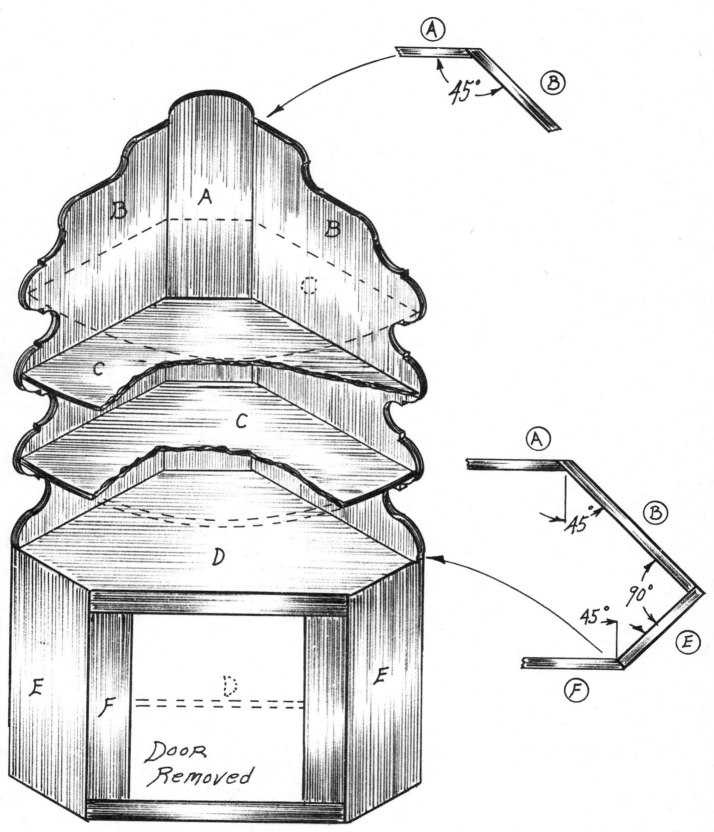

Fig. 3–54. Scallop-sided corner cupboard assembly

also has a cabinet with the same basic design. While the originals were not hand painted or decorated, the wide lower side panels lend themselves to symbolic designs.

Material

Cherry, basswood, or select clear pine.

Material List

	Part	Number	Size
A	Back	1	1" x 6½" x ¹/₁₆"
B	Side	2	1⁵/₈" x 6¹/₈" x ¹/₁₆"
C	Top Shelf	3	3¼" x 1½" x ¹/₁₆"
D	Bottom Shelf	3	3¼" x 1⁹/₁₆" x ¹/₁₆"
E	Return	2	³/₄" x 2¹/₂" x ¹/₁₆"
F	Frame Stiles	2	2" x ³/₈" x ¹/₁₆"
	Frame Rails	2	2⁹/₁₆" x ¹/₄" x ¹/₁₆"
G	Door	1	2" x 1³/₄" x ¹/₈"

Construction

1. Note the assembly top view in the bottom of figure 3–53. Notice the part numbers and assembly sequence. The sides (B) join the back (A) at a 45 degree angle; the sides (B) and the lower return (E) form a 90 degree angle. The lower return (E) joins the front frame (F) on a 45 degree angle. Shelf C has a rounded front while shelf D has the compound angle front.

2. Lay out and cut the back (A) and the sides (B) to shape and size. Mark for the shelves (C and D) (see fig. 3–53). Glue the sides to the back.

3. Lay out and cut the shelves to suggested shape and size. Glue the shelves to the sides and back. Cut compatible side angles on the lower returns (E). Glue the lower returns to the sides and bottom shelf. Make the front frame (F). It is best to make this frame slightly over-size and sand fit it between the lower returns. Glue the finished frame to the lower returns and the bottom shelf.

4. Make a double panel door (G). Hinge the door to the front frame with scale size H and L hinges.

Finish

Sand the entire cabinet smooth removing all traces of glue. Stain or paint to a color of choice. Hand paint designs if preferred. Cover with several coats of lacquer or similar finish. For an aged, painted effect follow the directions given for the "Bride's Chest" or the "Old Country Child's Chair."

SECTION FOUR

Victorian Furnishings

The Victorian period began with the coronation of Queen Victoria in 1837—hence the name. Characterized by scrolls, turns, gilt, and embellishment, authorities claim that Victorian styles were borrowed or copied from earlier classical interpretations, ranging from formal French classic to homespun, country-style Gothic.

The primary influences, French and English, can be further broken into several subdivisions. The French include rococo, baroque, Empire, Louis IV, or art nouveau and the English, Gothic, Renaissance, and Elizabethan. Added to all this is the American influence and interpretation, which produced yet another imprint.

The starting period of Victorianism in America closely followed the Early American period and continued right up to the beginning of World War II. While original Victorian furnishings are the mainstay of modern-day antiques, they are also the prototypes for modern reproductions. The volume and scope of this furniture style is an endless as the imagination.

Every species of wood was employed in the construction of Victorian furnishings, although walnut, oak, and mahogany were the favorites. Very often several different woods would be used together for dark and light contrast. Red, blue, gold, or purple brocades; polished marble; heavy tiers of moldings; and inlaid veneers were some of the trappings of Victorianism.

Victorian styling is a mixed blending of overly embellished classical form and newly invented mechanical production. New innovations such as sofa beds, synthetic materials, recliner chairs, and simulated wood were used by a mass producing industry that fell in love with the band saw. The old town craftsman who made individual furniture slowly gave way to the newly devised power assembly lines that turned out thousands of identical interchangeable pieces. Furnishings were no longer sold from the maker's shop, but instead from furniture stores that all carried, more or less, the same stock items.

This section was designed to cover as much of the American Victorian range as possible within limited pages. Some pieces will offer elaborate scrollwork based more on the French influence, while other miniature reproductions border on the early 1900 domestic versions. Mostly, the following miniature furnishings were designed for a turn-of-the-century Victorian room setting or for the Victorian house featured in *Building Masterpiece Miniatures* (Harrisburg, PA: Stackpole Books, 1980). Each reproduction offers full-size patterns for the required pieces, plus a detailed construction or assembly drawing showing how the parts are fitted together.

10

Bedroom Group

SERPENTINE-FRONT CHEST OF DRAWERS

The following miniature chest of drawers is designed with a curved serpentine front, common to late nineteenth- or early twentieth-century furniture. The curved fronts are made from a single piece of stock, and then cut into the required pieces. A half-round file is suggested for making the rounds.

Materials

Any of the hardwood species will suffice, although walnut is preferred.

Material List

	Part	Number	Size
A	Side	2	$1^5/8'' \times 2^7/8'' \times 1/8''$
B	Back	1	$3^1/8'' \times 2^7/8'' \times 1/16''$
C	Divider	3	$3'' \times 1^5/8'' \times 1/8''$
		1	$3'' \times 1^5/8'' \times 1/4''$
D	Top	1	$4'' \times 2'' \times 1/16''$
E	Drawer Front	3	$3'' \times 3/4'' \times 1/16''$
F	Drawer Side	6	$1^1/4'' \times 3/4'' \times 1/16''$
G	Drawer Back	3	$2^3/4'' \times 3/4'' \times 1/16''$
H	Drawer Bottom	3	$2^3/4'' \times 1^1/8'' \times 1/16''$
I	Feet	4	$5/16''$ dia. oval x $7/8''$
J	Bracket	2	$1/4'' \times 3/16'' \times 2^1/2''$
K	Mirror Backer	1	$2^3/4'' \times 1^1/2'' \times 1/16''$

Construction

1. Lay out and cut sides (A), back (B), divider (C), and top (D) to suggested shapes and sizes. Cut a rabbet on the rear edges of the sides (A). Glue the drawer dividers (C) between the sides (A), as noted in the pattern drawing. Glue the top (D) to the sides (A), back (B), and top divider (C).

Fig. 4–1. Victorian bedroom group

Fig. 4–2. Serpentine-front chest of drawers

2. Make the three drawer units. Cut the drawer front (E) to suggested size and shape. Cut a rabbet on each end as noted in figure 4–3. Glue drawer sides (F) into these rabbets. Glue drawer back (G) to drawer sides (F). Fit and glue drawer bottom (H) between drawer front (E), side (F), and back (G). Sand fit each completed drawer to its space in the dresser.

3. Make the four small molded feet (I). See "Construction Notes" for suggested methods. Glue feet (I) to the bottom divider (C).

4. Mirror. The mirror brackets (J) also have a serpentine profile (see "Construction Notes"). Lay out and cut brackets (J) to suggested shape and size. Drill $1/8$-inch-diameter holes in the bottoms. Glue a small piece of $1/8$-inch dowel into these holes allowing $1/4$-inch tenon extensions.

Cut the mirror backing (K) to suggested shape and size. The rail and stile frames should

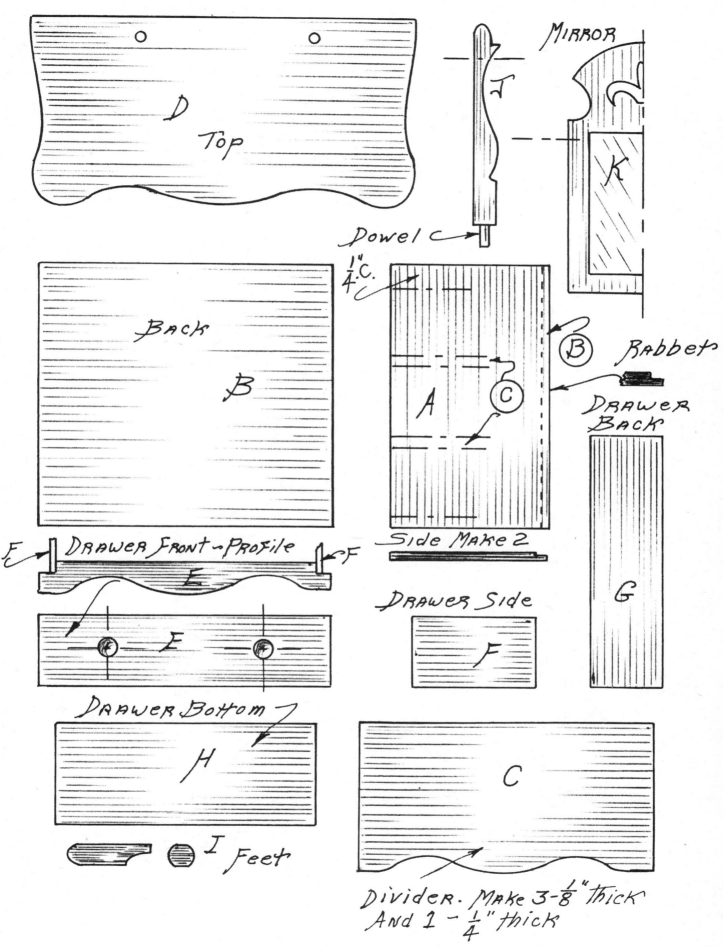

Fig. 4–3. Serpentine-front chest of drawers pattern

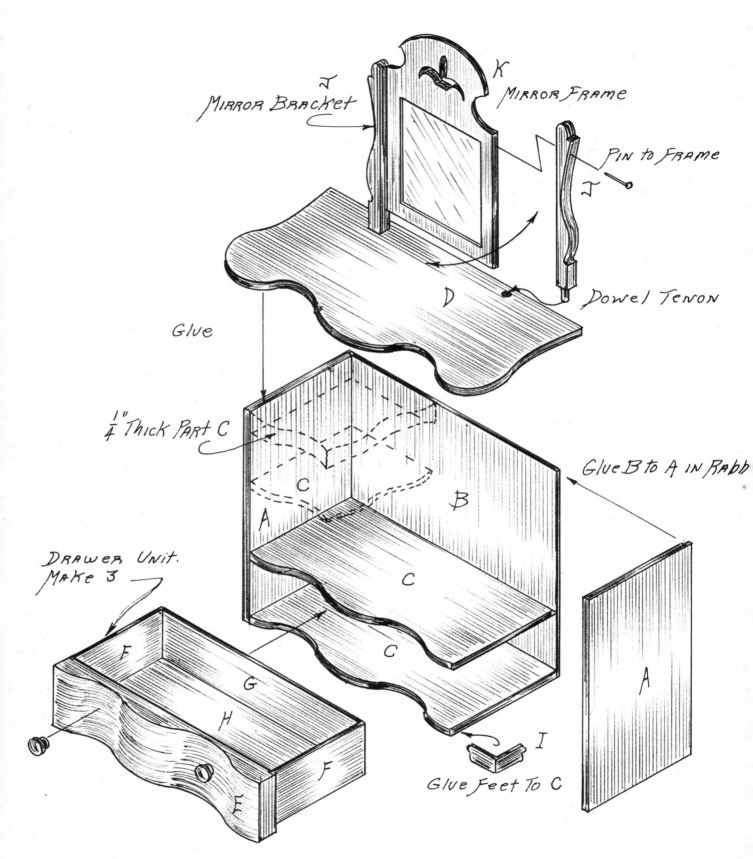

MIRROR BRACKET J

K MIRROR FRAME

PIN to FRAME

J

Dowel Tenon

D

Glue

1/4" Thick Part C

Glue B to A in Rabb

C

A

B

C

C

DRAWER Unit.
Make 3

F

G

H

F

F

E

E

I

Glue Feet To C

A

Fig. 4–4. Serpentine-front chest of drawers assembly

208

be added to a $1/16$-inch backer stock (see "Construction Notes" on raised panels). Install a small, $1/16$-inch-thick mirror into the space provided. Drill $1/8$-inch-diameter holes into the top (D) as shown in figure 4–3. Insert the dowel tenons on the mirror brackets (J) into these holes. Suspend mirror (K) between brackets (J) with small pins. The mirror should be adjustable to angle-tilt.

Finish

Remove all traces of glue. Sand the entire chest smooth. No stain is used except on pine or basswood. Cover with a high-gloss finish. Install scale-size drawer pulls.

NIGHTSTAND OR WASHSTAND

This particular nightstand is a direct descendant of its Early American counterpart. The style lines are very similar. Since many of its functional characteristics remain, the nightstand continued to be a useful furnishing into the Victorian era. The serpentine unit at the top can contain a mirror or a single towel bar.

Materials

Walnut, cherry, maple, mahogany, basswood, or pine. Walnut is preferred.

Fig. 4–5. Nightstand or washstand

Material List

	Part	Number	Size
A	Side	2	$1\frac{1}{4}$" x $2\frac{1}{2}$" x $1/8$"
B	Back	1	$2\frac{1}{2}$" x $2\frac{1}{2}$" x $1/16$"
C	Bottom	1	$2\frac{3}{8}$" x $1\frac{3}{16}$" x $1/16$"
D	Top Rail	1	$2\frac{3}{4}$" x $3/16$" x $1/16$"
E	Mid Rail	1	$2\frac{3}{8}$" x $3/16$" x $1/16$"
F	End Stile	2	2" x $3/16$" x $1/16$"
G	Mid Stile	1	$1\frac{3}{8}$" x $3/16$" x $1/16$"
H	Skirt	1	$2\frac{3}{4}$" x $5/16$" x $1/16$"
I	Drawer Rail	1	$1\frac{1}{8}$" x $3/16$" x $1/16$"
J	Door	2	$1\frac{1}{8}$" x $1\frac{3}{8}$" x $1/8$"
K	Top Drawer Front	1	$2\frac{3}{8}$" x $3/8$" x $1/16$"
L	Top Drawer Side	2	$1\frac{1}{8}$" x $3/8$" x $1/16$"
M	Top Drawer Back	1	$2\frac{1}{4}$" x $3/8$" x $1/16$"
N	Top Drawer Bottom	1	$1\frac{1}{16}$" x $2\frac{1}{4}$" x $1/16$"
O	Side Drawer Front	2	$1\frac{1}{8}$" x $5/8$" x $1/16$"
P	Side Drawer Side	4	$1\frac{1}{8}$" x $5/8$" x $1/16$"
Q	Side Drawer Back	2	1" x $5/8$" x $1/16$"
R	Side Drawer Bottom	2	1" x 1" x $1/16$"
S	Top	1	$1\frac{1}{2}$" x 3" x $1/16$"
T	Bracket	2	$3/4$" x $2\frac{1}{8}$" x $3/32$"
U	Mirror Back	1	$1\frac{5}{8}$" x $2\frac{1}{8}$" x $1/16$"

Construction

1. Lay out and cut the sides (A), back (B), and bottom (C). Glue sides (A) to back (B).

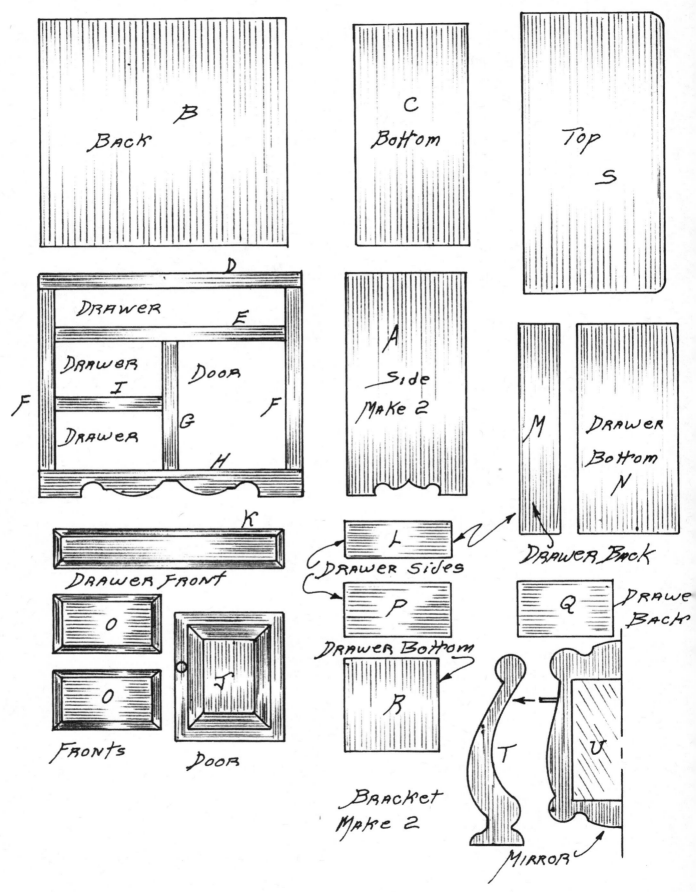

Fig. 4–6. Nightstand or washstand pattern

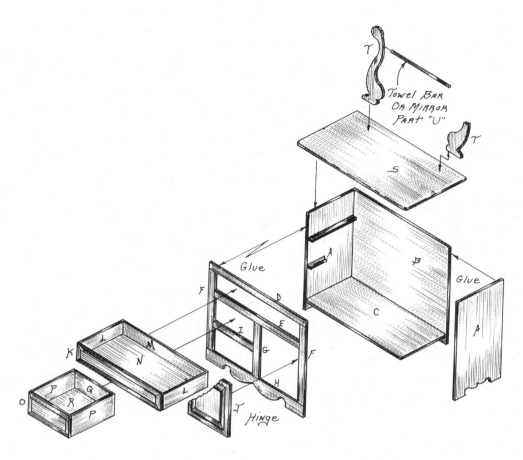

Fig. 4–7. Nightstand or washstand assembly

Insert and glue bottom (C) between sides (A) and back (B).

2. Lay out and cut the front frames (D, E, F, G, H, I). Glue the frame parts to each other and to the sides (A). See figure 4–7 for ·size and placement.

3. Make a door unit (J) to fit the door opening. Make two small drawer units to fit the drawer openings marked. Glue the drawer sides (P) to the drawer fronts (O). Glue the drawer back (Q) to the sides (P). Insert and glue drawer bottoms (R) between fronts (O), sides (P), and back (Q). Sand fit the drawer units to the spaces. Make drawer guides from scrap stock. Glue the left-hand guides to sides (A). Glue the right-hand guides between frame (G) and back (B).

4. Make the large top drawer. Glue sides (L) to front (K). Glue drawer back (M) to sides (L). Insert and glue drawer bottom (N) between front (K), sides (L), and back (M). Sand fit the drawer to its opening. Make drawer guides from scrap stock. Glue these guides to washstand sides (A).

5. Cut the top (S) to suggested shape and size. Glue the top to the sides (A), back (B), and frame (D). Lay out and cut brackets (T) to shape (see "Construction Notes"). The brackets (T) are then attached to the top (S) with 1/8-inch-diameter dowels or tenons or they can be glued on directly. If a mirror is to be used, lay out and cut frame (U) to shape and size. The frame (U) is attached to the brackets (T) with a dowel or pins. If a towel bar is desired, drill a 1/8-inch-diameter hole through brackets (T). Insert a 1/8-inch-diameter dowel between the brackets.

Finish

Sand the entire miniature smooth, removing

Fig. 4–8. Marble-top table

all traces of glue. No stain is recommended except over pine or basswood. Cover with a high-gloss finish. Attach required drawer pulls. Attach the door unit with scale-size hinges.

MARBLE-TOP TABLE

The small occasional table was used in almost every room of a Victorian home. These tables came in all shapes and sizes. Some were designed to hold and feature a single decorative object, while others were as large as kitchen tables. Common features of these tables were the decorative legs and the highly polished marble tops. The following miniature is a composite of such table styling.

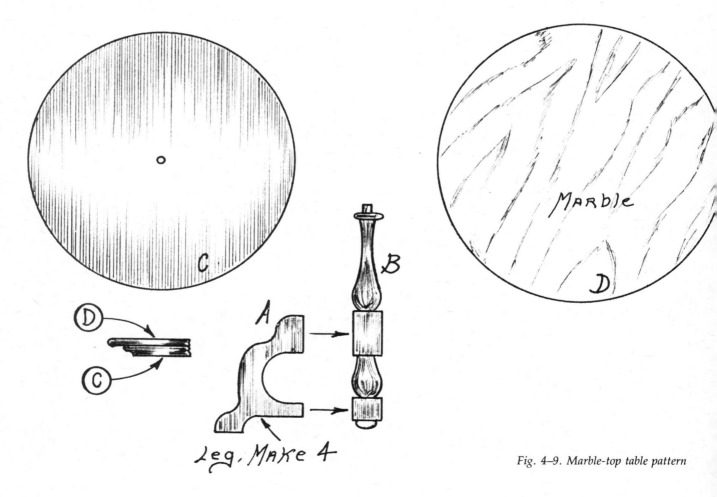

Leg. Make 4

Fig. 4–9. Marble-top table pattern

Materials

The wood can be walnut, maple, cherry, or basswood. Walnut is preferred. The tabletop can be made from Du Pont Corian[R], plastic, or marble-style formica or similar material.

Material List

	Part	Number	Size
A	Scroll Leg	4	1" x 1³/₈" x ¹/₁₆"
B	Stem	1	⁵/₁₆" dia. x 2¹/₂"
C	Wood Top	1	2⁵/₈" dia. x ¹/₈"
D	Marble Top	1	3" dia. x ¹/₈"

Construction

1. Lay out and cut the four legs (see "Construction Notes" for "Scroll or Scallop Legs").

2. Lathe-turn the wood tabletop (C). Or instead of cutting the wood and marble separately, glue the marble top to the wood stock and rough cut both the tabletop (C) and the marble top (D) in one step. (Note the marble top is slightly larger than the wood top. The combination top can be finish sanded while still on the lathe. When completed, drill a blind mortise hole in the bottom of the tabletop (C).

3. Lathe-turn the center spindle (B). Make a dowel-like tenon on the top of the spindle to fit the mortise hole in the tabletop (C). Glue the legs (A) to the spindle (B). Glue the tenon on the spindle (B) into the mortise hole in the tabletop (C).

Finish

Remove all traces of glue. Cover wood parts with a high-gloss finish. No staining is recommended except over softwoods like pine or basswood.

BRASS CRIB

Many different styles and forms of brass beds were found in the Victorian period. The following miniature reproduction is designed as a child's crib. The required brass can be

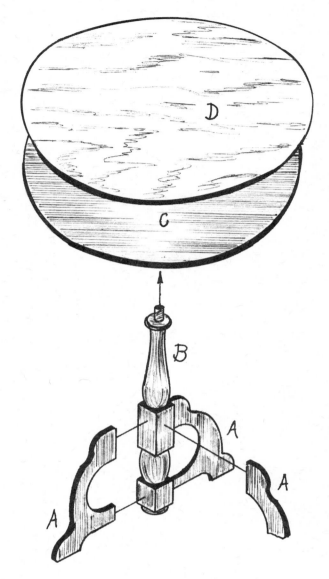

Fig. 4–10. Marble-top table assembly

purchased in hobby shops or model railroad outlets in tube or solid lengths.

Material

The various units are made on a wooden jig. The footboards and headboards are duplicates as are the two side rails.

Material List

	Part	Number	Size
A	Bed Post	4	¹/₈" dia. x 3¹/₄" brass tube

B	Side rail	4	$1/16''$ dia. x 3'' brass tube	E	Scroll	4	$1/32''$ dia. x $1^5/8''$ brass wire
C	Foot/Head Rail	4	$1/16''$ dia. x $1^3/4''$ brass tube	F	Finial	4	$1/8''$ to $3/32''$ dia. brass balls
D	Spoke	32	$1/32''$ dia. x $1^1/2''$ brass wire	G	Feet	4	$3/32''$ dia. door pulls

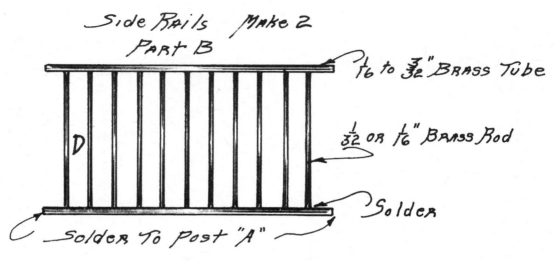

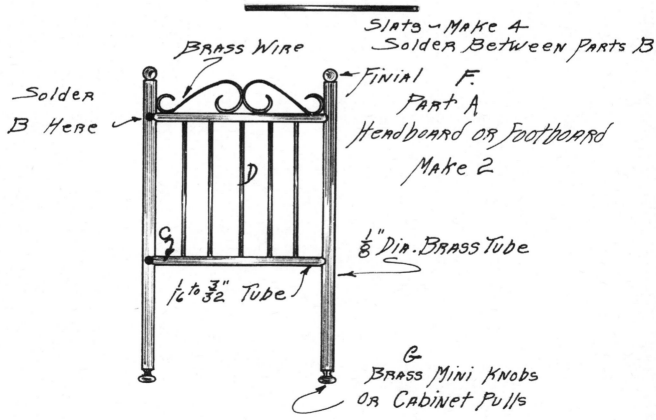

Fig. 4–11. Brass crib pattern

214

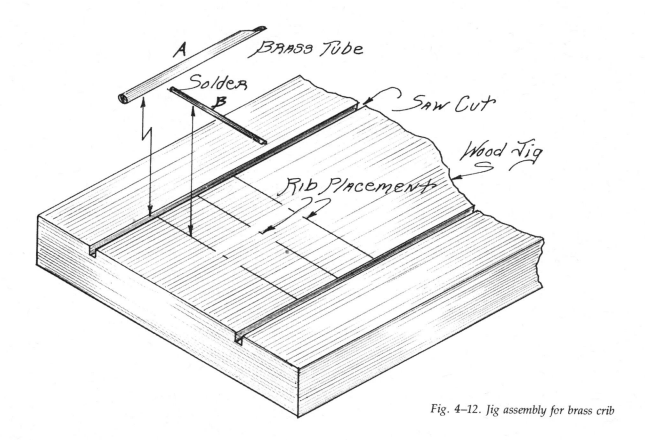

Fig. 4–12. Jig assembly for brass crib

Construction

1. Lay out a wood jig to receive the various parts of the headboard and footboard assembly. Cut the post stock (A) and rail tubing (B) to the required lengths. File fit the rails (B) to the shape of the posts. Solder the rails (B) to the posts (A). Cut the upright stile rounds (D) to size. Solder the stiles (D) to the rails (B). Make two top scrolls (E) from brass wire. Solder the scrolls (E) to the top rail (B). (Note: small parts such as the upright stiles and scrolls can be held in place on the wood jig with staples so they can be soldered without moving.) Solder round brass balls or finials (F) to the post tops (A). Solder brass miniature doorknobs or cabinet pulls to the post bottoms for feet (G).

2. Side rails. Cut the horizontal rails (C) to size. Cut the vertical stiles (D) to suggested size. Set these parts in place on a wood jig and solder the stiles to the rails. When the sides are

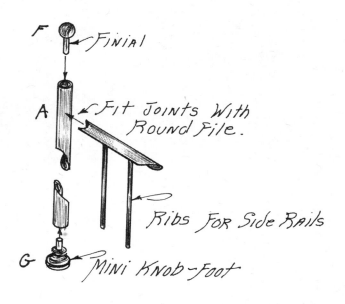

Fig. 4–13. Tube joint construction

completed, solder them to the headboards and footboards.

3. Cross slats can be made from 1/16-inch-diameter rod or 1/8-inch flat stock. Solder several cross slats between the bottom side rails. These slats will hold the mattress.

Finish

File and smooth off all solder joints. Polish the brass with fine steel wool. A coat of clear lacquer will preserve the bright brass. Make a mattress for the crib.

MASTER BED

Most Victorian beds were bulky with ornate posts and headboards. Their mass implied that they would be solid, substantial, long-lasting pieces of furniture. The following reproduction was developed from several prototypes of Victorian styling.

Materials

All stock is walnut.

Fig. 4–14. Master bed

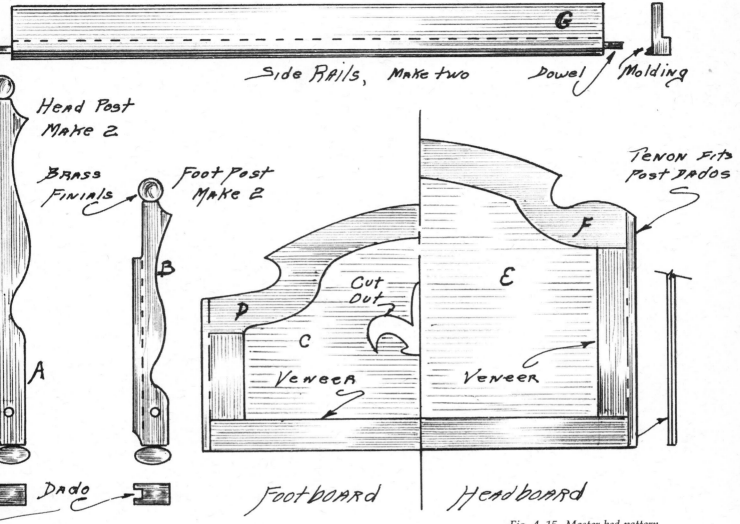

Side Rails, Make two   Dowel   Molding

Head Post Make 2

Brass Finials

Foot Post Make 2

B

A

Dado

Cut Out

D

C

Veneer

E

F

Veneer

Tenon Fits Post Dados

Footboard   Headboard

Fig. 4–15. Master bed pattern

Material List

	Part	Number	Size
A	Head Post	2	$3/8'' \times 4'' \times 3/16''$
B	Foot Post	2	$3/8'' \times 2^3/4'' \times 3/16''$
C	Footboard	1	$4^1/2'' \times 2^3/4'' \times 1/16''$
D	Footboard Trim	1	$4^1/2'' \times 2^3/4'' \times 1/16''$
E	Headboard	1	$4^1/2'' \times 3^1/2'' \times 1/16''$
F	Headboard Trim	1	$4^1/2'' \times 3^1/2'' \times 1/16''$
G	Side Rail	2	$5/8'' \times 6^1/4'' \times 1/16''$
H	Bed Slat	5	$5'' \times 1/8'' \times 1/16''$

Construction

1. Lay out and cut the foot posts (B) and head posts (A) to shape and size (see "Con-struction Notes" for details). Cut a 1/8-inch dado into all four posts as marked in figure 4–15.

2. Lay out and cut the headboard. This headboard is made in two stages with E as a solid backer piece and F added as a type of veneer (see figure 4–16). (The "Construction Notes" on raised-panel doors gives instruction for similar detailing.) Insert and glue the head-board assembly tenon into the headpost dadoes.

3. Lay out and cut the footboard. Follow the same procedure as outlined for the headboard assembly. The backing board (C) is solid and the veneer (D) is added on.

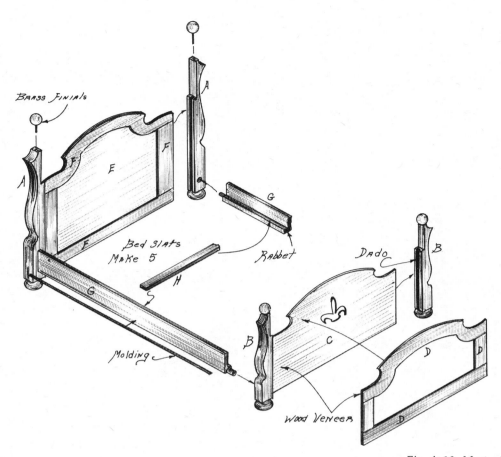

Fig. 4–16. Master bed assembly

4. Lay out and cut the side rails (G). See rabbet cut detail in figure 4–15. Drill a ⅛-inch-diameter hole into the ends of the side rails. Glue a section of ⅛-inch-round dowel into these holes, allowing ¼ inch to extend as a tenon. Drill matching holes into the headboard and footboard assembly as marked in figure 4–15. Glue the side rail dowels into the post holes. Cut five or six cross slats. Insert the slats and glue them between the side rails on the rabbets.

Finish

Sand the entire reproduction smooth. Remove all traces of glue. Stain softwoods. Cover with a high-gloss finish.

Make a scale-size box spring from a sponge or styrofoam block. Make a miniature mattress to fit (see "Construction Notes"). Make two pillows.

SINGLE BED

The highlights of the following miniature are the upholstered headboard and the blanket roll on the footboard. This bed can be made as a double bed by just increasing the width of the headboard or footboard (fig. 4–15).

Materials

Any hardwood, but walnut is preferred. Felt, velvet, or satin can be used for upholstering.

Fig. 4–17. Single bed with upholstered blanket roll and headboard

Material List

	Part	Number	Size
A	Head Post	2	$3\frac{1}{4}$" x $\frac{1}{4}$" x $\frac{1}{4}$"
B	Foot Post	2	2" x $\frac{1}{4}$" x $\frac{1}{4}$"
C	Headboard	1	$3\frac{1}{4}$" x $3\frac{1}{2}$" x $\frac{1}{16}$"
D	Footboard	1	$3\frac{1}{4}$" x 1" x $\frac{1}{16}$"
	Blanket Roll	1	$\frac{3}{8}$" dia. x 2" dowel
E	Side Rail	2	$1\frac{1}{4}$" x 6" x $\frac{3}{16}$"
F	Molding	1	24 lin. inch x $\frac{3}{32}$" molding
G	Felt	1	$1\frac{1}{2}$" x 2" (cloth)
		1	$1\frac{1}{4}$" x 2" (cloth)
H	Bed Slat	5	$3\frac{1}{2}$" x $\frac{1}{8}$" x $\frac{1}{16}$"

Construction

Follow figure 4–16 for assembly instruction.

1. Cut the stock for the head posts (A) and foot posts (B). (See "Construction Notes" for techniques.) Shape the posts to the suggested design and sizes.

2. Lay out and cut the stock for the headboard (C) and footboard (D). Make the required tenons on the headboard (C) and footboard (D). Sand all scrolls smooth. Mark the area to be upholstered on the headboard. Cut shop-made moldings with mitered joints for around this area. Glue a patch of fabric to the area and cover the edges with the moldings.

3. Cut a piece of dowel for the footboard blanket roll. Cut a slot in the bottom edge of the dowel so the top of the footboard will fit into it. Glue fabric around the dowel and glue the dowel to the top of the footboard. Shop-made or purchased wood or brass finials can be attached to the dowel ends.

4. Glue the completed headboard and footboard to the previously made posts. Lay out and cut the side rails (E). The rails are made in the shape of the letter L with rabbet cuts (see detail fig. 4–17). Drill $\frac{1}{8}$-inch-diameter holes in the edges of the side rails and glue a piece of $\frac{1}{8}$-inch-diameter dowel into the holes, allowing $\frac{1}{4}$-inch projections. Drill matching dowels

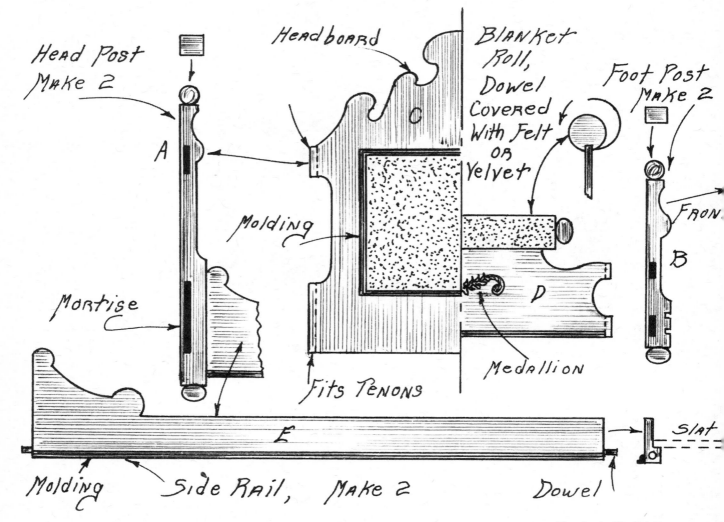

Fig. 4–18. Single bed pattern

into the head posts and foot posts. Glue the side rails dowels into the posts. Make and install five or six cross slats.

Finish

Remove all traces of glue. Cover entire reproduction with several coats of high-gloss finish. No staining is suggested. Complete with a styrofoam box spring and stuffed mattress and pillow.

BRASS BED

The brass bed has been made in almost every shape and design possible. At one time they were mass-produced and were an inexpensive item. Today they are sought as valuable antiques for Victorian furniture collectors.

Material

All stock is brass shapes, available in most hobby, miniature, or model railroad outlets. All fastenings are made by soldering. Decorative brass finials can be purchased in many hobby outlets in the shape of rounds, ovals, or decorative turns.

Material List

	Part	Number	Size
A	Bed Post	2	1/8" dia. x 5" brass tube

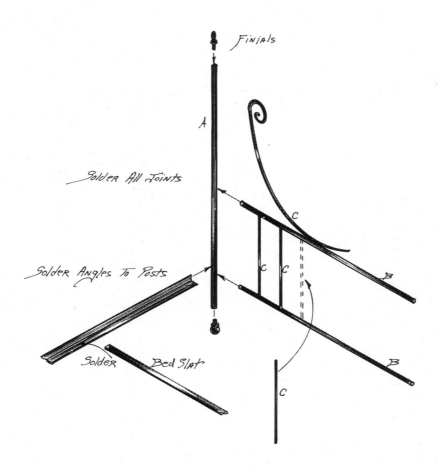

Finials

Solder All Joints

Solder Angles To Posts

Solder   Bed Slat

A

C

C   C

B

B

C

Fig. 4–19. Brass bed

A–1	Foot Post	2	1/8″ dia. x 3 3/8″ brass tube
B	Rail	4	3/32″ dia. x 3 7/8″ brass tube
C	Spoke	12	1/16″ dia. x 1 5/8″ brass wire
C–1	Headboard Scroll	1	1/16″ dia. x 6″ brass wire or rod
D	Scroll	4	3/64″ x 2 1/2″ brass wire
E	Side Rail	2	3/16″ x 3/16″ x 6″ brass angles

Construction

1. Make a wood jig and lay out all the shapes, turns, pieces, and joints. Make the headboard and footboard following this process. Cut the brass tubes for the posts (A) and rails (B). Mount these to the wood jig with tape, pins, or bent-over nails. Cut out and mount the stiles (C) between the rails (B). Solder rails (B) to posts (A), and stiles (C) to rails (B). Make the rounds and scrolls (D). Solder these scrolls wherever they touch other brass parts.

Make brass finials by lathe-turning brass rounds or by soldering brass scale-size door or drawer knobs (pulls) to the open ends the head and foot posts.

2. After the headboard and footboard are made, cut the side rail angles. Solder the side angles to the head posts and foot posts with the angle flange in toward the bed center. Make five or six mattress slats from brass flats or from thin wood stock. If brass slats are used, solder these slats to the angle flanges. If wood slats are used, glue the wood to the angle flanges.

Finish

Polish the finished bed with very fine steel wool. The high sheen can be preserved with a coat of brushing lacquer.

221

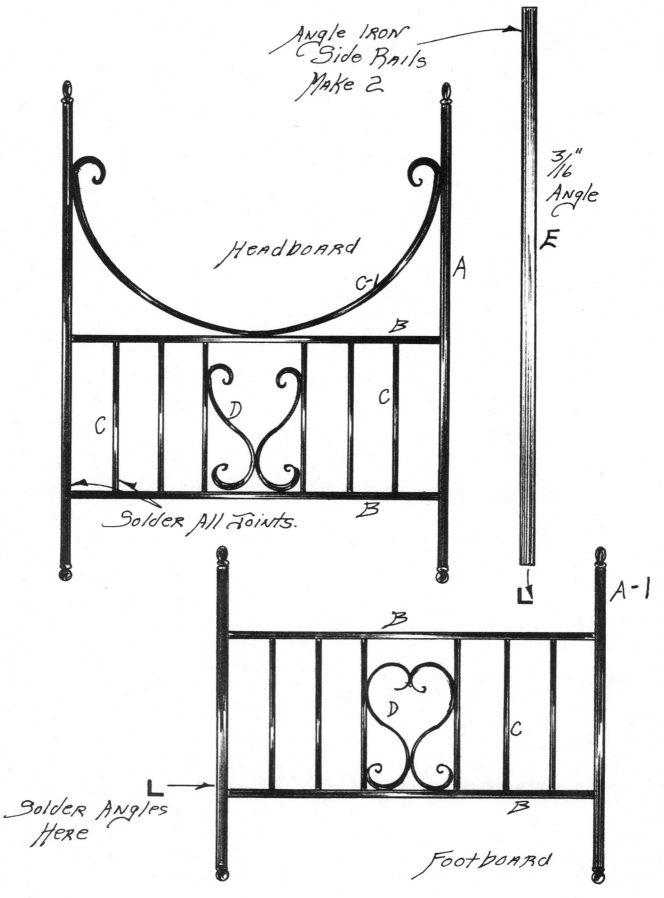

Angle Iron
Side Rails
Make 2

Headboard

C-1

A

B

C

C

D

Solder All Joints.

B

3/16" Angle

E

L

A-1

B

D

C

Solder Angles
Here

L

B

Footboard

Fig. 4–20. Brass bed

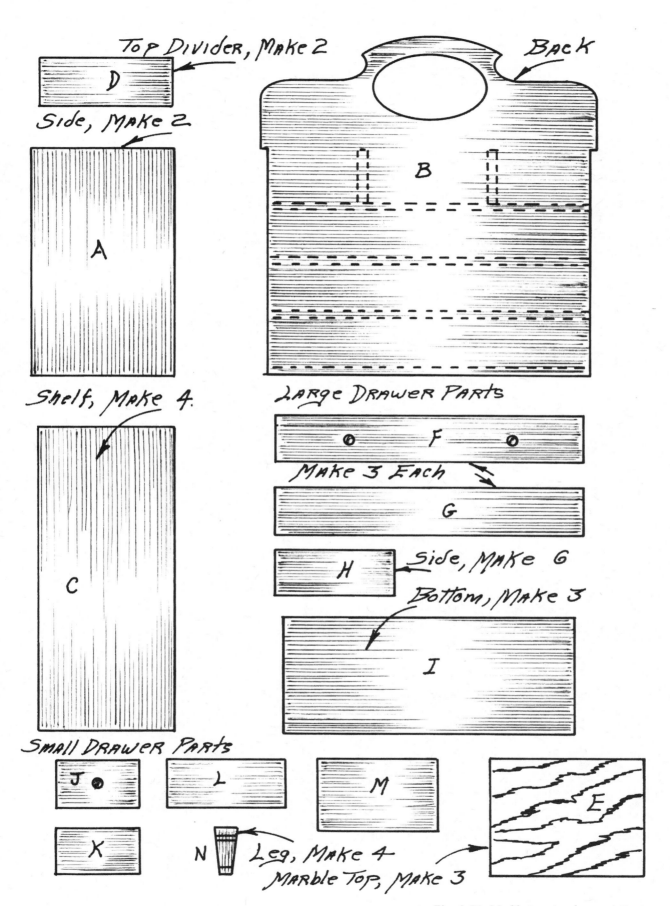

Top Divider, Make 2

D

Back

Side, Make 2

A

B

Shelf, Make 4.

C

Large Drawer Parts

F

Make 3 Each

G

H   Side, Make 6

Bottom, Make 3

I

Small Drawer Parts

J

L

M

E

K

N   Leg, Make 4

Marble Top, Make 3

Fig. 4–21. Marble-top step dresser pattern

223

Make a mattress and pillows for the bed. See "Construction Notes" for patterns for bed mattress and pillows.

MARBLE-TOP STEP DRESSER

This dresser has two small step drawers with a recessed top between an oval, inlaid mirror. This dresser is typical of the turn-of-the-century Victorian furnishings which were popular between 1890 and 1930.

Material

Walnut, cherry, birch, or basswood.

Material List

	Part	Number	Size
A	Side	2	$1^{1}/_{2}$" x $2^{1}/_{2}$" x $^{1}/_{8}$"
B	Back	1	$3^{1}/_{2}$" x $3^{3}/_{4}$" x $^{1}/_{16}$"
C	Shelf	4	$1^{7}/_{16}$" x $3^{1}/_{4}$" x $^{1}/_{16}$"
D	Divider	2	$1^{7}/_{16}$" x $^{1}/_{2}$" x $^{1}/_{8}$"
E	Top	3	$1^{5}/_{8}$" x $1^{1}/_{4}$" x $^{3}/_{32}$" marble
F	Large Drawer Front	3	$3^{1}/_{4}$" x $^{1}/_{2}$" x $^{1}/_{16}$"
G	Large Drawer Back	3	$3^{1}/_{4}$" x $^{1}/_{2}$" x $^{1}/_{16}$"
H	Large Drawer Side	6	$1^{1}/_{4}$" x $^{1}/_{2}$" x $^{1}/_{16}$"
I	Large Drawer Bottom	3	$3^{1}/_{8}$" x $1^{1}/_{4}$" x $^{1}/_{16}$"
J	Small Drawer Front	2	$^{7}/_{8}$" x $^{1}/_{2}$" x $^{1}/_{16}$"

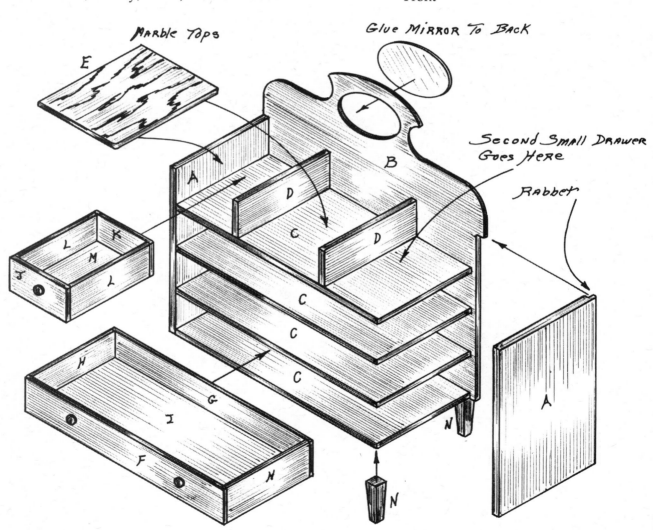

Marble Tops

Glue Mirror to Back

Second Small Drawer Goes Here

Rabbet

Fig. 4–22. Marble-top step dresser assembly

K	Small Drawer Back	2	$7/8'' \times 1/2'' \times 1/16''$
L	Small Drawer Side	4	$1^{1}/4'' \times 1/2'' \times 1/16''$
M	Small Drawer Bottom	2	$1^{1}/4'' \times 3/4'' \times 1/16''$
N	Leg	4	$1/4''$ dia. x $1/2''$

Construction

1. Lay out and cut the sides (A), back (B), shelves (C), and top divider (D). Cut a $1/16$-by-$1/16$-inch rabbet on the rear inside edges of the sides. Glue the back into the rabbets cut into the sides. Glue the shelves between the sides and to the back (see fig. 4–21 for location).

Glue the top dividers (D) to the top shelf (see fig. 4–21 for location). The top dividers form the step for the small drawers, and the recessed marble top is between the two dividers.

2. Make three large drawers to fit the openings, using parts F, G, H, and I. See "Construction Notes" for suggested techniques on drawer construction.

Make two small drawers from parts J, K, L, and M. Sand fit the drawers to the openings.

3. Cut the marble tops (E). Glue one marble top to the top shelf in between the dividers. Glue the other two marble tops on top of the sides and dividers. Glue a piece of mirror behind the cutout oval in the back.

Finish

Sand the entire miniature reproduction smooth removing all traces of glue. Stain to a color of choice. Cover with several coats of lacquer or similar finish. Finish off with a coat of paste wax.

11

Kitchen Group

The furnishings in Victorian kitchens matched the available technology. Many late 1800 and early 1900 kitchens had wood or gas stoves, iceboxes, a soapstone or china sink, and a small dinette set. When electricity became a way of life, the refrigerator and washing machine were added.

The kitchen was used for food preparation and casual dining. A formal dining room was used for full family, company, and evening meals.

Almost every Victorian household had a pantry which contained cabinets for stocking food and storing dishes and cooking utensils. The other walls were often lined with pots, pans, and vessels of every description.

The following miniature reproductions were developed for an early 1900 Victorian kitchen and pantry.

PANTRY CABINET

Many Victorian pantry cabinets contained see-through glass doors on the top units with wainscot batten-type doors on the bottom units. The following offering does not have a given length because it was designed as a typical unit to fit any size space available. Make the length to suit your space.

Material

All stock is $1/8$-inch oak, maple, cherry, or basswood. Oak is preferred. Glass panels for the top units can be craft sheet plastic, or $1/32$-inch sheet glass.

The sizes given for the pantry are only general or typical guide lines. They can be adjusted to fit any size desired; longer or shorter, wider

Fig. 4–23. Victorian kitchen

Fig. 4–24. Pantry cupboard

or narrower, shorter or taller. Because this pantry is a suggestion and not a set pattern size, no material list is given but general dimensions are given in the working drawing.

Construction

1. Lay out and cut the side pieces. These are 8 inches long, 3/4 inch wide at the top, and 1⅞ inches wide at the bottom. Cut the required shelving 3/4-inch wide for the top unit, and 1⅞ inches wide for the bottom unit. The spacing between the shelves is optional. The top cabinet section is 3½ inches high, and the bottom cabinet section is 2⅝ inches high. Glue the shelving between the two side pieces (see figure 4–25).

2. Lay out and cut the top cabinet section rails and stiles. Glue the cabinet framing in

place. Cut out the lower section cabinet rails and stiles to size and glue these in place as suggested in figure 4–25. Make a counter top 2⅛ inches wide and glue this in place. Note: the counter top can be marble if preferred.

3. Glass doors. Make the required number of door frames using half-lap joints (see "Construction Notes" for suggested techniques). Fit each door to a matching cabinet space. Attach the door frames to the top cabinet spaces with scale-size hinges. The plastic or glass should be applied after the doors are finished and installed.

4. Lower unit doors. The lower doors are made of one solid piece of stock cut to the correct size, with the grain running vertical. Score the door face to resemble scale-size 3 or 4-inch wainscoting. Scoring can be done with a knife, screwdriver, or awl. Attach the doors to

the spaces with scale-size hinges. Attach brass cabinet pulls (handles) to all doors.

Finish

The Victorian-style pantry cabinet has a very high-gloss finish. No stain is suggested except for basswood which is stained and then finished as any other species.

When completed, the top shelving can be stocked with scale-size canned goods, dishes, or miniature condiments. Install the completed pantry against one solid wall. Scale-size food-stuffs can be placed on the counter if desired. Pots, pans, or cookware can be hung on the other walls of the pantry.

KITCHEN TABLE

The round pedestal table was often the mainstay of the Victorian kitchen. This table was used for informal dining, food prepara-tion, and as a part-time counter. This miniature reproduction was developed from the oak de-sign popular at the turn of the century.

Material

Oak, maple, cherry, walnut. Oak is pre-ferred.

Material List

	Part	Number	Size
A	Leg	2	$2^5/_8$" x $^5/_{16}$" x $^5/_{16}$"
B	Stem	1	$^1/_2$" diameter x $2^3/_8$"
C	Top	1	3" diameter x $^1/_8$"

Construction

1. Lay out and cut the base legs (A). Cut the half-lap joint into the two matching legs. Glue the legs together in the shape of a cross.

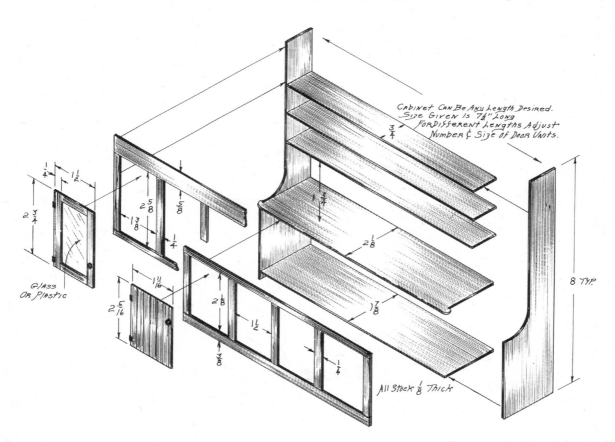

Fig. 4–25. Pantry cabinet assembly

Fig. 4–26. Kitchen table

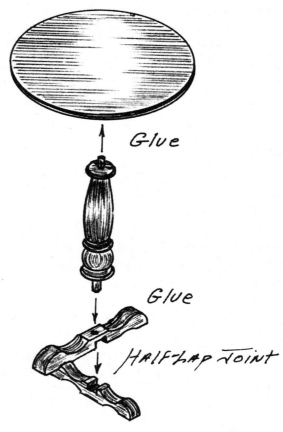

Fig. 4–27. Kitchen table pattern

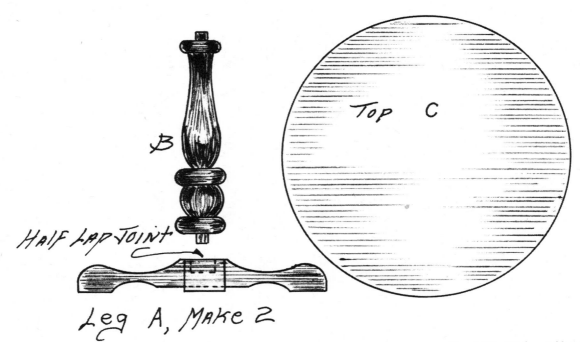

Leg A, Make 2

Fig. 4–28. Kitchen table assembly

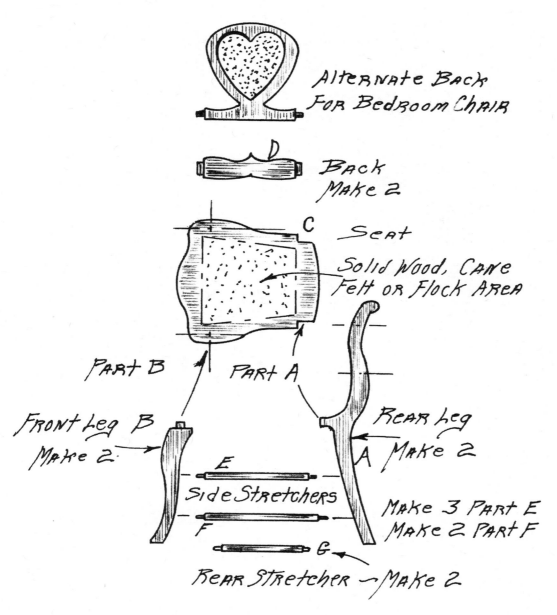

Fig. 4–29. Kitchen chair pattern

2. Lay out the main pedestal (B). Turn this pedestal to shape on a lathe or with an electric drill. Leave round tenons on the top and bottom ends. Drill a matching mortise holes into the crossed base legs. Glue the pedestal to the crossed legs.

3. Lay out and cut the round tabletop (C). Drill a blind mortise hole into the bottom center. Glue the top pedestal tenon into this hole.

Finish

No stain is recommended. A very high-gloss finish should be used to accent the wood grain.

KITCHEN CHAIR

The basic kitchen chair can be used with a little modification in the dining room or as a boudoir chair. See note on alternate back and seat design.

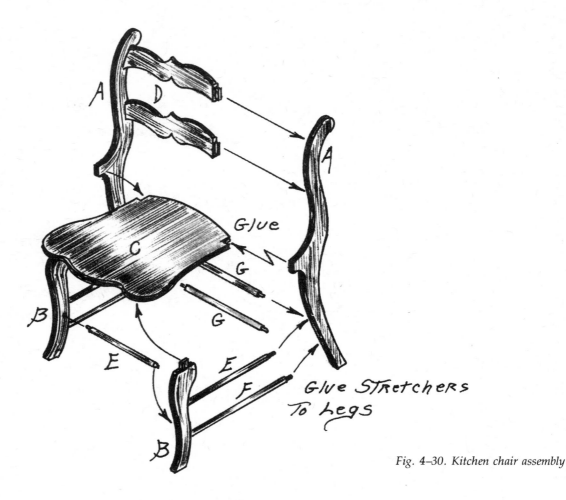

Fig. 4–30. Kitchen chair assembly

Material

Material List

	Part	Number	Size
A	Rear Leg	2	$2^3/_4'' \times {}^5/_8'' \times {}^1/_8''$
B	Front Leg	2	$1^1/_2'' \times {}^1/_2'' \times {}^1/_8''$
C	Seat	1	$1^3/_8'' \times 1^1/_2'' \times {}^3/_{32}''$
D	Back Slat	2	$1^1/_8'' \times {}^1/_4'' \times {}^1/_{16}''$
E	Stretcher	3	${}^1/_8''$ dia. x $1^1/_4''$
F	Stretcher	2	${}^1/_8''$ dia. x $1^3/_8''$
G	Rear Stretcher	2	${}^1/_8''$ dia. x $1''$
H	Alternate Back	1	$1'' \times 1'' \times {}^1/_{16}''$

Construction

1. Lay out, cut, and form rear and front chair legs (A and B). See "Construction Notes" for suggested techniques. Drill $^1/_{16}$-inch-diameter mortise holes for the stretchers (E, F, and G) as shown on figure 4–29.

2. Lay out and cut the chair seat (C) notching it as shown to receive the rear legs (A). Lay out and cut stretchers (E, F, G) and back (D or H). Glue the rear stretchers (G) and back (D or H) to rear legs as you attach the legs to the chair seat (C) at the notches.

Drill small mounting mortise holes in the bottom of the seat for the front legs. Drill mortise holes in the front legs for the front stretcher (G). Glue the front and side stretchers into the front legs. Secure the other ends of the side stretchers into the mortise holes on the rear legs as the front leg tenons are glued into the notches on the chair seat.

3. Alternate seat and back. If a boudoir or formal dining room chair is desired, use the decorative back piece (H) in place of the slats (D). Both the seat and the back piece of a formal chair should have upholstered insets. These can be flocked, satin, felt, or velvet.

Finish

No stain is used for the kitchen-style chairs. However, a stain is used for more formal chairs. Cover either with a high-gloss finish.

ICEBOX

The icebox was considered an example of modern technology at the time of its invention. The top tray, which held the block of ice, had a rubber hose to draw the water from the melting ice into a pan at the bottom of the box. This water pan had to be emptied once a day, and more often during hot weather. Below the ice chamber, food was stored on racks. The cool air from the ice filtered down and surrounded the food, keeping it fresh for a few days at best. The icebox was insulated to keep the cool air contained. Most often the box interior was metal while the exterior was polished oak.

Material

Oak is preferred although maple, cherry, basswood, or walnut can be used.

Material List

	Part	Number	Size
A	Side	2	$1^3/4''$ x 5'' x $^1/16''$
B	Stile	4	$^1/4''$ x 5'' x $^1/16''$
C	Rail	6	$1^1/4''$ x $^1/4''$ x $^1/16''$
D	Front Stile	2	$^3/16''$ x 5'' x $^1/16''$
E	Front Rail	2	$^3/16''$ x $1^5/8''$ x $^1/16''$
F	Skirt	1	$^5/8''$ x $1^5/8''$ x $^1/16''$
G	Back	1	$1^7/8''$ x 5'' x $^1/16''$
H	Top	1	2'' x $2^3/8''$ x $^1/16''$
J	Top Door	1	$1^5/8''$ x $1^5/16''$ x $^1/16''$
K	Bottom Door	1	$1^5/8''$ x $2^3/4''$ x $^1/16''$
L	Top Door Stile	2	$1^7/16''$ x $^3/16''$ x $^1/16''$
M	Bottom Door Stile	2	$2^7/16''$ x $^3/16''$ x $^1/16''$
N	Door Rail	4	$1^3/8''$ x $^3/16''$ x $^1/16''$
O	Rack	2	$1^3/4''$ x $1^1/2''$ x $^1/32''$ wire
P	Ice Pan	1	2'' x $1^7/8''$ thin sheet metal
Q	Water Tray	1	$2^1/4''$ x $1^3/4''$ thin sheet metal
R	Metal Liner	1	$5^1/8''$ x $7^3/4''$ thin sheet metal

Construction

1. Lay out and cut the sides (A), stiles, (B), rails, (C), and back (G). Cut a $^1/16$-by-$^1/8$-inch

Fig. 4–31. Icebox

233

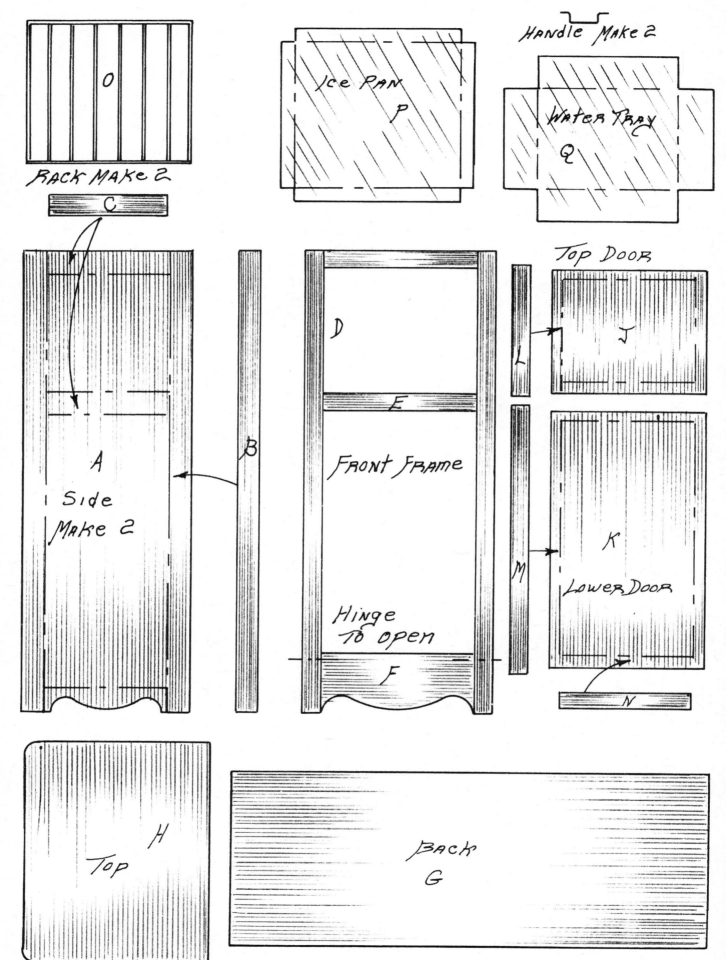

Fig. 4–32. Icebox pattern

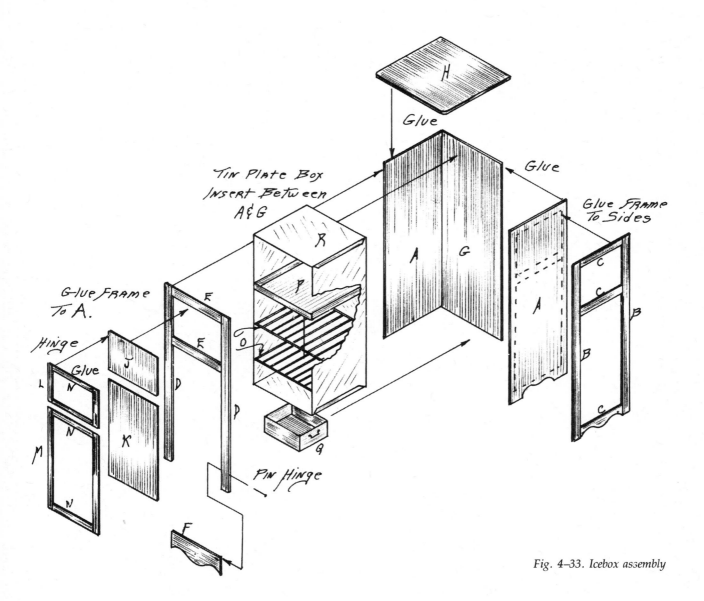

Fig. 4–33. Icebox assembly

rabbet into the back edges of the sides. Glue the side stiles and rails to the sides making panels. Glue the back into the rabbets on the sides (see fig. 4–33).

2. Metal pattern. Lay out and cut the metal liner. See figure 4–34 for full-size pattern. Make the open metal pan from 22- or 24-gauge tin plate. Solder the corner tabs together. Insert the metal box liner into the U formed by parts A and G. The metal liner can be glued in place if preferred. Make the suggested ice pan (P) and racks (O). Solder these parts in place in the metal liner (see fig. 4–34 for location). The open

racks can be made from paper clip wire or similar material.

3. Lay out and cut the front door frame (D, E, F). Glue the frame parts to the sides. Hinge part F in place (see detail, fig. 4–33). Make the top (H) to size and glue it to the sides, front frame, and back.

4. Lay out and cut the door stock (J, K, L, M, N). Make the required overset door frames. Fasten the door units to the icebox with scale-size hinges. Cut a normal-scale hinge such as a Houseworks H hinge in half. Bend one side of this hinge to match the degree of door offset.

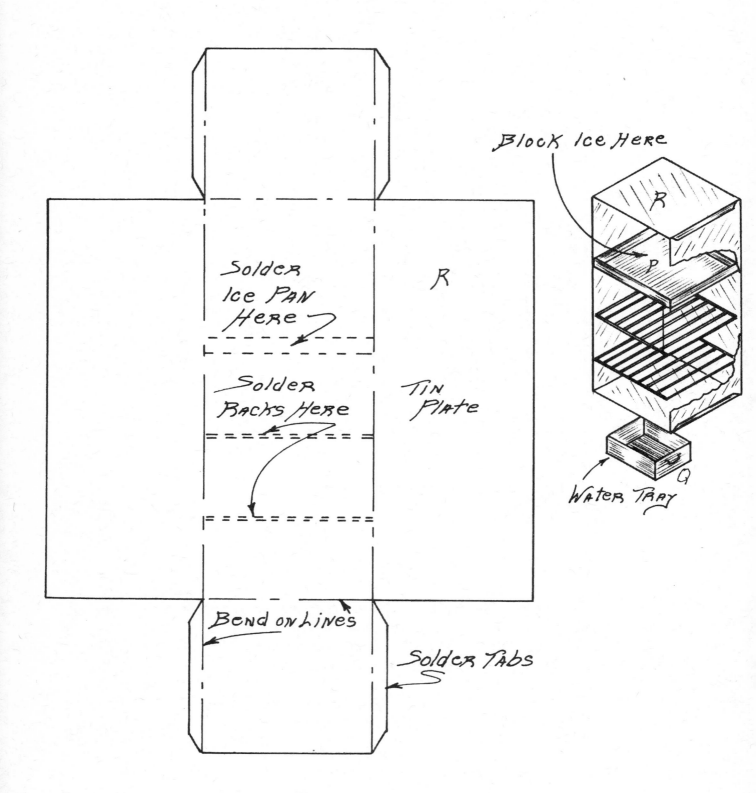

Block Ice Here

Solder
Ice Pan
Here

R

Solder
Backs Here

Tin
Plate

Bend on Lines

Solder Tabs

Water Tray

Q

R

P

Fig. 4–34. Icebox metal interior pattern

Make two locking door handles. Fasten the handles to the doors and frames.

5. Make the metal water tray (Q). Solder the corner tabs together (see fig. 4–34 for pattern). Insert the pan under the metal lining where part F closes.

Finish

Cover the icebox with a clear high-gloss finish. No stain is recommended except over basswood. Scale-size food, ice, and beverages can be purchased for the interior. Attach ice tongs to a hook on the box exterior.

12

Dining Room Group

DINING ROOM TABLE

The following miniature dining room table can be made to any suitable size. The patterns given are for an average size table. If a different width or length is desired, adjustments will be required. The tabletop will overhang the rectangle box by the amount shown regardless of overall table size.

Material

Walnut, cherry, maple, or basswood. Walnut is preferred.

Material List

	Part	Number	Size
A	Leg	4	1" x 3" x $^{1}/_{8}$"
B	Side	2	$^{3}/_{8}$" x 5$^{1}/_{4}$" x $^{1}/_{8}$"
C	Side	2	$^{3}/_{8}$" x 2$^{5}/_{8}$" x $^{1}/_{8}$"
D	Tabletop	1	3$^{1}/_{2}$" x 6$^{1}/_{2}$" x $^{3}/_{16}$"

Construction

1. Lay out and cut the legs (A) (see "Construction Notes"). Shape and sand the legs. Lay out and cut the table boards (B and C). Glue these parts into a rectangle. Glue and pin the legs to the corners of this rectangle, setting them at a 45 degree angle.

2. Lay out and cut the tabletop (D). Sand the top and edges smooth. Glue the tabletop to the table board assembly.

Finish

Remove all traces of glue. Finish sand and cover table with a high-gloss finish. No stain is required over hardwoods but may be required if basswood is used.

BONNET-TOP CHINA CABINET

This curved-front cabinet was often used to store the special Sunday dinner china. At times a similar cabinet was employed in the living room or study to protect, yet display, valuable glass or other art objects. This miniature reproduction can be used anywhere in a Victorian-style house, but was primarily designed for the dining room.

Material

Walnut, cherry, maple, or basswood. Walnut is preferred.

Material List

	Part	Number	Size
A	Side	2	1½″ x 4½″ x ⅛″

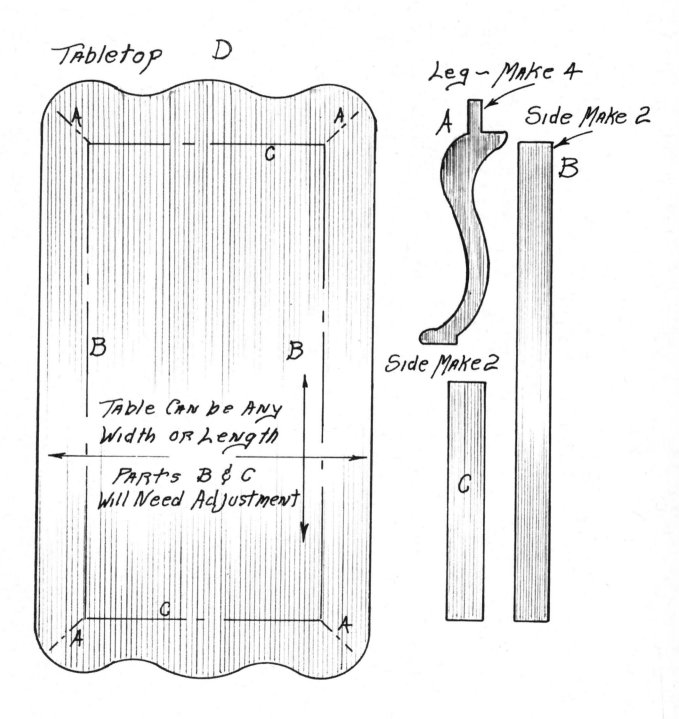

Fig. 4–36. Dining room table pattern

240

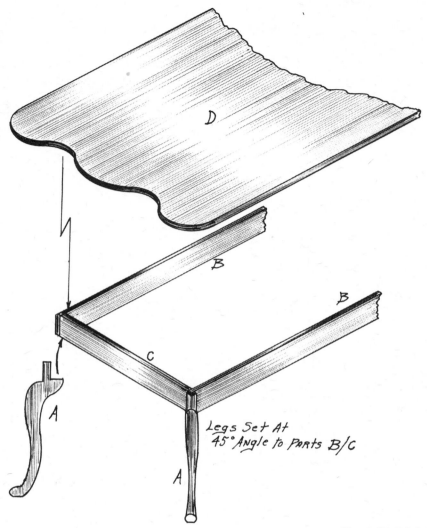

Fig. 4–37. Dining room table assembly

B	Back	1	3¼″ x 4½″ x ¹/₁₆″
C	Top/Bottom	2	2″ x 3³/₁₆″ x ¹/₁₆″
D	Bonnet	1	1″ x 3¾″ x 2″
E	Shelf	3	1⅞″ x 3⅛″ x ¹/₁₆″
F	Front Leg	2	¾″ x 1¼″ x ⁵/₃₂″
G	Rear Leg	2	¼″ x ¼″ x 1″
H	Door	2	1¾″ x 4¼″ x ⅛″

Construction

1. Lay out and cut the sides (A), back (B), and top and bottom (C). Cut the required ¹/₁₆-by-⅛-inch rabbets into the rear edges of the sides and top and bottom. Glue the back into the rabbets on the sides. Glue the top and bottom to the sides and back.

2. Lay out and cut the bonnet top to shape and size (see ''Construction Notes'' for methods). Glue the bonnet top to the top (C) keeping the rear edges flush.

3. Lay out and cut the shelves (E). Glue the shelves between the sides in equal spaces. Make the legs (F and G) (see ''Construction Notes'' for suggestions). Glue and pin the finished legs to the bottom (C). The front legs are set on a 45 degree angle while the rear legs are set square.

4. Make the pair of curved doors. The door curves match the curve shown on the shelves, therefore, the door stiles must be cut out in a similar round. Since bent wood has a tendency

241

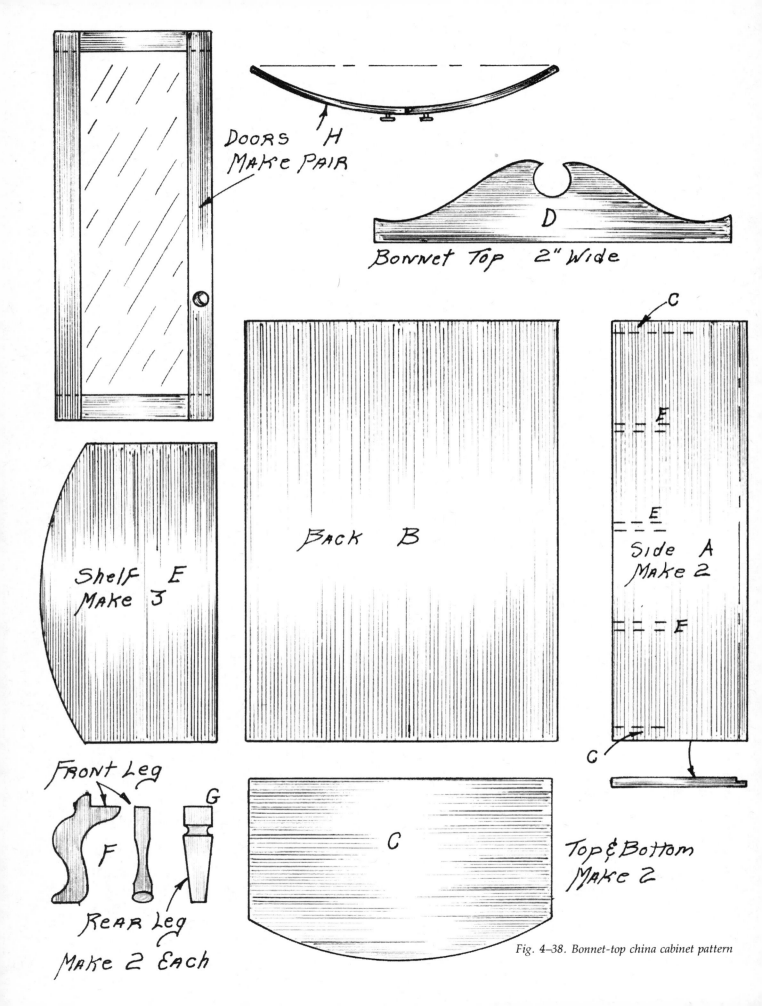

DOORS MAKE PAIR

H

BONNET TOP 2" WIDE

D

C

BACK B

Side A Make 2

E

E

E

C

Shelf E Make 3

FRONT LEG

F G

REAR LEG

Make 2 Each

C

Top & Bottom Make 2

Fig. 4–38. Bonnet-top china cabinet pattern

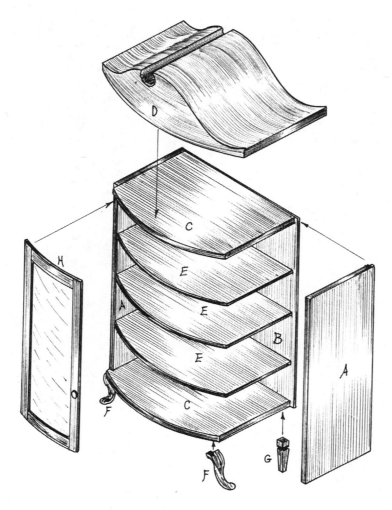

Fig. 4–39. Bonnet-top china cabinet assembly

to return to a prebent form, it is recommended that the door tops and bottoms be cut on the suggested bends rather than bent to shape.

Cut out the required rails and stiles (H). Make two matching doors, a right and a left. Use half-lap joints at the corners. Sand fit the completed doors to the openings. Glue a piece of thin glass or heavy gauge craft plastic over the doors. Attach the doors to the tops and bottoms with pins or hinges.

Finish

Remove all traces of glue. Sand the entire reproduction smooth. Cover with a high-gloss finish. Stain is not recommended except over basswood or pine woods.

KAS

Very often the one feature missing in a Victorian house was adequate closet space. In order to provide storage facilities, a cabinet called a kas was employed. This cabinet was not a Victorian invention, but was adopted from Early American times. This basic type of furnishing went under several different names; wardrobe, armoire, master chest, and portable closet. While the kas was found mainly in bedrooms, it was also used in other rooms, sometimes using glass doors in place of solid wood ones. The following miniature was developed for use in Victorian-style dining rooms, living rooms, or bedrooms.

Fig. 4–40. Kas

Materials

Walnut, cherry, maple, basswood, or pine. Walnut is preferred.

Material List

	Part	Number	Size
A	Side	2	1½" x 5½" x ⅛"
B	Back	1	3¼" x 5½" x 1/16"
C	Shelf	3	1 7/16" x 3⅛" x ⅛"
D	Center Shelf	1	1¾" x 3¼" x 3/16"
E	Crown	1	⅞" x 4" x 2"
F	Drawer Front	2	3" x ¾" x 1/16"
G	Drawer Back	2	3" x ¾" x 1/16"
H	Drawer Side	4	1¼" x ¾" x 1/16"
I	Drawer Bottom	2	2⅞" x 1⅛" x 1/16"
J	Door Backer	2	1½" x 3½" x 1/16"
K	Door Stiles	4	3/16" x 3½" x 1/16"
L	Door Header	2	⅝" x 1⅛" x ⅛"
M	Door Rail	2	3/16" x 1⅛" x 1/16"

Construction

1. Lay out and cut the sides (A), back (B), shelves (C and D). Cut a 1/16-by-1/16-inch rabbet on the rear edges of the sides. Glue the back into these rabbets. Glue the shelves (C) between the sides and to the back as shown in figure 4–41. Glue the center shelf in place.

2. Lay out and cut the crown (E) (see "Construction Notes"). Glue the crown to the sides, back, and top shelf.

3. Make two drawers to fit the openings. Sand fit the drawers in place. Install scale-size drawer pulls.

4. Make two panel doors, a right and a left. (Glass may be used if the furnishing is to be used in the living room or dining room.) Cut a solid piece (J) to size. Cut K, L, and M to shape and size and glue them to the solid backer (J) as shown in figure 4–41. Sand fit the doors in place. Attach doors to kas with pins or hinges. Attach scale-size door pulls.

Finish

Remove all traces of glue. Sand smooth.

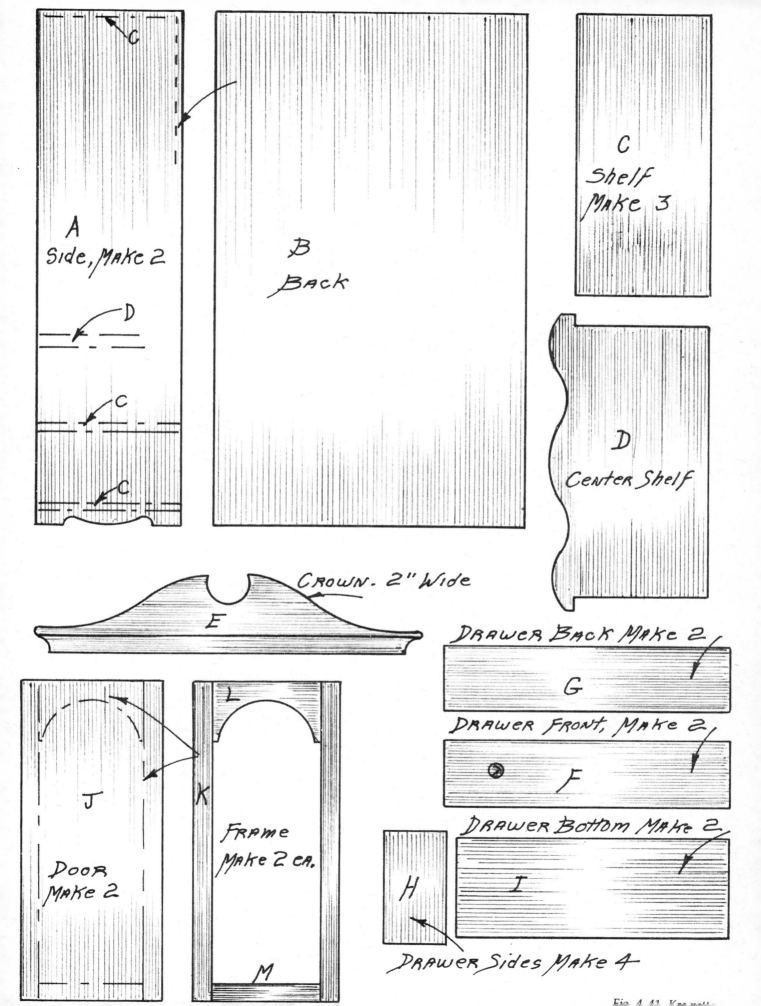

C

A
Side, Make 2

D

C

C

B
Back

C
Shelf
Make 3

D
Center Shelf

CROWN. 2" Wide

E

DRAWER BACK MAKE 2

G

DRAWER FRONT, MAKE 2

F

DRAWER BOTTOM MAKE 2

H

I

J

K

Door
Make 2

Frame
Make 2 ea.

L

M

DRAWER SIDES MAKE 4

Fig. 4-11. Kennett

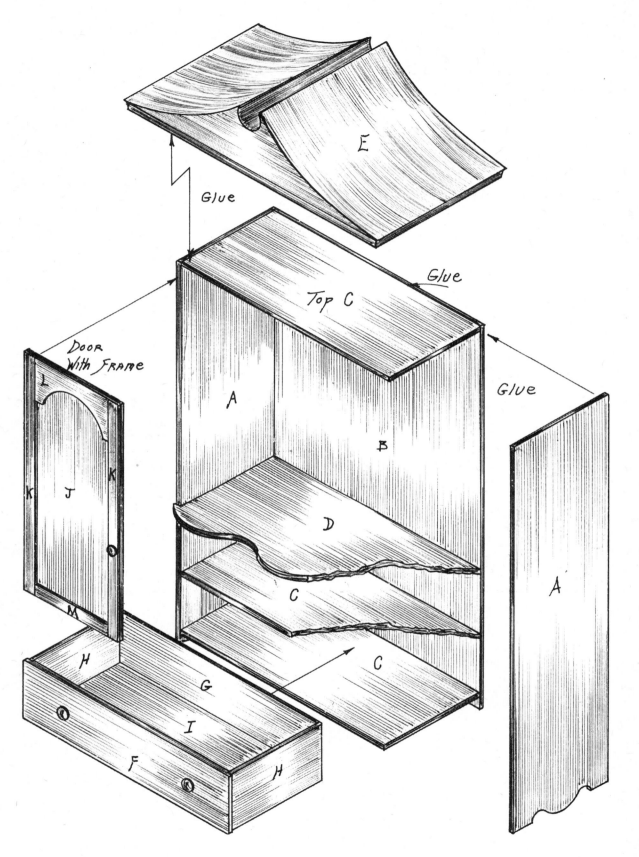

Glue

E

Glue

Top C

Door
With Frame

L

A

B

Glue

K

K

J

D

A

O

C

M

C

H

G

O

I

F

H

Fig. 4–42. Kas assembly

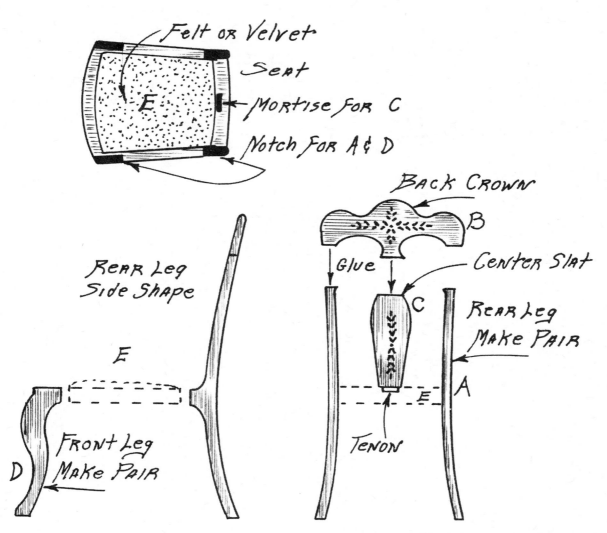

Fig. 4–43. Dining room chair pattern

Cover with a high-gloss finish. Stain is not recommended except over basswood or pine.

FORMAL DINING ROOM CHAIRS

The Victorian dining room was reserved for the day's main meal, company, or special occasions. The large table was surrounded by several ornate, upholstered chairs. The following miniature was designed from a composite of many Victorian-style chairs. It is not as ornate as some examples, or as plain as kitchen chairs. It represents a good example of early twentieth century, middle class Victorianism.

Materials

Same species as the dining room table. Walnut is preferred. Upholstery fabric can be velvet, felt, flock, or satin.

Material List

	Part	Number	Size
A	Rear Leg	2	$1/2''$ x $3^3/8''$ x $1/8''$
B	Crown	1	$5/8''$ x $1^1/2''$ x $1/16''$
C	Center Slat	1	$7/16''$ x $1^1/16''$ x $1/16''$
D	Front Leg	2	$3/4''$ x $1^1/2''$ x $1/8''$
E	Seat	1	$1^3/8''$ x $1^1/2''$ x $3/16''$

Construction

1. Lay out and cut the rear legs (A). See

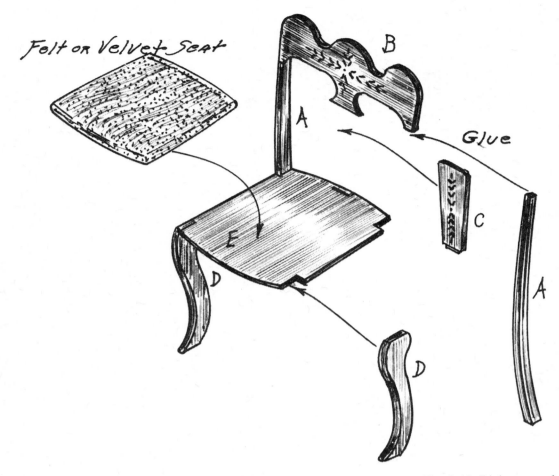

Felt or Velvet Seat

Glue

Fig. 4-44. Dining room chair assembly

"Construction Notes" for simplified instructions. Lay out and cut the crown (B). Sand fit the crown to the rear legs to achieve a blending. Lay out and cut the center slat (C). Cut a small tenon extension on the bottom of the center slat. It is best to cut the center slat slightly oversize and fit it into place by sanding.

2. Lay out and cut the front legs (D). Cut out the wood seat (E). Cut a mortise slot in the rear of the seat in order to receive the tenon on the center slat. Notch the seat where the front and rear legs will be attached. Glue the front and rear legs into the notches on the seat. Sand blend the legs and seat together. Sand fit the center slat between the crown and the seat.

Finish

Sand the entire chair smooth, blending all interlocking parts together. Carve in the decorations on the crown and center slat. Small brass findings can be glued to these areas if preferred.

Cover the chair with a high-gloss finish. No stain is recommended except over basswood or pine. Cut a cardboard seat to match the area shown in figure 4–43. Lay a very small amount of cotton or similar upholstering material over the cardboard. Cover this with felt, satin, velvet, or other selected material. Glue the upholstered seat to the wood seat. (If the chair seat is to be flocked, apply the flocking glue to the seat and blow the flocking material onto the wet glue.)

Glossary

Apron: (1) a piece of horizontal trim or molding installed just under the window sill. (2) a section of horizontal stock used to join furniture legs and support tabletops.

Balloon-style: a rounded, enlarged top resembling a type of inflated balloon used for the backs of chairs and rockers.

Ball rasp: a ball-shaped metal bit that cuts wood via a file or rasp teeth cut into the ball.

Bank pin: a small ½-inch straight pin, often called "sequin" pins, used to hold stock together or as a hinge pin.

Batten door: a door made up of individual vertical boards held together with horizontal and angle cleats called Z battens. Such doors can be full-size entrance doors or small cabinet doors.

Bevel: see chamfer

Blind hole: a hole drilled only part way through the stock.

Blind drill: to drill only part way through the stock.

Block front: a style of dresser which has the front of the drawers stacked in block alignment.

Bootjack: a V-type notch cut into a board.

Butt: (1) a simple right-angle joint where pieces of stock come together; (2) the term used for door hinges.

C Clamp: a threaded clamp made in the form of a C with an arm that descends to an anvil.

Cabriole: a curved, footed furniture leg used in Queen Anne and Chippendale furnishings.

Caddy: carrier or holder.

Casing: the trim around a door, window, or mirror.

Chamfer: to cut away the edge of a board on an angle.

Child guard: in the mammy-type bench or rocker, an assembly placed into mounting holes that prevents a child from rolling out as the bench is rocked.

Chuck: the end member of a drill (or lathe) that holds the cutting bit. Most often has three jaws that open and close with a chuck key.

Circle template: a plastic sheet containing several circles of different sizes. Example: $1/16$-inch diameter up to 3-inch diameter in units of $1/16$ inch or $1/8$ inch.

Commode: a low cabinet or chest containing drawers or doors. A movable stand or cupboard which contains a washbowl.

Copper flashing: a sheet metal used to seal fireplace or chimney to the roof proper. A metal used to make dry sinks.

Cornice: the top trim of a building or furnishing that marks the meeting of walls (sides) and roof (top). Contains the soffit, fascia, and moldings.

Counterbore: larger hole drilled over a smaller hole to allow a bolt or screw head to sit below the surface.

Countersink: cut the edges of a hole to take the slope or fit of a flathead screw. Most often cut at a 60 degree angle.

Cyma curve: a profile made from a part concave and part convex curve. Most common in crown moldings. Used to create the normal skirt board of Colonial furnishing styles.

Dado: a recess or U shaped groove cut into one board to receive and support another board at a right angle.

Dado, blind: a dado that stops short of the board's end or edge.

Dado saw: a combination of two circular saw blades and assorted inset cutters, used to cut out various width dadoes.

Dentil: a molding resembling small wooden blocks that project like a row of teeth.

Dowel: a presized hardwood round stock. Example: $1/8$-inch dowel would be a round stock, $1/8$ inch in diameter, most often of maple or birch.

Dough trough: a small, wooden box or bin used to hold rising dough.

Dresser: a common term used to describe a chest of drawers used in bedrooms, or a large kitchen or dining room cupboard.

Escutcheon pin: a nail or pin with a round or decorative head.

Fascia: in cornice work, the horizontal face board. In cabinet work, the board on top of the cabinets that touches the ceiling.

Finger drill: a small drill holder that fits between two fingers for turning, contains small chuck to hold bits.

Fifty/fifty (50/50) solder: half lead, half tin solder. Can be solid or hollow core with acid fill.

Finish nail: a series of nails that have small heads that can be set (driven) below the surface of the stock and thereby be filled and smoothed over.

Fly-bracket: a small, turning cleat set into a table apron which supports a drop leaf when in the open position.

Fusible webbing: a glue-type material used in sewing that sets under heat from an iron.

Gate-leg: a gate-like leg assembly that swings out to support the extended leaf.

Glaze: a mixture of half flat black paint and half thinner which is wiped on furnishings during finishing to "age" them.

Half-lap joint: a right angle or joint formed by removing one-half of the thickness from the two pieces of stock to be joined. Allows a larger surface for fastening.

Highboy: a high chest of drawers very often set on a lowboy type of base.

High-chest: a high or large stacked series of drawers.

Jig: the construction of a pattern or frame to hold stock in a fixed position during assembly. Most often used when several units of the same size and style are required.

Kas: a very large, closet-like chest containing doors and drawers for storage, most often a bedroom piece.

Kerf: the slot or cut made by the saw teeth.

Lathe: a machine containing a head and tail stock which supports and turns material. Used to turn (cut) circular shapes or turnings.

Lathe chisel: a series of cutting chisels used to create turnings on a lathe.

Lathe turning: the stock cut on a lathe.

Mammy bench: a term given to a double seat deacon's bench that rocks. Often used with a child guard.

Medallion: a large oval or circular design used as decoration for rooms or furnishings.

Millwork: the term used to describe products made in lumber mills or woodworking plants, moldings, door and window frames, sash units, stairwork, or mantels.

Miter: a right angle made up of two 45-degree angle cuts.

Miter joint: an angle cut joint where two members join each other, most often at 45 degree angles. Used to joint two irregular shapes such as moldings.

Molding: wood millwork that cuts a design or curved edge into long, narrow strips.

Molding, Bed: a molding commonly used for right angle meetings such as walls and ceilings or sides and tops.

Molding, Chair rail: a millwork product used to divide a normal wall at chair back height.

Molding, Cove: a molding with a concave profile, for example a quarter of a circle or round.

Molding, Crown: a series of moldings with part concave and part convex profiles, a cyma curve for example.

Molding, Quarter Round: a series of moldings that represent a quarter of a circle.

Molding, Scotia: a series of moldings that represent the interior shape of a quarter round, for example smaller cove moldings.

Mortise: a hole or recess made to receive a tenon.

Mullions: the wood member where two or more window units are jointed together.

Muntin: the vertical and horizontal members dividing a window sash into various size panes of glass. In a eight-over-eight window sash unit the muntins divide the sash proper into eight individual panes of glass.

Muntin insert: wood members that are installed in order to give the appearance of individual panes of glass in windows or in furnishings.

Nail block: an extra block of stock installed in order to reinforce a joint. Sometimes called a glue-block.

Pegged: using hardwood dowels to join wooden members together.

Plumb: exactly perpendicular or vertical.

Pie safe: a furnishing made of wood and metal panels used to store pies or other pastry. Metal panels most often pierced to allow air circulation.

Pin hinge: refers to a pin used to hinge a cabinet-type door.

Rabbet: a recess or L-shaped groove cut into one board to join another board at a right angle.

Rake: the trim that runs parallel to the roof slope which forms the finish between the roof and house side, furnishing sides and tops, or incline roof angle and front.

Rake trim: the stock making up the rake, fascia, and moldings used along gable ends; trim itself could be molded in furnishings.

Rail: horizontal pieces of a door, window, or cabinet.

Resaw: to recut normal lumberyard stock to achieve thin widths and thicknesses.

Rip fence: a table saw fixture attached to the tabletop that allows ripping to a given size or line.

Router: a hand-held electrical tool that turns at a high rate of speed and uses assorted bits and cutters to make molded edges, rabbets, or mortises.

Rushing: the weaving of a fiber material for chair seats. Rush weeds are used in full-size chairs, waxed line is used for miniature-size chairs.

Sash: the framework containing the window panes and any muntins. In furnishings, cabinet doors are called sash units if they contain panes of glass and muntins. Normal double-hung windows would have two sash units, top and bottom.

Scale: a ruler.

Scallop: a series of arcs much like a scallop seashell edge.

Ship lap: another name for half-lap joint.

Soffit: the flat, underside, horizontal trim members that fit between the house wall and the fascia boards. Or in furnishings, members that fit between side(s) and roof bonnets.

Splay: to spread out, increase angle. The angle of a chair leg as it descends from the seat to the floor.

Stile: vertical side pieces of a door, window, or cabinet.

Stretchers: wooden members used to reinforce and hold legs at a proper distance from each other.

Sunburst: any carved or painted design that resembles a full- or half-circle sunburst, often with rays or dividing lines starting from a central point.

T-square: a tool used in drafting to create straight horizontal lines. The seat upon which the triangles ride.

Tenon: in joinery, a male projection on the end of a wood member that fits into a female mortise.

Tester (bed): head piece, a canopy over a bed.

Triangle: plastic triangles of any size. Used to make vertical lines in drafting. Most common, 45-degree and 60-degree/30-degree angles.

Wainscoting: woodwork installed in dwellings on interior walls in a vertical, horizontal, or raised panel construction. Most often installed only part way up a wall to chair-rail height.

White glue: polyvinyl or white liquid glue.

Wood filler: material used to fill in holes or voids in cabinet stock; material used to fill open grain pores before finishing.

Index

Page numbers in italics refer to illustrations